D0956002

3 0600 00183 8466

The Dream Beside Me

Other books by CAROL TRAYNOR WILLIAMS

Elements of Research: A Guidebook for Writers
(with Gary K. Wolfe)

The Dream Beside Me

The Movies and the Children of the Forties

Carol Traynor Williams

Rutherford • Madison • Teaneck
Fairleigh Dickinson University Press
London: Associated University Presses

© 1980 by Associated University Presses, Inc.

Associated University Presses, Inc.
Cranbury, New Jersey 08512

Associated University Presses
Magdalen House
136-148 Tooley Street
London SE1 2TT, England

Library of Congress Cataloging in Publication Data

Williams, Carol T   1935-
   The dream beside me.

   Bibliography: p.
   Includes index.
      1. Womin in moving-pictures.   2.   Moving-pictures--
United States.   I.   Title.
PN1995.9.W6W5   791.43'0909'352   78-66858
ISBN 0-8386-2290-9

To all of us who are going through this now, not know-ing how it's all going to end . . .

And to my father

Gerald Aloysius Traynor
October 22, 1896-August 11, 1974

this book is dedicated.

Long ago and far away
I dreamed a dream one day
And now that dream is here
Beside me. . . .
—Jerome Kern and Ira Gershwin,
  "Long Ago and Far Away,"
  from *Cover Girl* (1944)

. . . a splendid ship's funnel, showing from behind the clothes-line as something in a scrambled picture—Find what the Sailor Has Hidden—that the finder cannot unsee once it has been seen.

—Vladimir Nabokov, *Speak, Memory*

Contents

9

Preface
"The Movies, Like Waking Dreams . . ." *

When I was working on this book, my mother began thumbing through the books about movies I was using to revive my memories. (I think she was trying to figure out why I was treating movies as I used to treat books.) Turning the pages of *Hollywood at War*, she began to comment:

> *Destination Tokyo*—I'll never forget the ending of that one, when the submarine slipped through the nets in Tokyo Bay. . . . *A Guy Named Joe*—that had that beautiful song, "I'll Get By." . . . *Bomber's Moon*. . . .*Crash Dive*. . . . *Eagle Squadron*. . . . *The Very Thought of You*—oh, I went to see that one just to hear Dennis Morgan sing "The Very Thought of You," and he never did. They only played it on the radio in the car, do you remember?

Now, my mother is no film freak. She did not go to the movies between *Butch Cassidy and the Sundance Kid* when it first came out, and *The Sting* in the summer of 1975 (she likes Paul Newman); and it was some thirty years since she saw

---

*Harvey R. Greenberg, M.D., *The Movies on Your Mind* (New York: Saturday Review Press, E.P. Dutton & Co., 1975), p. 3.

The Very Thought of You. There I was, full of memories about Elizabeth Taylor's wearing a powder blue taffeta dress when she was Jane Powell's bridesmaid, and Jane's wearing jonquil yellow organdy when she was Elizabeth's bridesmaid. There I was, writing a book about why the movies and movie stars I had seen as a child in the 1940s had embedded themselves in me as deeply as—well, at least as deeply as "The Star Spangled Banner." And without any of my recalling, reviewing, and researching—without even trying—there was my mother, topping me. Over the past two years or so, I have talked forties movies with more people than, anymore, I can count, and in these talks, again and again, I have been topped.

There was the worldly woman who upon hearing *Gone with the Wind,*" went into its opening paragraph: "Scarlett O'Hara was not beautiful, but men seldom realized it when caught by her charm as the Tarleton twins were. In her face . . ." There was the scholar who confessed he had fled the scholar's convention for the Navy Yard because he had never gotten over the war movies of his boyhood, or playing Mr. Roberts in his high school play. There was the woman I had known for years who startled and chastened me with her virtually total recall of almost every forties movie I could name, and then some. There was the linguist who sang the songs from the forties movies of her childhood, even ones like "Put 'em in a Box and Tie 'em with a Ribbon and Throw 'em in the Deep Blue Sea" (Doris Day, *Romance on the High Seas,* 1948). And more, whose dreams—as Doris Day might sing—matched mine, and lying beside mine now, still do.

So now I know that the movies of my girlhood mattered so much not because of me but because movies were especially important to everyone in the war years of the forties. Historians tell me that it was gas rationing and blackouts that changed my mother and father from New York theatergoers to hometown New Jersey moviegoers. It was; yet in memory it seems more a foggy, suffusing fear and war "fever," a preoccupation with the war, that kept people like my parents

close to home. In *Thank Your Lucky Stars* (1943), Eddie
Cantor sang about avoiding "nonessential spending":

> We're staying home tonight
> My baby and me,
> Having a patriotic time. . . .

More than movies before or after, those of the war years
seem now to have been more memorable and more influential, because they were more of a communal rite. We went
together, we on "The Home Front," and we saw the boys being brave in battle and the women being brave at home. And
at the intermission, before the B-movie, we bought war
bonds, or at least ten-cent war stamps. (Radio was at least as
comforting, but like our television sets today, radio was in
our homes, and could not create the community of the movie
show.) After the war, as before, there were other things to
do, other calls on our time and money, a life more to live than
to escape from.

Movies also changed in the postwar years. No longer did
they represent communality, but rather the shadows and
strains of "readjustment" not entirely hidden under "the
best years of our lives." The conventions in the very conventional movies of the war years cracked in the postwar era; one
convention became unconventionality: Show a Jew
"passing"; show a Negro Pinky. . . . Where was the comfort
in that? Was *that* entertainment?

Thus, I can see now that as a child of both the wartime and
the postwar forties, my moviegoing was a social and not an
aesthetic event. I went to *the movies* first as a child attached
to parents who rationalized "suitable" films; for after my
first one *Woman of the Year* with Hepburn and Tracy when I
was six, I became an addict, begging to come along every Friday night. Later I went to the movies as a dating teenager,
one who in every generation is part of a social rite, rather
than "audience." And as an adolescent, I changed precisely
when my world changed, after the war was over, and when

movies changed as profoundly, if as secretly, as America changed.

In 1946-47, at the age of about eleven, I was allowed to go to the movies with my girl friends on Saturday afternoons. A few years later, it became Friday or Saturday night dates, and finally I could even go on holy Sunday afternoons. (Going to the movies after going to church was hard for my mother to swallow. If she had known that as soon as she did allow it, my girl friend Norma and I began skipping church, to have the collection plate money for the box office. . . .)

It was a complex ritual enacted on those predating Saturday afternoons in the small movie theater—the Rivoli—in that small New Jersey town. The boys sat in one section, the girls in another. The boys made one or two exploratory, tantalizing trips up and down the aisles ("going for candy"), then fanned out in our zone. It never went the other way. It was as unthought of that we girls go and sit with boys as that we boys and girls would do the social things we were doing—were there to do—without a movie moving along out there in front of us.

A boy was "serious" if he wanted to sit next to a particular girl. With admiration now, I recall Tommy, the object both of my love and that of my very best girl friend, Florence. One Saturday afternoon Tommy came and asked to sit between Florence and me. When his hand slipped under the arm of the seat and took mine, I was triumphant. As soon as Florence and I were alone, walking home in the winter dark after we had passed Tommy's corner, I announced, "He held my hand."

And Florence—of course—replied, "He held *my* hand."

And this went on in the dark in front of a screen full of Gene Autry or "Wild Bill" Elliot in "The Western," a serial starring Superman or Brenda Starr, the "News of the Week," previews, the B-movie, and finally the feature. I wonder now that all these moving pictures even registered, much less influenced. But, of course, they did; for as Graham Greene wrote of books and his "lost childhood,"

Perhaps it is only in childhood that books have any deep influence on our lives. In later life we admire, we are entertained, we may modify some views we already hold, but we are more likely to find in books merely a confirmation of what is in our minds already.

If Greene had been a typical child of the American forties like me, he might have added movies to books. He might even have substituted them.

In her autobiography *A Different Woman*, Jane Howard muses in awe and rue on why, at the age of thirty-six, she can still remember that Alan Ladd disliked lamb chops. In her autobiography, *Laughing All the Way,* Barbara Howar recalls her sister's birth in 1946 as a hospital crowded with war brides, all of whom looked to eleven-year-old Barbara "like Jeanne Crain, their long, wavy hair held back by pink or blue ribbons depending on the sex of the baby." To *Nabokov's Dark Cinema*, on the influence of films (mainly prewar and European) on Vladimir Nabokov, Alfred Appel, Jr., grafted a first chapter about the war movies of his American forties boyhood. The psychoanalyst Harvey R. Greenberg dedicates *The Movies on Your Mind* to his personal "affliction" from childhood, "the movies of *my* mind."

Alices. Jane Howard, Barbara Howar, the woman who recites *Gone with the Wind*, me. . . . But also Alfred Appel, Jr., Harvey R. Greenberg, the man who acted Mr. Roberts, and so on. We are all like that child of the forties, Alice, in the movie *Alice Doesn't Live Here Anymore*, who as a child is certain she can sing "You'll Never Know" better than Alice Faye does in *Hello Frisco, Hello* (1943), and as an adult learns—slowly—that she is no more Alice Faye than men are "protectors," and that that's O.K. "I'm as good as—I am," she finally says of her singing, content. After that, she can accept a man, David (Kris Kristofferson), in spite of the deep, painful, scary ways in which they differ, because he has learned to say, "I love you and I want you to be happy," and has offered something from himself. He will give up his ranch, if she wants so much to get back to Monterey. Monterey, where she was the child dreaming she was Alice Faye, Scarlett against the backdrop of burning Atlanta, and Dorothy on the yellow brick road. At the end of the movie it looks as if Alice may be forgetting Monterey and accepting the ranch and stardom in the piano bars of nearby Tucson. Maybe. Ellen Burstyn who played Alice said that the writers did not know how to end the movie, and finally took Kristofferson's suggestion, "I love you and I want you to be happy." But, she says, "we don't say definitely that they are getting married . . . . I think any way we ended it would have been partly unsatisfactory because this movie is about something we're all going through right now, and nobody knows how it's all going to end."

That last line of Burstyn's tells why her movie is my book. Alice is a child of the forties, and the movie is a parody of its fantasies, but it is a loving, respectful, complex parody, from its romantic beginning to its climax in the lovers' unromantically desperate, noisy battle and ironically shy, Dale Evans-Roy Rogers clinch in a two-bit, clinking and chattering Tucson cafe. *Alice* begins as the romances of the forties do, with its credits unfolding in lipstick-fuchsia on baby-blue satin. The soundtrack washes us in Alice Faye's "You'll Never Know," lush as baby-blue satin. The hazy orange opening scene re-creates the *Gone with the Wind* setting in which Rhett embraces Scarlett on a country road against the smoke of burning Atlanta. ("Gee, I remember that scene as the *end* of *Gone with the Wind*," says a girl child of the forties.) *Alice* re-creates *GWTW*, that is, until an eight-year-old Alice appears on the road, walking out of the infernal smoke overblown just enough for parody, and transforms *Gone with the Wind* into *The Wizard of Oz*. Until she speaks, that is, and wipes nostalgia out with, "I can sing better than Alice Faye any day. If anybody doesn't like that, they can shove it up their ass."

This is *Alice's* forties *cum* seventies opening, and Ellen Burstyn's words, " 'this movie is about something we're all

going through right now, and nobody knows how it's all going to end,' " is its seventies theme and mine. The something
we are all going through is shaping our most intimate connections, those we have with the men and women we love. At
best (*Alice* and I propose), these connections have both
equality and intimacy, but not the thorny, segregating equality of militancy, and not the intimacy of rape.

Who among us Alices did not thrill when Rhett Butler
swept Scarlett up the stairs into the dark? And in these few
years of our liberation, who among women Alices have never
felt that surge of pure rage at an injustice done us only
because we are women? Margaret Mitchell connected
Scarlett's passion when surrendering to Rhett to the "dizzy
sweet . . . cold hate" Scarlett felt when she shot the Yankee
come to rape her and Tara. Mitchell, of course, was right; the
connection is primal.

But I think we are learning that the connection is not innate. The entwining of love and hate is deeply rooted in men
and women both, and not only in children of the forties. But
from all the talks with other Alices over these past few years,
I begin to conclude, hoping it is so, that we are sloughing
Rhett and Scarlett off—and Othello, for whom love is possession, and his Desdemona, who agrees. And sloughing off the
enraged couplings that for a lot of us succeeded romance—if
Alice doesn't live here anymore, neither, it seems, do Bob,
Carol, and Ted. And finally, perhaps we are ready now to
move on from the newest confusions of "big bad wolves,"
"male buddies," or the lovely girl, born in 1951, who in
1978, cried, "Most of all, I wish I could be asexual. . . ."

Yet they are all there in our lives' passages, in Alice's as in
mine: The myths, the images, the icons, the archetypes, and
the "favorites." If that home of our childhood can be
reconstructed, that hazy home with the fog machine just off
stage and the soundtrack singing of unreachable love, then
we may know more about how to move on, and where we can
go if we leave our Montereys, our Taras. In 1959, when the
set of Tara was dismantled, David O. Selznick said, " 'Once

photographed, life here is ended. It is almost symbolic of Hollywood. Tara had no rooms inside. It was just a facade.' ''*

But Selznick was wrong. Tara was not just a facade. The dream was real and shaping, and now it is here beside us. I cannot deny it; I do not want to retreat to it. If we explore it—if we find what the Sailor Has Hidden—we may learn and cherish what we like of ourselves in it, and free ourselves from what hurts us.

*Quoted in Gavin Lambert, *GWTW: The Making of Gone with the Wind* (Boston: Atlantic Monthly Press, Little, Brown and Company, 1973), p. 216.

Acknowledgments

For permission to reproduce, I acknowledge Warner Brothers Music: "We're Staying Home Tonight (My Baby and Me)" and "Love Isn't Born (It's Made)" by Arthur Schwartz and Frank Loesser (1943), and "It's Magic" by Sammy Cahn and Jules Styne (1948); G. P. Putnam's Sons, for the excerpt from the Rosalind Russell interview in *Hollywood Speaks*! by Mike Steen (British rights: Roberta Kent, WB Agency, New York, N.Y.); and I particularly thank the T.B. Harms Company for their permission to reproduce the lyrics from "Long Ago and Far Away" by Jerome Kern and Ira Gershwin ©Copyright 1944 T.B. Harms Company. Copyright Renewed. This Arrangement ©Copyright 1974 T.B. Harms Company); and Eve Merriam for her permission to quote from her poem "The Coward," ©Copyright 1946, used in both the play and the film, *Home of the Brave*.

Fans of the 1940s movies remember Greer Garson's gregarious Academy Awards speech in 1942. I will be more restrained; but as with all works that reach for complex and deeply felt things, such as the men-women connections, there are many to thank, and more acknowledgment than can be written.

For help in the final stage of the book, I thank my editor, Ronald Roth, and the copy editor, Ellen Gordon.

Over the four years of the book's writing, I am, first, grateful to my resources for forties films, particularly to Susan Dalton, Film Archivest, and to the Wisconsin Center for Film and Theatre Research at the State Historical Society of Wisconsin in Madison, Wisconsin; and to the Library of Congress and American Film Institute and their staffs. I thank the National Endowment for the Humanities for the Summer Stipend that allowed me to work in the Library of Congress; my university, Roosevelt University, and particularly its Dean of Faculties Milton Greenberg, for nominating me for the Stipend; and the Dean of my college, Lee Porter, for his contributions in his scholarly field of adult psychology and for his friendship.

Some other colleagues contributed recommendations to the NEH grant proposal; some offered films; tapes, or information in all the fields this book touches—film, psychology, Women's Studies, popular cultural history; some read drafts. Some people from many places and times in my life were interviewed or answered my questionnaire. Some contributed bed and board and "ears" and feedback as I viewed films and wrote drafts of the book in Madison, Wisconsin; Washington, D.C.; Cape May, New Jersey; Southwest Harbor, Maine; and Chicago, Illinois. Some supported it by supporting me—with confidence, child care, typewriters on a Maine island. . . . Some made this book happen by caring about it when it was very young and, in its "trivial, nostalgic" image, not a child I planned to nurture. To you, and to strangers in airplane conversations, students in my classes, and colleagues at Popular Culture Association, Modern Language Association, Women's Studies, and film conferences, who responded to papers drawn from the book in progress, I can only offer an insufficient thank you, and the hope that you enjoy our book.

I also thank Dick Allen, Ray Browne, Ruth Carrington, John Cawelti, Priscilla Davidson, Dave Feldman, Ginny Fry, the late J. Ralph Gleason, Rosemary Hake, Dan Headrick, Garth Jowett, Stuart Kaminsky, John and Mimi Lyons, J. Fred MacDonald, Jack Metzgar, Pat Novick, Marjorie Robinson, Rob and Sherry Russell, Herman Schuchman, Anne Scott, Bernard Sherman, June Sochen, Joyce Soloman,

Joan Frech Stonesifer, John Thomas, Eleanor and Rhys Williams, and Kary K. Wolfe.

Some more must have particular thanks:

Kathrine Taylor Rood: My mentor, who, even when we are not together in Tuscanny, is always with me, as I try to write and try to be an adult.

My mother, Maria Rogstad Traynor. The book makes clear her importance to my study of films of the 1940s, but it does not reveal the care of her grandchildren, her cooking, cleaning, and other necessaries as I wrote in our home in Maine; and, more important, it does not acknowledge that without her belief in my abilities, this girl child of the 1940s probably would not have even gone to college.

Gary K. Wolfe, my colleague at Roosevelt University, who bore the drafts, and who at crucial times understood *The Dream Beside Me* better than I did.

Most of all, Joe Williams, my husband, because he was—and is—"chief parent"; and, more important, because for eighteen years he has understood my abilities, sometimes better than I.

And finally, Joe, Megan Kathrine, and Christopher Williams: my third generation. There are my father and my mother and Kathrine; there are all of us who, in the words of Ellen Burstyn in my Preface, are going through this, not knowing how it is all going to end; and there are the children, young men and young women, who we hope can learn to love.

Carol Traynor Williams
Chicago, Illinois

Introduction
Through the Fog Machine:
Views of the Forties

The content of any popular art is exactly what the whole body
of folkways makes it.
                              —an anonymous Hollywood actor[1]

Movie stars were so much more influential . . . than our
mothers and teachers were. And their values were, in many
cases, extreme opposites.
                              —an interviewee, born 1924

In *The Crucial Decade—And After: America, 1945-1960*,
the historian Eric Goldman uses the food we ate during that
period as a sign of change: less macaroni and cheese and
more meat dinners after the war than before. But Goldman
does not mention movies. Joseph C. Goulden's recent history
The Best Years: 1945-1950 is welcome because it isolates the
postwar from both the wartime forties and the Eisenhower
fifties. But except in its opening, which uses *The Best Years
of Our Lives* metonymously for the era, Goulden's book also
ignores movies. It seems still so, as Garth Jowett says in the
Preface to his *Film: The Democratic Art*, that "the importance of the motion picture as a major socializing agency . . .
has never received the serious attention it deserves, and

American social and cultural history has suffered as a result.''[2]

Recent studies, such as Jowett's and Robert Sklar's *Movie-Made America*, are important because they place movies in the social field, establishing films—those frivolous entertainments—as reflectors and shapers of American history. But in doing this, perhaps inevitably, they reduce the movies themselves to types and trends, and hence sometimes to distortions, as when Sklar writing on films of the forties, limits himself to the type of film he likes (*"film noir"*).

Psychological film studies are even less developed.[3] Back in 1916, Hugo Münsterberg published *The Photoplay: A Psychological Study,* about how the womblike atmosphere of the movie house and the fantastical ambience of "the movies" give the photoplay a unique influential power. But then, as now, movies were not taken very seriously,[4] Lenin in 1920, and Pope Pius XI in 1936, took movies seriously as influences; and in 1950, in *The Great Audience*, Gilbert Seldes, a pioneer in taking the popular arts seriously, tried to get us to ask "the new questions [that] come up" as soon as we see that our "mass media are creative"; creative, that is, not in the making of their formulaic products, but in their "influence": "They create their own audience, making people over; they create the climate of feeling in which all of us live."[5] But just as Seldes writing on the influence, and hence the responsibility of television, was an early voice in a lonely place, so was he unable to call up any study of how movies affect us, especially the young, who have always dominated the audience for movies. There is Martha Wolfenstein's and Nathan Leites' *Movies: A Psychological Study* (also 1950), and little else that is equally informed on movies and psychology.

Thus, current films study could be historical, sociological, and psychological. But until very recently, it has been almost wholly aesthetic, and particularly, *auteuristic*. To Andrew Sarris, who was typical, the stars, the stories, the ambience, and other stuff of movies that to Wolfenstein and Leites illuminate us and our culture were only "malleable material" for the film artist, who was usually the director.[6] It is not insignificant that in the later seventies Sarris has discovered the stars, and has recanted. Yet, still, little has come from Parker Tyler's call in 1947, for film studies of that which "register[s] vaguely, obliquely, unconsciously" on the "large mass," which, because it is a mass, is "critically inarticulate."[7]

This paucity of analysis is understandable. Psychological studies are not easy, or at least they should not be. Where does one find that which registered unconsciously, especially in the long ago? And how do my old, oblique registrations relate to yours? Such studies must speculate, and one must sympathize with the psychiatrist Jarl Dyrud's concern about the "reductionist quality [of] so many of [the] pseudo-explanations" coming from the contemporary "diffusion of psychoanalysis into popular culture."[8] The argument that movies are psychological and social indicators and influences is not won by speculation such as this:

> Would it be pushing the connection too far to say that depersonalized sexuality, constantly stimulated, provokes the kind of schizophrenic divorce from human reality that makes men able to become killing machines?

> The bomb dropped on Hiroshima was named Gilda.[9]

Yes, it would be pushing the connection too far; and no, the bomb was dropped on Hiroshima before the movie *Gilda* was released. It was the first atomic bomb detonated in peacetime that was named "Gilda" and decorated with Rita Hayworth's picture.

This is an unusually bad example (at least I hope it is); yet psychological movie study is prone to the unsound connection. To be informed in their speculation, social psychologists of film have to learn about—and look at—many movies, and many popular movies are as bad as Andrew Sarris thinks they are. On the other hand, these psychologists also have to understand the culture in which their artifacts were made, and in addition, they must recognize that in studying the effects of movies, they are, in the words of I.A. Jarvie, in the "classic anthropological posture of being a participant observer." Thus, as Jarvie says of his book *Towards a Sociology of the Cinema* (in America, *Movies and Society*), "on occasion, the argument is anthropological, like any other field report."[10]

Sorting the participant "I" from the observer is especially hard to do with our childhoods. Understanding how we are shaped by forces we hardly recognized is hard enough. But if we get that understanding, it is even harder to keep it pure of distortion by what we know now. Separation and synthesis have to be juggled continuously. Now, for example, it seems clear that the stalwart matriarchs in the wartime forties movies—the Mrs. Minivers—were not the Ma Joads of *The Grapes of Wrath* so much as they were Claire Boothe Luce's bitch-*Women* in patriotic refuge. But I am certain I never noticed that as a child and loving daughter. Tracing the path back to oblique and unconscious understandings is an odyssey in the fog. I did not notice this because almost no one was telling my parents, much less me. In the forties, Parker Tyler's mass had no choice but to be critically inarticulate; there were probably less than a handful of people in the country who saw anything in the movies to articulate. So far as I can tell, the first culture study to use popular movies was David Riesman's *The Lonely Crowd*, written in the late forties.[11] Those who read the few American movie critics who took movies seriously in the forties—James Agee and Manny Farber, in particular—might have seen how they were shaped, even by the B-movies. But relatively few moviegoers read Agee and Farber, and even fewer of us children did so. Who among ordinary moviegoers took seriously *Two Guys from Milwaukee* and *Till the End of Time* (1946)?

Andrew Sarris criticized Wolfenstein and Leites for resurrecting these two movies, among other "bad" popular movies. But *Till the End of Time*, a movie about the problems of war veterans, reveals 1946 America, and its stars are a representative troika of forties icons: Guy Madison, the Apollonian heartthrob; Dorothy McGuire, "Claudia," the All-American child-wife; and Robert Mitchum, the misfit and rebel in postwar America. When we compare postwar to wartime forties movies, even the musical comedy programmer *Two Guys from Milwaukee* reveals changing admirations and antipathies.

Popular movies can do this precisely because they are not intended as art. A time is revealed by its conventions; or in Lawrence Alloway's words, the "typical patterns of recurrence" and the "iconography" reveal more than "individual creativity."[12] For the conventions and patterns are the form of the myths: the formulas of a culture, reflecting its dreams, and, later, ours. In our time, the prevalent myth of the forties is something we might call the "*That's Entertainment* myth": the movie version of the larger myth that as the October 1971 *Esquire* cover announced, the forties were "the last time America was happy."

The *That's Entertainment* myth runs something along the foggy lines that forties movies all sparkled, glowed, and gripped like the *That's Entertainment* movies and Richard Schickel's TV documentary, *"You Must Remember This": Hollywood in the Forties.* These anthologies are made of entertaining and dramatic moments from many movies, strung like bright beads. In reality, as anyone who remembers the forties knows, the whole of most forties movies would have a contemporary audience squirming or stupified. We take what we need from forties movies to make the myth we need, that the forties were the last time America was happy (or we extract to create the myth that the fifties were the last "happy days," and so on).

In 1974, *Meet Me in St. Louis*, one of nostalgia's favorites from the forties, wearied my mother, me, my Margaret O'Brien-age daughter and, it seemed, everyone else in the audience. (It was an ordinary audience, mainly kids and parents, in a small-town movie house in Maine.) But neither my mother nor I remember being bored when we saw it in

1944; quite the contrary. Then, the simpler, slower-paced movies were conventional, and are my memory's favorites. The more complex, surprising, and fast-paced movies—those that most of us, including me, now prefer—were then the unconventional. There were many movies like *Meet Me in St. Louis* and *Mrs. Miniver*, and few like *The Big Sleep*, until the postwar forties when the surprises of the war years became conventional. In general, Hollywood in the wartime forties now seems reprise after reprise of Judy Garland crooning "The Boy Next Door," closeup, her eyes rounded and her eyebrows arched to make her look like a "Cover Girl," her lips so fat and Technicolor-red that it is them, not the Garland eyes, that seem to fill the screen. But then such lips looked natural—on glamour girls. Hollywood in the war years seems drenched in Margaret O'Brien's tears; yet memory and forties polls agree that in the forties Margaret O'Brien was a superstar.*

Today, wartime forties movies are hours of slipping through jungles, sifting across Saharas, slogging through Europe, and ploughing across the Atlantic or Pacific, before the excitement of slipping through the submarine nets in Tokyo harbor. They are mind-softening expanses of sun-suffering aquamarine water, and Esther Williams crawling through it, crimson-lipped, white-teethed, round-eyed, sunstruck. The Esther Williams segments of the *That's Entertainment* movies are hilariously funny to younger people—and to us who, when pressed, remember that we loved those watery holocausts when they originally erupted. When my college roommate was a child, Esther Williams was her model because she made being tall and liking to swim look glamorous. I too saw Esther Williams movies religiously, and G.I.s voted *Bathing Beauty*, the first of her epics, their favorite movie of 1943-44. But when I read James Agee now—for, of course, I did not then—I see that he viewed

*See the "Subjective Typology" of forties "Superstars," "Dependable Leads," "Blond Starlets," and others in the Appendix.

Esther Williams movies as we cynics do now. Of *Bathing Beauty*, Agee wrote,

> I could not resist the wish that Metro-Goldwyn-Mayer had topped its aquatic climax—a huge pool full of girls, fountains, and spouts of flame—by suddenly draining the tank and ending the show with the entire company writhing like goldfish on a rug.[13]

And of movie musicals of 1943 in general, Agee wrote as I do in the seventies: They "gave perhaps twenty seconds of genuine pleasure with each two hours of annihilation."[14]

But viewed only from Agee's perspective, the forties are as much distorted as if we look back with only our own, similarly glazed eyes; and they are more distorted by ignoring the movies and players who, like Esther Williams, were popular then, than by turning studio directors into *auteurs* and dependable leads such as John Wayne into icons. For it is easier to see when the present is too much with the past, than it is to learn from movies and movie players that are never mentioned. Today, I cannot imagine anyone writing about, say, *The Song of Bernadette* (1943), and ignoring the changes in values and life rhythm that make that box-office bonanza of the forties a bore now. Interpreting *Bernadette* thus might cast at least a glimmer of historical insight. But the movie is hardly ever mentioned either in film histories or general histories of the forties. Much less are the implications explored in the fact that *Bernadette* and *This is the Army* were much more popular in 1943 than *Mission to Moscow, Sahara, The Fallen Sparrow,* and *The Cat People*, all favorites of today's historians or cineasts.[15]

In its discussion of forties movies, Robert Sklar's *Movie-Made America* is entirely Sklar on *"film noir* [or] psychological thrillers": the films of Hitchcock, Fritz Lang, Robert Siodmak, Preston Sturges' comedies, and the melodramas of Bette Davis, Joan Crawford, et al. According to Sklar, these are the films of the forties that share the "feelings of claustrophobia and entrapment" that are the "hallmark" of *film noir*.[16] Perhaps so; but such feelings were not the hallmark of forties films in general, or of forties life. There was bleakness, and there were twisted psyches. There was *film noir*, and it does speak to our time. Does it matter then if the forties are implied to be all *noir*? It does.

Just as it matters that Barbara Deming's *Running Away from Myself: A dream portrait of America drawn from the films of the forties* (1969) implies that Betty Hutton's Texas Guinan film biography, *Incendiary Blonde* (1945), was an Electra movie; or that the intentionally entertaining *The Maltese Falcon* and the psychological clinker *The Chase* (Michele Morgan and Robert Cummings, 1946) had the same psychological effect as the seriously psychological hit *Pride of the Marines*. And just as it matters that histories of the forties rarely note that at the box office and in the popularity polls, Bing Crosby and Abbott and Costello always topped Bette Davis, Humphrey Bogart, and our other forties icons;[17] and that in 1946, after *To Have and Have Not* and *The Big Sleep*, Bacall and Bogart were numbers twenty-seven and twenty-eight (respectively) at the box office.

Who now looks at the B-movie for social signals and psychological effect? Yet in the forties we saw a B-movie with almost every feature, and we saw the Bs in the context of entertainment rather than uplift, because Hollywood bothered less to be patriotic about these sixty-minute programmers. Thus, however formulaic, the Bs may be the most realistic, and hence, in some ways, the most revealing of forties films; and also perhaps the most influential on us children (who favored them[18]) because we experienced them so purely.

Similarly ignored are the movies and players from what might be called the "Radio City Music Hall genre," because they often premiered at that movie palace of palaces, the talisman of hope opened in the darkest days of the Great Depression. Cherishing Ida Lupino's smoky voice and Ann Sheridan's cheery leer, we have forgotten the "Queen of Radio City Music Hall,"[19] Greer Garson. In the definitive history, *Hollywood in the Forties*, Charles Higham and Joel Greenberg dismiss Garson's movies with one word, "glutinous."[20] But in the forties Lupino and Sheridan were only dependable leads, and Garson and her consort Walter Pidgeon were immensely popular (but only during the war years[21]). In my memory they are the king and queen—more exactly, the Mother and Father—of my Hollywood youth.

Now I can see how witty Ann Sheridan is in *Thank Your Lucky Stars*, in her slinky white jersey gown and that hallmark of the forties, the snood, the chastity belt of the hair.* Surrounded by a gaggle of ingenues in this variety show for warriors and war workers, Sheridan sings Arthur Schwartz's and Frank Loesser's "Love Isn't Born, It's Made":

Love isn't born
On an April morn.
Love isn't born—
It's made.

When he says, come up
And see my antique jade,
Remember,
Love isn't born—
It's made. . . .

Each refrain of "It's made" gets a close-up cheery leer from Ann Sheridan. As a child I did not notice, nor even remember the number. But now I wonder: how could my unconscious miss that message that love and money go together?

What I did remember from the forties was Ann Sheridan, the true-blue American girl friend and wife of Ronald Reagan, the All-American boy, in *King's Row* (1941); Ann Sheridan, the patriotic war worker in *Wings for the Eagle*

---

*It is nostalgia's myth that the snood became popular because Veronica Lake, with her long blonde fall, helped safety-conscious war plant foremen promote it. But, in reality, it became popular because of *Gone with the Wind*, when, after their war was lost, Vivien Leigh and Olivia de Havilland wore snoods to plow Tara's fields.

(1942),* and the brave Norwegian Resistance fighter in *Edge of Darkness* (1943). Today these movies are as ignored as are Greer Garson and Walter Pidgeon, and it is the flag-wavers of Bette Davis, Joan Crawford, Rosalind Russell, Katharine Hepburn, Ginger Rogers, Ida Lupino, and the other movie actresses of the forties who are popular now because they looked somewhat liberated then. Ironically enough, these movies are also neglected by the most popular feminist film historians, Molly Haskell in *From Reverence to Rape: The Treatment of Women in the Movies,* and Marjorie Rosen in *Popcorn Venus: Women, Movies and the American Dream.* It may be as silly as Higham and Greenberg suggest, to cast Joan Crawford as a French partisan named Michele De La Becque in *Reunion in France* (1942),[22] or to make Katharine Hepburn a Chinese named Jade in *Dragon Seed* (1944). But the fact remains that besides Bette Davis' *Beyond the Forest,* Crawford's *Humoresque,* or any of the other "women's films" popular today, moviegoers of the forties saw more women's films about the brave nurses at Bataan, the brave WAFs in England, the brave partisans, and the brave women on the American home front.

Most of us did not grow up on a diet of *Mourning Becomes Electra* (Rosalind Russell, 1947). Many of us, like me, were not even allowed to see those "unpleasant" movies. We were nourished by Mrs. Miniver or by Irene Dunne as an American who marries a British soldier, in *The White Cliffs of Dover* (1944), the film of an improbably popular poem, *The White Cliffs.*[23] In an America listening through Edward R. Murrow et al., to England under the blitz, Alice Duer Miller's poem became popular after it was read on the radio by one of the first ladies of the theater, Lynn Fontanne; for first ladies of the theater meant more then than they do now, as did radio, slim volumes of poetry, and England.

---

*The priority of war workers' morale took Sheridan and Dennis Morgan to *Wings for the Eagle,* and away from *Casablanca,* in which they had been slated to play the roles of Ilsa Lund and Victor Laszlo. Their co-star as Rick would have been another popular actor of war heroes, Ronald Reagan.

Many of us saw, and never forgot, Bette Davis in *Watch on the Rhine* (1943); few of us saw her in *Mr. Skeffington* (1944), and if we did, we generally found it talky and boring. We grew up not only on Rosalind Russell in those boss lady roles in which she pretended to hate men, but also on her *Flight for Freedom* (1943), in which she wore beautifully flowing Jean Louis costumes and played an aviatrix and American agent modeled on Amelia Earhart, who in 1937 went down in Japanese waters, and, never found, became a legend during my girlhood. In retrospect and overview, the most liberated and capable women in forties movies look to be some of these patriotic heroines who are now generally ignored by cineasts and feminists alike. And they were the women we took most seriously—not for their costumes, but for The War, the most important thing in all our lives. Thus, it seems that Rosen, Haskell, et al. are looking at the wrong women's films for early spurs to the liberation of women in my generation. It was the schlocky, formulaic, ubiquitous propaganda pictures in which the woman was heroine instead of merely leading lady that, if anything, planted the seeds of adventure and achievement in us young girls. I can see that now; and I can see that, besides the influence of the war, a major reason why these movies were memorable is that conventional, formulaic stories are clearest to children.

I remember being baffled, and thus bored by much in *Lady in the Dark* (1944), a movie I now see as indicative of how I got to be me. In the forties I preferred Ginger Rogers' "home front" melodramas, such as *Tender Comrade* (1943) and *I'll Be Seeing You* (1944), to her "executive," her dumb lady in the dark, who psychoanalysis turns into an "enchantress." But at the time, James Agee saw *Tender Comrade* as a symptom of one of the "archetypical national diseases," the American homemaker:

A mass of women, frightening to conceive of, and the women's magazines, and the movies must have created each other mutually to belong so wholly to each other; and when you see a film such as [*Tender Comrade*] you have seen the end. What God hath joined together, let no man put asunder.[24]

To anyone who does not remember love in the forties, Agee's judgment may seem quirky; it certainly does to me now. Yet its soundness in terms of the forties is indicated by a young man of the time, Wallace Markfield, who exploring how the movies affected him in a 1967 *Saturday Evening Post* piece, " 'Play It Again, Sam'—And Again," apologizes for his feelings about those sturdy war wives and sweethearts:

> I don't mean to be vindictive. . . . [but] a lot of us have never forgiven them for being the good wives and girls named Jo who, simpering and whimpering, sent us—and Sonny Tufts—off to war.[25]

Ginger Rogers' name in *Tender Comrade* was Jo, although it was Robert Ryan, and not Sonny Tufts who she sent to the war. I have gone back to *Tender Comrade* now, and Rogers' Jo neither simpers nor whimpers. In fact, she even fights—if mildly—for her notion that "wives are a little bit smart too." That is important in seeing the forties clearly. But it is also at least as important to recognize that men of the forties found her "frightening to conceive of," and, a quarter of a century later, unforgivable.

There is a good deal more to be said about the wartime attitude of men toward their women. Veterans of World War I remember soldiers in that war favoring Prohibition to safeguard their women, and the attitude of soldiers in World War II toward the girls they left behind seems to have been similarly complex. In this introduction to looking back at the forties, I only want to say that we distort both past and present if we study the past simply through our interests and values. I doubt that in the thirties and forties, Daddy Warbucks struck even many grown-ups in the way he was portrayed in the seventies on Broadway, as a symbol of the hidden, omnipotent moneybags behind F. D. R. and the New

Deal for the common people. Nor, did we take our movies then as we take those same movies now. We did not take them as today's serious cynics or cineasts do. But, unconsciously and obliquely, we took them as seriously as one takes one's life.

It is hard enough to figure how we were influenced by Ginger Rogers' Electra in a Technicolor musical, *Lady in the Dark*. But it will be even harder if we forget that we were baffled by the Freudianism in *Lady in the Dark*, and rapt by the romance.

Notes

1. Quoted in Leo C. Rosten, *Hollywood: The Movie Colony, The Movie Makers* (New York: Harcourt, Brace, 1941), p. 351. Rosten's classic sociological study of Hollywood is partially based on over 4,000 questionnaires sent to movie producers, actors, directors, writers, editors, cinematographers, et al. Of the sixty-five actors who responded to the invitation to " 'comment on the content of American movies today,' " only two were "neutral" (fifty-one were favorable). It was one of the two neutral, anonymous actors who created that succinct definition of popular culture some thirty-five years ago.

2. Garth Jowett, for the American Film Institute. *Film: The Democratic Art* (Boston: Little, Brown & Co., 1976), p. ix.

3. There are numerous behavioral studies; that is, studies generally limited in intention and nonspeculative. "The Effect of Cinema Attendance on the Behaviour of Adolescents as Seen by Their Contemporaries" is typical. W. D. Wall and W. A. Simpson and their associates learned that movies influence the dress, hair styles, and surface behavior of thirteen to seventeen year-olds in Britain, girls more than boys. But they conclude—properly for a team of sociologists—that their statistics cannot prove a "carry-over . . . to a more subtle incorporation of ways of thinking about the self through reverie and daydreams." (*British Journal of Educational Psychology*, 1949, pp. 19, 53-61; the quotation is from p. 61.)

4. Shortly after *The Photoplay: A Psychological Study* was published, Münsterberg died. Robert Sklar, in *Movie-Made America: A Social History of American Movies* (New York: Random House, 1975), suggests that *The Photoplay* did not have the impact it should have, because of the virulent anti-Germanism of the time. (p. 125) It is interesting to speculate whether, if the popular, but German-born Harvard professor had published *The Photoplay* a few years earlier or later, psychological study of popular movies might by now have grown beyond the embryo phase. Retitled *The Film, The Photoplay* was reprinted by Dover in 1970.

5. Gilbert Seldes, *The Great Audience* (New York: The Viking Press, 1950), pp. 3-4.

6. "Pop Go the Movies," *The Primal Screen: Essays on Film and Related Subjects* (New York: Simon and Schuster, 1973), pp. 72-73; 78. Frank McConnell, *The Spoken Seen: Film and The Romantic Imagination* (Baltimore: The Johns Hopkins Press, 1975), particularly Chapter Six, makes a rare countercase for the role of movie "stars" in the aesthetic of film.

7. Parker Tyler, *Magic and Myth of the Movies* (New York: Henry Holt, 1947), p. viiii.

8. Jarl Dyrud, "Toward a Science of the Passions," *Saturday Review,* February 21, 1976, p. 26.

9. Marsha McCreadie, editor, *The American Movie Goddess* (New York: John Wiley, 1973), p. 32.

10. I.A. Jarvie, *Towards a Sociology of the Cinema: A Comparative Essay on the Structure and Function of a Major Entertainment Industry* (London: Routledge and Kegan Paul, 1970), p. xviii. The American edition is *Movies and Society* (New York: Basic Books, 1970).

11. David Riesman, *The Lonely Crowd: A Study of Changing American Values.* Abridged edition with 1969 Preface (New Haven: Yale University Press, 1973), pp. 1x-1xi. Riesman says that he was introduced to the movies as social reflections and influences by his first collaborator on *The Lonely Crowd*, Reuel Denney, who went on to write a pioneer popular culture study, *The Astonished Muse* (1957).

12. Lawrence Alloway, *Violent America: The Movies, 1946-1964* (New York: The Museum of Modern Art, 1971), pp. 12, 41. Alloway's is an historic text because in its original form, an essay in *Encounter* in 1954, it helped establish movies in particular, and popular media in general, as intellectually respectable subjects.

13. James Agee *Agee on Film: Reviews and Comments by James Agee* (Boston: Beacon Press, 1964), p. 101.

14. Ibid., p. 67.

15. Box-office figures extrapolated from *Variety,* January 5, 1944, p. 54. cols. 2-4.

16. Robert Sklar, *Movie-Made America: A Social History of American Movies* (New York: Random House, 1975), pp. 253-55.

17. In "Explaining the Choice," his introduction to *The Films of The Forties* (Secaucus: The Citadel Press, 1975), Tony Thomas at least apologizes for omitting from his 100 forties films, any movies of top-ten stars Abbott and Costello, Gene Autry, Roy Rogers, Sonja Henie, Wallace Beery, and Esther Williams. (p. 3)

18. An American Institute of Public Opinion poll in 1940 showed that whereas people over eighteen preferred single features, those between six and seventeen preferred double features. Similar polls throughout the forties showed little change. *Motion Picture Herald,* August 10, 1940, in Leo Handel, *Hollywood Looks at Its Audience: A Report of Film Audience Research* (Urbana: University of Illinois Press, 1950), p. 131.

19. In February 1946, the Radio City Music Hall crowned Garson its "Queen," in honor of her seven Music Hall movies, which had run for a total of fifty-four weeks and played to more than eight million people. *Variety,* February 13, 1946, p. 55.

20. Charles Higham and Joel Greenberg, *Hollywood in the Forties* (New York: Paperback Library, 1970), p. 172.

21. For both Garson and Pidgeon, stardom began only with *Blossoms in the Dust* (1941), and superstardom after *Mrs. Miniver (Variety* used *Mrs. Miniver* as its example in a story on how to sell wartime starless movies: 22 July 1942, p. 5, col. 3) But after the Minivers of England became a timely symbol of true and family grit, Garson entered the top ten box-office stars, and Pidgeon was picked the favorite of *Women's Home Companion* readers polled in 1945 (reported in "Inside Stuff," *Variety,* May 30, 1945, p. 25). But their superstardom ended with the end of the war. She was Clark Gable's leading lady in his home-from-the-war vehicle, *Adventure* (1946), but it proved less memorable than its poster line, "Gable's Back! And Garson's Got Him!''; and a Pidgeon and Garson reunion in *Julia Misbehaves* (1948) was overshadowed by the beauty of their daughter, the sixteen-year-old Elizabeth Taylor.

22. Higham and Greenberg, *Hollywood in the Forties,* pp. 101-2.

23. Alice Duer Miller, *The White Cliffs* (New York: Coward-McCann, 1940). See William Manchester, *The Glory and the Dream: A Narrative History of America, 1932-1972* (Boston: Little, Brown & Co., 1973), Vol. 1, 263, on the popularity of *The White Cliffs.*

24. Agee, *Agee on Film,* pp. 90-91. The categorization, one of the "archetypical national diseases," is on p. 27, in Agee's review of *The Powers Girl* (1942), one of the several forties movies about the era's symbol of beauty, the fashion model.

25. *Saturday Evening Post,* Vol. 240, April 22, 1967, p. 75.

The Dream Beside Me

1
One or Two Alicias: The Role of Women in the Forties

Our marriage was headed for the rocks the minute she began
to write.

—*Old Acquaintance*, 1943

In *Lady in the Dark* (1944), Ginger Rogers plays a
magazine editor who is successful but unhappy. So she goes
to an analyst (Barry Sullivan), who concludes,

> You have to dominate all men. You have to prove to them
> that you're superior to them.
>
> *Liza* (Rogers): What's the answer?
>
> *Dr. Brooks:* (Sullivan) Perhaps some man who will
> dominate you.

And the picture's conclusion is the same as the analyst's. Liza
gives both her editorship and her hand to a dominating man,
her advertising manager.[1]

Analysis frees Liza from her compulsion to dominate men.
(It reveals to her that as a child she felt rejected by her

father.) Now, free, Liza takes up with a supremely macho movie star, Randy Curtis (Jon Hall), but she rejects him when he confides that he is "frightened and insecure inside." Today this seems a humanizing and liberating moment, but is was not made that way in the forties. In a dream near the end of the movie, the advertising manager, Charley Johnson (Ray Milland), sings Liza her dilemma: she must choose between being "the executive or the enchantress." (He really does *sing* that.) Liza's dream ends when she proclaims her choice: "I'm through with the magazine. I'm going to live my life as a *woman*." In this split between executives and enchantresses, and in the assumption that sexual relationships depend on domination, *Lady in the Dark* now seems a touchstone for the wartime forties love story.

It seemed that touchstone when, in 1976, the new star of *One Flew Over the Cuckoo's Nest*, Louise Fletcher, was interviewed. For some ten years before making *Cuckoo's Nest*, Louise Fletcher said, she had retired from acting in order to be a wife and mother, and all that time she had felt that " 'love' " only happened to her when she did things: " 'If my cake recipe failed, I felt like a failure.' " Only after " 'the women's movement came seeping through my pores, not my head,' " she said, did she " 'take the risk' "; and now, at the age of forty-one: " 'What a relief it is to find someone loves me for myself; not for what I do for him.' "[2]

What Louise Fletcher then said may reveal why it took her so long to free herself from the " 'built-in habit of performing for a man.' " At the age of eleven, she said, she saw the movie that made her want to be an actress:

> "I went to see Ginger Rogers in 'Lady in the Dark' and stayed in the movie house from 1 in the afternoon until 11 at night. I never left my seat. I never ate. I was paralyzed.

> "Although I knew the film had a tremendous impact on me, it wasn't until I was 28 that I really realized what it was about.

"Ginger Rogers plays a bitchy, uptight fashion editor who dreams out her fantasies, but her dreams are the opposite of what she appears to be in real life.

"I learned then that your life can appear to be one way to the people around you, when in reality it is quite the opposite."

Thus did Louise Fletcher learn to live the two-faced life, the lie by a sweet and sacrificial name that almost all women learn, and like Louise Fletcher, almost always with the help of Hollywood's romances. Fletcher's interview suggests no connection between *Lady in the Dark* and her grown-up life, which even in success, she calls a matter of "trying to cope with the problems of playing so many roles in life."

* * * * * * * * * *

"Joe, Where Was the Empire State Building in the Last Picture?"
or
". . . A Lot of Cheap Orders"

In the popular films of the forties the good life for good women was marriage, babies, and the "Home Beautiful."[3] For the ingenue, the right road was virginity, devotion to Mr. Right, patience if he dated a vamp, and oceanic understanding when he came to his senses. As late as January 1950 (and it could have been 1960), *Ladies Home Journal* advised young men not to attempt a kiss until at least the third date;[4] and reading that now, I recall that, yes, in my teenage years in the early fifties, the Third Date was as gospel as the Second Coming, and not much less important. A kiss was not only to build a dream on; it could create a crisis, and maybe even a catastrophe. A daughter's mother and father regularly translated a kiss into "making love," just as Janet's Mom and Pop did when she dated Dave, the handsome flyer (Eleanor Parker, Beulah Bondi, Henry Travers, and Dennis

Morgan in *The Very Thought of You*). At its zenith, a kiss could make a woman marry a man she did not "love," as in *Gone with the Wind*, when Rhett's burning kisses warm cold-hearted Scarlett to say yes, because she is tipsy.

Nor did all this virtue accrue only to the virgins. It characterized the matron as well, and even the lady executives. In *Tender Comrade*, Ruth Hussey plays a war wife whose husband flirted before the war, and, after he went to sea did not write her. Even so, when she makes a date with another man, she is roundly shamed by Ginger Rogers and their other housemates. No more leeway was given those sophisticated career women in their glamorous Jean Louis peplums and padded shoulders. It was *It Happened One Night* and the blankets between the beds all the way. The strongest boss ladies portrayed by Crawford, Colbert, Russell, et al, invariably ended up in the arms of Melvyn Douglas, John Wayne, or Fred MacMurray, vowing that it was better to be dominated than to dominate. In *Lunatics and Lovers*, Ted Sennett judges accurately that the " 'feminist' attitude [in career girl pictures] was really a sham: the 'liberated' lady . . . was obliged to reveal the femininity behind her iron corset and truculent manner."[5] But the contemporary feminist myth is that the career-women films of the forties were, as Marjorie Rosen says in *Popcorn Venus,* "ground breaking." Rosen says, "The film form did not forsake love as its central point of conflict, but oftentimes self-awareness, professional élan, and romance could exist side by side with the female as the healthy protagonist, the male as the needy one."[6] *Variety* put it more succinctly, reviewing Crawford and Melvyn Douglas' *They All Kissed the Bride* in 1942 as another in the "cycle of girl-immersed-in-biz vs. irresponsible mate."[7]

The implication that "healthy" women and "needy" men are model lovers needs exploring. But, first, it should be noted that these boss ladies are not strong. They are only stronger than weak men—until the finale when they suddenly capitulate to these dippy Milquetoasts and deflate the whole film. Or so it seems now. At the time, this was the happy ending we expected—and if romantic truth be told, still do. It is all summed up by Molly Haskell's description of Irene Dunne's *Together Again* (1944):

> . . . Irene Dunne's strength as the mayor of a small town alternates with her love for artist Charles Boyer, without the two elements either conflicting dramatically or coalescing. As mayor, she is effective and obviously happy, but Charles Coburn, playing the father of her dead husband, fears that she will lose her femininity in so authoritative a position, and with it her chances of remarriage. When he advises her to quit, she scoffs at his male egocentricity. "You're one of a dying race,"* she tells him. "Women can live perfectly well without men. But you're terrified of the idea that they can. If you lose your emotional power over women, you're lost." But it is to precisely that emotional power that she surrenders when, in the end, she forsakes her mayoralty to go off with Boyer.[8]

Actually, it is worse than Haskell says: Dunne's job and love do conflict dramatically; Boyer makes her choose. And by the end, a movie that by today's values began so promisingly (it was produced by Virginia Van Upp, one of the few women producers in the forties), associated everything connected with Dunne as mayor of Brookhaven, Vermont, with hypocrisy, repression, and bleakness, and associated everything about the French sculptor from New York, Boyer, with liberty, honesty, and gaiety. And the movie achieves this by using the romantic conventions so cleverly that I defy the most militant feminist to root against Boyer getting Dunne to do it his witty way.

Similarly, watching *Without Reservations* (1946) today, I still root for John Wayne. The only difference is that today I view myself as a snake facing the mongoose—or is it the other way around? In any case, it is shameful; for in *Without Reservations*, the man's man Marine Wayne tops the egghead

---

*The actual line is "You're a vanishing race."

who wrote a "progressive" postwar best-seller about One World, (Claudette Colbert). Wayne defends the pioneers who wiped out the nasty Indians and filled out no forms for Washington afterwards, but just looked at the big sky and, according to John Wayne, said, " 'Thanks, God, I'll take it from here." At the end, when Colbert gives up her ideas and wins Wayne with feminine wiles, she looks up at the ceiling of her Hollywood mansion and says—yup—"Thanks, God, I'll take it from here." Shameful.

The career-women films of the forties were summed up by Rosalind Russell, the first lady of forties boss ladies, in her interview published in *Hollywood Speaks! An Oral History.* Russell describes the endings of her twenty-three boss lady roles: "Finally, I settle down in a mosquito-ridden cottage with Fred MacMurray or Ray Milland in New Jersey." This interview bears reading by anyone who subscribes to the myth about ground-breaking career women in forties movies.

Russell: . . . The opening shot was always an air shot over New York. Then it would bleed into my suite of offices on the fortieth floor of Radio City. I would have the same desk and the same side chairs and bookcases. Out the window behind me was always a view of the Empire State Building, in order to identify the setting. I used to say to [cameraman] Joe Walker, "Joe where was the Empire State Building in the last picture?" which had only been a couple of months before. He would say, "I had it a little to the left." I'd say, "Well, this time throw it over on the right." Then I would say, "Blackie, how many telephones did we have last time?" He'd say, "You had about nine." So I'd say, "Well, throw in thirteen. This will be a big double *A* picture!" I would always open with about the same dialogue, give a lot of cheap orders.

During this era, I was invited to give a speech in San Francisco at the Business Women of America convention. . . . I was as nervous as I could be. I thought, "Well, for heaven's sake, say something you know a little about. . . ." So I thought, "Well, I'll talk about the career women." I said, "You go to nice offices, but I have one that's on the fortieth floor of the Radio City Music Hall Building! How many phones do you have? Two, three, four? I have twelve! And, I have an all-male staff who sit there as I give my orders. Fred MacMurray has been sitting there all that time with his hat down over his eyes. I spot him and say, 'Have you been listening to this meeting? Who are you? He says, 'I'm from the press.' Then I go out to have lunch with him. Then we go to my penthouse. I never do get back to the office. He says to me, 'You're really a wonderful woman underneath all this brashness, this executive ability of yours.' I sort of push him aside, and then I go to Europe .... I also go, later on, to my resort home, which is in the Adirondacks or Southampton. Finally, I settle down in a mosquito-ridden cottage with Fred MacMurray or Ray Milland in New Jersey. I don't know why you women work the way you do because. ..." I gave them plenty of laughs. ...

[interviewer]: When you married Frederick Brisson in 1941, your own career was not interrupted?

Russell: Well, it made a great difference in my planning of my life. Although Metro wanted me to sign another long-term contract, I said no. I wanted to free-lance because I wanted to have a family. I sure failed there with only one son, but a larger family was our intention. When a professional woman such as myself marries, you have to make the decision whether your marriage and family is first or second. My decision was that my family would come first regardless.[9]

Brilliant in her analysis of the conventions of her boss lady films, as herself (talking about addressing the "impress[ive]" women, or about her marriage and family), Rosalind Russell is blindly conventional, the stereotype forties woman.

"Go Ahead and Laugh . . ."

It seems appropriate, then, that the movie *Dance, Girls, Dance* was released in the first year of the forties. It just may be the last movie made before *Singin' in the Rain* (1952) even to hint that it was alright for the heroine to want a career as much as she wants the hero. *Dance, Girls, Dance* is a cult movie now because it was directed by Dorothy Arzner, the only woman director of the thirties and forties. Too young to see it in the forties, I initially found this movie disappointing when I saw it in the seventies, as I did all the favorites of today's feminists. I then realized that I knew these movies differently, and hence asked too much of them, and of women who, because they did not remember the forties, were unrestricted in seeing themselves in my real old movies.

Dance, Girls, Dance is only a 1940 R.K.O. programmer starring "shaky A" players Maureen O'Hara, Lucille Ball, and Louis Hayward. But although it is no exposé of American lust, it does have some bitter close-ups of the audience at the "burley" watching Judy O'Brien (O'Hara), the serious dancer who hates degrading herself, and some even more powerful close-ups of Lucille Ball, who plays Bubbles *cum* Tiger Lily White, who relishes being a sex object. It also has a haunting image, symbolic of "woman's role," and symbolically, this is the fade-out image in the film.

All the complications of the soap opera plot have been resolved. The heroine, Judy O'Brien, is at last secured in the arms of her hero, producer Steve Adams (Ralph Bellamy). Now that she has chosen him over the charming wastrel Jimmy Harris (Louis Hayward), Adams promises her stardom. And not only stardom but—marriage. "Go ahead and laugh, Judy O'Brien," nice guy Steve Adams says, holding her. The final frame is a close-up of her face against his chest.

But it is not a laughing face we see. It is remarkably subtle and complex (especially for Maureen O'Hara). The eyes are shadowed by the pain of love for the wastrel Jimmy from the upper class; her Bubbles, the friend from the old, poor days, hardened now by greed; for the dedicated dancing teacher played by Maria Ouspenskaya, run over by a New York bus early in the movie. The eyes are shadowed by degradation, whole burleys-ful of degradation. Yet the mouth is tentative, tempted to believe. It seems now a symbolic face of the forties, a time when the few liberated gestures were regularly belied by love-and-marriage endings and close-ups of pretty faces starry-eyed with dreams inevitably not of dancing but of serving in marriage.

Now I can see that, compared to later forties films, *Dance, Girls, Dance* offered at least shadowy respect for Judy O'Brien's career. A more typical forties movie is my childhood favorite *Cover Girl* (1944). In a good print still a dazzling dream of russet Rita Hayworth hair, perfect Cover Girl faces, gigantic red lips, wind-machine-blown chiffon, peacock, fuchsia, dubonnet, and electric blue . . ., it is so high, it is camp for seventies audiences, like the Busby Berkeley ramps from a white-clouded, sparkly-starred heaven, which, along with almost every other forties convention, *Cover Girl* appropriated. Its story also looks different now from the romance I remember of Rusty Parker (Hayworth) and Danny McGuire (Gene Kelly), in which he knew better than she did that she would not be happy as a Broadway star, but only as a dancer in his Brooklyn "jernt."

Now, and in large part thanks to that new, triumphant Technicolor, Hayworth's Rusty looks like the most beautiful girl in the world; also, a great dancer, and as nice as can be besides. But instead of winning stardom *and* happiness, Rusty is punished for being ambitious, and what is worse, more successful than Danny. In *Dance, Girls, Dance*, Judy O'Brien is at least given that last close-up. In *Cover Girl*, stardom brings Rusty to the brink of ruin: drunkenness (cute drunkenness, of course); hysteria: "This is what I wanted for me all my life—*isn't it*? (Voice rising and cracking on the final two words); and humiliation: the scorn even of Pop the night watchman, the God figure in show biz movies. Only after all this purgatory, and on the very verge of marrying a scion (Lee Bowman), is Rusty released, worthy at last to fulfill what everyone from Pop down in her life has decreed as her obligation: to love Danny the failure because he loves her. And with Danny, even though they are "out of the money," she is all dazzling Rita Hayworth smiles. "I feel," she says, "as if I belong." I loved that movie as a child.

Old Acquaintance (1943), a Bette Davis, Miriam Hopkins, and John Loder triangle, is a generally forgotten forties "woman's film." For me, it is another childhood favorite as newly ironic now as *Cover Girl.* For by the assumptions of the forties, Miriam Hopkins' Milly is a shallow, insensitive model of what a woman should not be. But by the feminist tenets of the seventies, Milly is a heroine. Inspired by her best friend Kit Marlowe (Davis), Milly, whose besetting flaw is envy, sets out to be a writer. Davis is a "serious" writer; but Milly, writing the potboiler romances that, as she says blithely, "people want," becomes rich and famous, so famous that an interviewer (Anne Revere), chancing upon Milly's husband Preston Drake (Loder) can ask, "Oh, do you work too?"

Milly revels in her money. As she returns from a shopping spree with gifts for both Kit and Preston, she resists Kit's disapproval, shouting happily, "I'm a very successful woman and I'm rich." We are supposed to take this as evidence of Milly's wrong-headedness; but by today's feminist standards, hers is the healthiest character in the film. Ironically, it is Davis—our very symbol of liberated womanhood—who scolds Milly for unmanning her husband by succeeding, and who cares for Preston and Milly and Preston's daughter Deidre, while Milly is off writing in Mexico. It is also Davis who sacrifices Preston, the man she loves who loves her, because Milly is her friend:

Kit: There are things that you just don't do if you want to live with yourself afterwards.

Preston: You mean that your friendship for Milly is greater than your love for me?

Kit: I know there are some things a man can't understand, but. . . .

And finally, in the last segment of the film, the middle-aged and still spinster Davis sacrifices her young love, Gig Young—to Deidre.

There is one small suggestion in the picture that Davis' sacrifices are other than heroic. When Loder asks her why she puts up with his wife, she tells him that her childhood was bleak enough that she clung to Milly's "perfect" family life. The implication there that Milly's model, Kit, is fundamentally the more dependent, has a great deal of potential for complex character development.* But how could such complexity stand a chance against the conventions of the wartime forties and the images of its stars? These alone virtually assured that the ordinary moviegoer would see Davis' sacrifices as noble, and thus that the moviemakers would not go far in hinting otherwise.

Davis' image was ridiculed even in the forties, but watching her in *Old Acquaintance* in the seventies—walking across a darkened, late-night hotel lobby to meet Loder and reject him, a fox jacket over a long black gown, touching her short, bobbed hair, smoking as only she smoked—I am awestruck, convinced now of the cliché I recall from our mothers: "there is no one like her." How could anything she did in a movie be other than heroic? It is less Davis' Kit Marlowe than Miriam Hopkins' Milly who should be our model in *Old Acquaintance*. But what chance has Hopkins' Milly against the Davis image? And now I also wonder if at some deep, very oblique level of consciousness, Davis did not convey that a woman could have ideas and still be attractive, could live by a personal, sometimes even an unpopular conviction, and still be glamorous. A man old enough to have been an adolescent in the early forties says that Bette Davis is the only woman movie star of the time who comes to mind as having been of the "caliber" of his favorites, Cagney, Bogart, Errol Flynn,

---

*It is interesting that in the play *Old Acquaintance*, Kit merely tells of her childhood adoration of Milly's family, and Milly, in turn, reveals that when they were children, she envied Kit's family life. Thus, John Van Druten, who with Lenore Coffee, adapted his play to the screen, added the note of Kit's dependency to the movie. Or did Lenore Coffee?

Cary Grant, Tyrone Power, and Edward G. Robinson: stars who had "tremendous impact, fuller careers and could carry pictures handily." Indeed, she had that power—in the forties, a "masculine" power—to do it her way, strongly, and still be attractive. Yet, it was so subliminal. On the surface she was always Kit Marlowe. It seems that this lady who sacrificed so abjectly in her forties films is admired as extravagantly as she is by today's feminists because they are as blinded by images as were we ordinary fans of the forties.

We are prone to this blindness about movies and television shows and similar things which "don't really matter," and which we do not analyze as we do wars and viruses. In *Popcorn Venus*, for example, Marjorie Rosen sees Ingrid Bergman in *Spellbound* (1945) as a positive role model for working women.[10] (Bergman plays a psychiatrist who cures Gregory Peck of amnesia, a guilt complex, and a murder conviction.) I also remembered Bergman in *Spellbound* as a capable, in-control professional. I wondered: might this be the popular film of the forties that showed a woman respected as an equal among men? But when I reviewed *Spellbound*, as with other films of my childhood, I found in those oblique shadows something more complex than either my memories or current myths have it.

Thus, in *Spellbound*, Bergman's colleagues are less interested in Dr. Constance Petersen's expertise than they are intrigued by the question of when Constance "the glacier" will unfreeze. After she does fall for Peck, her colleagues have only scorn for her, for mixing feelings with psychoanalysis. There is something to be said for their scorn. On the other hand, her treatment of Peck is proved correct, and, in her showdown with her colleague the killer (Leo G. Carroll), she is as cool as Gary Cooper when, with Carroll's gun on her, she walks across and out of the room, psychoanalyzing as she goes why he will not shoot her. On the other hand, her role of a psychiatrist who jumps back and forth between smooching with Peck and analyzing him could not have done much to recommend women to the profes-

The Role of Women in the Forties

sion. On the other hand, her Dr. Constance Petersen is an iconoclast, unbending before the scorn of her colleagues. On the other hand, the movie ends with smooching, and the impression that it was only Bergman's love for Peck that gave her insight and courage. But, finally, is a meld of love and our minds not the goal?

Notorious (1946) suggests even more a comparison of Bergman with the present Amazons of forties "strong women," Bette Davis, Joan Crawford, Rosalind Russell, et al. As a career model, Bergman is generally as ambiguous as her Dr. Constance Petersen (what does Ilsa do for a living while she and Rick are having their idyll in Paris?) But I wonder now if she may not have shaped us children in another area in which, consciously or not, girls and boys adopt models, the area of sexuality. Looking over the field, I wonder if Bergman was not even unique among forties movie actresses in being this positive sexual influence. Except perhaps for Bacall.

Until I saw *Notorious* in the midseventies, I remembered Bergman and Cary Grant's long kiss around the telephone, that kiss which in 1946 was touted as censor bait, as intensely and mutually realistic. Not so. It is only Bergman who acts aroused, and—another surprise for a forties movie—she is startlingly erotic: open-mouthed, touching, moving, breathy, warm, whereas Grant is close-mouthed, rigid. At least partly, this may be because of his role, a common one in the forties, in which he is required to distrust her. He is a stalwart American undercover agent and she is a loose woman, the daughter of a Nazi, drinking heavily and consorting with unsavories. But, since the plot has him falling for her, he should have unbent a little around the telephone.

Cary Grant never unbent. I would never have thought that; I had never questioned the Cary Grant image until I reviewed *Notorious*. But now I see that not once in any love scene—and I have looked at a lot of them since *Notorious*—did Cary Grant give. To Pauline Kael he is "the male love object" and "the most publicly seduced male the world has known," and that is the Grant image. For Kael, Grant's reserve is exciting, "sex with mystery," and according to her, he is the catalyst of Bergman's sexuality: "She was never again as sexy as in that famous scene in 'Notorious' . . . ."[11] But, *chacun* . . .; I cannot cite, and in my conversations I cannot find anyone who can cite, an aroused Cary Grant love scene (not even in *Every Girl Should Be Married* [1948] with his new young bride Betsy Drake). To men as well as women of the forties (and before and after), Grant seems to epitomize "class." One man with whom I talked said that Cary Grant was his model of models because Grant was handsome, and in his wit and grace, "beyond sex." Watching Grant with Katharine Hepburn in *Holiday* (1938) and *The Philadelphia Story* (1940) is particularly spooky, because she seems his counterpart in good looks, wit, grace, and asexuality. No one, it seems, wants to argue that Bergman did not also have class. But she seems to have more of it because she was also sexual. Unlike Grant and Hepburn, Bergman fills her part in a love story with promise. Let me define: class and sexuality together equal sensuality; and this sensuality seems now, among forties movie actresses, unique in Bergman. Nor is it that common in men. Given a romantic story and the right partner, Humphrey Bogart can be sensual in the way Bergman is. He is sensual in *Casablanca,* and Kael, when she labels Bergman's sexiness in *Notorious* unique, ignores her Ilsa. Bergman's Alicia Huberman in *Notorious* differs only in the details from Ilsa Lund. Both women appear unfaithful to the men they love, but are in reality ideally warm and true forties women. Thus, *Notorious* suggests a key to the "classic" *Casablanca*. Skeptical though he may be of her virtue, rigid though he tries to be, Bergman's lover in *Casablanca* responds to her sexually.

In *Movies: A Psychological Study,* Martha Wolfenstein and Nathan Leites draw a revealing analogy when they point out that the plots of Hollywood love dramas of the forties often turn on "toning down" a vamp's sexiness, whereas the plots of the forties comedies are busy about "infusing sex" into characters played by Irene Dunne, Claudette Colbert, June Allyson, and others who appear as if they haven't got "too much."[12] The antithesis may be more obvious when the vamp is Rita Hayworth's Gilda, rather than Bergman's subtle Ilsa or Alicia. But it is just as real: it seems that Bergman would have smiled away all those conventions that kept Irene Dunne preening down her too-long nose at Charles Boyer. A question like this cannot be answered with certainty, but I wonder now if Bergman did not teach us subliminally that the answer to how to be a happy woman lay neither in the vamp's aggressive hardness nor in that of the career woman, nor in the opposite: the negative hardness of an all-enduring Ma, matriarch of the American "Home Beautiful." Did Bergman teach us instead that loving sexuality is the ideal? Did she teach us that the humanistic values of dignity and integrity ("class") could, and should, be melded with sexuality?

Perhaps. But if she did project this positive image of a sensual woman to nice girls like me, she did it against odds. Children are not keen to subtleties (although they may be unconsciously); and sensuality is not sensual unless it is subtle. And in addition, Bergman was not generally one of our "favorites." It is hard to keep in mind now, but *Casablanca* was her first hit. After her American debut in *Intermezzo*, in 1939, she was third lead behind Spencer Tracy and Lana Turner in *Dr. Jekyll and Mr. Hyde* (1941), and made two other lesser features: *Rage in Heaven* and *Adam Had Four Sons* (both 1941). How many who admire her so in *Casablanca* remember what a surprise she was originally? In his "Introductory Note" to Howard Koch's *Casablanca: Script and Legend*, the late Ralph J. Gleason wrote, "Bergman, well, all she had to do was to let those eyes fill with tears and the world was at her feet"; and *"Casablanca* was the film of my generation's youth, just as Bogart was the man and Ingrid Bergman the woman."[13] I should not dispute Ralph Gleason's memories, but it was an adult who wrote his fan note from hindsight. In the forties, Bergman toiled in *For Whom the Bell Tolls* (1943), *Gaslight* (1944), *Spellbound,*

Saratoga Trunk (released in 1945 but made in 1943), and was most popular playing a nun opposite Bing Crosby's Father in *The Bells of St. Mary's* (1945). After *Notorious*, her postwar movies were disappointments: *Arch of Triumph* (1948), *Under Capricorn* (1949), and even *Joan of Arc* (1948), after a hit on Broadway the year before in Maxwell Anderson's *Joan of Lorraine*. It was a string of embarrassments that probably left her ripe for the novel postwar Italian realist director Roberto Rossellini. In the forties no one was at Bergman's feet, like all actors and actresses at the studios, she was only as good as her last picture.

To us girls especially, she seemed nondescript. She was not an out-of-reach superstar, such as Bette Davis or Greer Garson, but neither was she young enough, or American enough, to play our ingenues. Nor did she look like the conventional forties glamour girl. We valued beauty above everything in a woman (except, of course, virtue), and by forties standards, Bergman was not beautiful. Men who were grown then seem generally to recall her as "good-looking," although, if they were youthful G.I. Joes, not with the enthusiasm they remember Betty Grable, Esther Williams, et al. But a man who was a teenager in the war years recollects Bergman as "big and bovine," and a woman who was a child then says,

> The fan magazines told us that Bergman never wore makeup—not even lipstick—and instead of being impressed favorably by that piece of intelligence, I was appalled: How could anyone be glamorous without fire-red lipstick? And if anybody needed it, it was surely that dumb old Bergman who had an icky nose and fat lips.

This same woman found Bergman compelling when both were older. "After seeing *Aimez-Vous Brahms?* 1961), I began to play Bergman myself," she says. "I was scared to be forty until I saw her and discovered that it was not only okay to be that old, but that it also carried a lot of advantages."

Today, we can see Bergman's films of the forties as a *corpus*, and it seems that Ilsa, Hemingway's Maria, Cleo in

Saratoga Trunk, Alicia Huberman, and the other Bergman women could have communicated a subliminal message to girls like me, the opposite of what we were getting from our mothers, ministers, and magazines: the vital information that honest, enjoyed sexuality should be one of our ideals. If Bergman did convey this message, even a little, perhaps she countered all those boss ladies who started out strong, ended up servient, and were sexless all along the way.

Good-Tough Girls

After I discovered Bergman in *Notorious* in 1975, I began to wonder if there were others like her, forties movie actresses who might have shaped our sexuality before we knew we had it. For the record—since this (like Cary Grant) must be a matter of taste—I find no other Bergman, although I cannot wholly dismiss Lauren Bacall. Other critics, such as Pauline Kael in her *New Yorker* profile of Cary Grant and Marjorie Rosen in *Popcorn Venus*, have rated the sensuality of forties actress. Kael could find none, granting Bergman only a "deep, emotional" voice.[14] But Rosen's candidates—Bergman in *Casablanca*, Jennifer Jones in *Duel in the Sun* (1946), Bacall, Ann Sheridan, Hayworth, and Hedy Lamarr[15] are at least candidates, unlike Kael's sitting ducks, Joan Crawford, Katharine Hepburn, Irene Dunne, and Myrna Loy. Lamarr, Sheridan, and Hayworth, along with Dorothy Lamour, Veronica Lake, Paulette Goddard, Betty Grable, and the others, listed in the "Subjective Typology" as "Sultry 'Face' Pinups" or "Ladies—but" may have been beautiful, wholesomely attractive, or even sexy. But were any of them sensual; that is, suggestive of sexuality as a human value?

Marlene Dietrich was openly sexual, and perhaps even sensual to a limited number of Americans, but at least to American girls, she was alien, as alien as the assumptions in *The Blue Angel*, which few of us saw in the forties. As

Pauline Kael wrote in a recent review of Dietrich's *Dishonored* (1931), "she seems always to come from another planet, and to be the only inhabitant of it."[16] Patricia Neal had enough class and mature sexuality in Ayn Rand's *The Fountainhead* (1949) to overcome perhaps the most immature "adult" love story ever written. But this seems mainly because she and her co-star, Gary Cooper, were falling in love as they made the film. Jennifer Jones looks now like the warmest of the virgins, promisingly sensual in her ingenue parts in *Since You Went Away* (1944), *Love Letters* (1945), *Portrait of Jennie* (1948), and others. But in *Duel in the Sun*, with the promise exposed, Jones is embarrassing. (Later, she appears sensual in her lady roles, as in *Love Is a Many-Splendored Thing*, [1955], and *The Man in the Gray Flannel Suit* [1956]. But again, as in the forties, the image is tainted by embarrassing sexpots such as *Ruby Gentry* [1952]. Finally, in the late forties, Ava Gardner's loving could be every bit as cheerfully sexy as Bacall's with Bogart, especially when Gardner had Gable (*The Hucksters* (1947); *Lone Star* (1952); *Mogambo* (1953). But, at least in the forties, neither Gardner nor Bacall, much less Hayworth or Jennifer Jones, was ever the sexual *lady* Bergman was. And we were girls taught to "try to be ladies," not vamps.

Like everyone else, Bacall had less class than Bergman, and a cooler, more androgynous, more "seventies" kind of sexuality. Or so it seems now. Her screen roles and her not-very-private life as Bogart's woman, both of which began in 1944, give her the image of a forties good tough girl, like Ava Gardner but more refined, classier, and hence homier. At the time, Bacall was no more a model than Bergman, at least consciously. But watching her now with Bogart in *To Have and Have Not* (1944), *The Big Sleep* (1946), *Dark Passage* (1947), and *Key Largo* (1948), the girl I remember almost not at all in those often confusing, always dreary melodramas, is witty and resilient, loyal, resourceful, courageous, and sensual, in complex, seventies kind of movies. In her movies without

Bogart, such as *Confidential Agent* (1945; Charles Boyer), she was panned, and rightly; she was an amateur.

Marjorie Rosen and other feminists see the career girls in forties films as ground-breaking, and I have suggested that the patriot roles may have been even more influential. In *The Popular Arts*, Stuart Hall and Paddy Whannel add another model, the "black thriller," which, they say, is one of the few genres in forties film in which the heroine "achieved anything like equality with the hero." But their only examples of the genre, (which is familiar to film noir,) are *To Have and Have Not* and *The Big Sleep*, and as they concede, their argument depends on the assumption that the Bogart-Bacall relationship is special and irrelevant either to the characters that Bogart and Bacall play or to the plots of these "conventional . . . private-eye film[s]."[17] At least *The Big Sleep* has more going for it then just the Bogart-Bacall relationsip vitalizing the formula. Yet there seems no doubt that this relationship has a great deal to do with the popularity of these films—now. It is easy to overstate, as Joan Mellen does in *Big Bad Wolves: Masculinity in the American Film:*

> Bogart and Bacall carry off what Marlon Brando and . . . Maria Schneider fail to achieve in *Last Tango in Paris* (1973): an experience in the present, free both of the legacy of personal repression and of the varieties of social oppression that distort people and make their interactions so painful. Bogart and Bacall do indeed "come without touching," as Brando and Schneider had put it. . . .

Bogart would have been embarrassed.

Still, Mellen does well to highlight the closing exchange between Bogart and Bacall in *The Big Sleep:*

Bogart: "What's wrong with you?"
Bacall: "Nothing you can't fix."

And she does well to add that "What is striking is here is that this is true in every sense. . . . They face each other with no need for the obligatory kiss, and the film is over." In the forties, none of Bogart's and Bacall's movies was that popular, especially with us children. How influential, then, was the "equality" between Bogart and Bacall in their films?

Molly Haskell on Bergman and Bogart, and Bacall and Bogart, suggests why the latter seem better mated than Rick and Ilsa by contemporary values. In *From Reverence to Rape,* Haskell points out that is it not to Hemingway's "machismo" heroics that Bogart's Harry Morgan ("Steve") commits himself at the end of *To Have and Have Not,* but to Bacall's "Slim"—after she has "'prove[n] herself' by playing it his way, by showing her physical courage or competence."

Thus, says Haskell, Harry's "heroism, for which he will win no medals, is to have accepted the consequences of heterosexual love." Rick, on the other hand, makes the "easiest" choice, walking away with his buddy, Louis.[19]

Given *Casablanca*'s propagandistic intention, and despite Bergman's having said that her fate in the film was not decided until the last minute,[20] Rick seems to have no choice but to give Ilsa back to Victor Laszlo. But Bogart's happy ending with Claude Rains must have had its effect on our final impression of Bogart and Bergman as lovers. The end of *To Have and Have Not,* like that of *Casablanca,* focuses on Bogart's decision to join the fight against Fascism, and on his rescuing a male friend; in *To Have and Have Not,* it is Walter Brennan's childlike alcoholic, Eddie, the counterpart to Rains' Louis. Harry Morgan's decision to join up with "Slim" is played down and cool, in the style of their romance. But Morgan does not join "Slim" and adds her to the family of himself and Eddie. It did not—it could not—seem romantic then, at least not to those of us growing up on *Old Acquaintance* and *Casablanca.* But now its love, as friendly as it is sexy, looks good.

The Big Sleep is even more contemporary, less a "black thriller" than a black comedy, at home today with the works of Jules Feiffer and Joseph Heller. The plot is so chaotic that when the time came to end it, no one could figure out how to, not even Raymond Chandler, who wrote the mystery on which the film was based. Who had done it? As one of the scriptwriters, Leigh Brackett, later said, "who cared?"[21] *The Big Sleep* flaunts its plot *manqué*—one of its most "seventies" characteristics—by running through its denouement at the speed of a silent movie.

If the film as a whole is so confused, why should we expect clarity in Vivian (Bacall)? As in *To Have and Have Not,* in *The Big Sleep*, she is at once Philip Marlowe's strong right staff and toughly independent thorn. But because her allegiance is so (untypically) murky until the end, when she makes it clear that she would give her life for him, understanding their relationship in any conventional forties way is the last thing a seventies viewer would take on—as is understanding the film. I do not even remember *The Big Sleep* from the forties; if I did see it, I probably forgot it at once because it was so confusing. Now I can see its bits with liberated women (and despite the Christopher Columbus attitude of present feminists, so, at the time did *Variety*[22]): Dorothy Malone's bookstore clerk, who has a brief encounter with Bogart that is all good, sexual fun; and Joy Barlowe's taxi driver, who looks like any forties Cover Girl, but responds to Bogart's command to follow that car with no-questions-asked competence, and when at the end of the ride, he tries to flirt with her, blisters him.

Then there is the scene, which looks now like one of the best in any movie, in which Bogart and Bacall show up at the apartment of two-bit gangster Louis Jean Heydt. They appear separately, at cross-purposes, although, naturally enough in this movie, neither purpose is clear. In an episode that now recalls Jules Feiffer's *Little Murders* and the routines of Mike Nichols and Elaine May, Bogart and Bacall's squabbling mingles with the nagging of Heydt's greedy girl friend Agnes (Sonia Darrin), Bogart's staccato put-downs of Heydt's machismo and guns, and the farcical gun tussling reminiscent of Humbert Humbert's wrestling with his *doppelgänger* Clare Quilty in *Lolita.* Then the doorbell rings, Heydt answers it, and is scored with bullets. They freeze, the men and women who have been in control up to then, Bogart and Bacall and little nagging Agnes. They stand stock still, shocked, impotent.

No one in *The Big Sleep* is spared. At the end, no man or woman comes out all clean and wise; and in fact, it may be the most egalitarian movie made in the forties, and the most avant-garde.

Yet, such a bleak last word on *The Big Sleep* is inappropriate; for at the end of the movie, confused, confusing Bacall competently saves Bogart's life, and because of her movie-long ambiguity, turns the conventional happy ending into a classic revelation. Her final act places *The Big Sleep* in that small group of forties films that depict loving, and reasonably equal relationships between men and women. Some others in this small number are Bogart and Bacall's *To Have and Have Not, Dark Passage*, and *Key Largo*; Bogart and Bergman's *Casablanca*; and Bogart and Mary Astor's *Across the Pacific* (1942), like *Casablanca*, a formulaic espionage film in which there is no reason for an unconventionally equal romantic relationship—except the kind of dialogue and denouement that Humphrey Bogart seems to have inspired.

The drift is clear: Bogart is the key. In *The Spoken Seen: Film and the Romantic Imagination,* Frank D. McConnell says that Bogart's " 'existential' . . . . absurd man is man exclusively as *victim* of the world's mechanism, a victim whose sad irony reminds us that even in defeat there remain the possibilities of a self-mistrustful honor and dignity."[23] This represents the common view of Bogart's contemporary appeal; but at least in the forties films in which he was a romantic hero, it seems subtly different. It seems not so much endurance of victimization as in-control *choice* to discard old power games. Thus, it looks now as if the man assured enough to shrug off power is half of most, if not all, of the few reasonably healthy sexual relationships on the forties screen. What equality there was between men and women in the films I saw as a child came almost wholly from the personality of one man, who was not one of our "favorites," and furthermore, this equality touched only the personal relationship between him and his woman. In professional relationships between men and women (except perhaps for spying), inequity was intensified by the economic and political facts of forties life, which I doubt any girl-child recognized, much less questioned.

"Creatures of Habit"

It is easy for us to see how the war made women a commodity. David Hinshaw's *The Home Front*, published in 1943, states that "the war is directly serving to speed the complete emancipation of women . . . . in part because the depression failures had taken some conceit out of the human male animal."[24] But Hinshaw's optimism, read now, does not ring true in memory. Indeed, looking back, the wartime attitude toward women seems better caught by a Pittsburgh theater manager, who when he discovered that most of his customers were unescorted women, sent Hollywood the message, " 'Sex up the beautiful hunks of men.' "[25]

When the men went to war, the women replaced them or filled the new jobs the war created. They were the better workers. Forming 36 percent of the labor force, women worked faster, required less supervision, had less accidents, did less damage to tools and material, and were more content.[26] And this despite the fact that their paychecks were, quite illegally, lower than a man's pay for the same work,[27] and that the typical explanation for the women's success on the assembly line seems to have been that they had " 'less initiative' " and were " 'creatures of habit.' "[28]

By June 1945, 95 percent of women war workers wanted to

stay on their jobs after the war was over.[29] But there was a problem: the more than 11,000,000 male veterans who needed jobs. If the women did not go home, economic chaos loomed—and more ominously, social and psychological chaos. Advertising, popular magazines, newspapers, radio, and Hollywood all responded to the potential crisis with barrages of propaganda, and in the year after V-J Day, more than 2,160,000 women went home. (Dr. Spock was waiting. The first edition of *Baby and Child Care* came out in 1946, stressing to the postwar baby boomers, as it did to me in 1961, the mother's importance as guardian of a potential genius—if baby got her full attention.) In 1945-46, the percentage of women in the labor force dropped from 36 percent to 29 percent. There was another side to the story. Of the women who went to work during the war, about two-thirds did not go home. In November 1946, 16,600,000 were still working. The 3.5 percent net gain in percentage of women in the labor force during the war years, almost equaled the increase between 1900 and 1940.[30] But if in June 1945, 95 percent of the working women wanted to keep working, and one-third of the total could be convinced to retire, the propagandists for Home Beautiful could be proud.

I did not know any of this then. But in discovering it now, I feel no antagonism toward the soldiers—I wonder if anyone who grew up during the war could. When Chris Jones (Robert Ryan) goes overseas in *Tender Comrade* (1943), he promises his wife Jo (Ginger Rogers) that when he returns, they will leave Los Angeles and return to "Shale City," where his job is being held for him. In their last moments together, Chris and Jo plan their vegetable garden, a few chickens, the barbecue, and "that kid" they want. As in so many movies of this kind so often written off as "sentimental," Chris Jones is killed in action, unknowing that on his last leave he begat Chris Jones, Jr., who at the end of the movie, his mother is vowing to bring up according to his father's dreams of a better world. It appears easy now to dismiss movies such as *Tender Comrade*. But when *I* look back at these movies, the facts of World War II life on which their plots turn, remain facts of dead human beings, women without husbands, and children without fathers. More moving now after all these years Chris Jones, Jr., the Ivory Soap baby burbling into the camera in the last frame of *Tender Comrade*, looks more bereft now than ever he could have when I wept for him in 1943.

In *Pride of the Marines* (1945), a popular film, and hence it can be presumed, a representative and likely an influential one, the end-of-the-war attitudes of veterans are expressed, and those of America about her veterans are reflected, in a scene that even someone who was only a ten-year-old girl-child in 1945 is tempted to judge more powerful today, after the passage of the fifties, the sixties, and the seventies, than it was in 1945. In a Veterans Hospital in California, the wounded soldiers voice their fears about getting jobs, their bitterness toward the employers who broke their promises to hold jobs for them, and finally, a general bitterness and some fear—eerily like the "paranoia of the seventies"—directed at the country they served, that now makes them feel undesirable and impotent. Who's running America? they ask. Who will run it after the war is over? Will we control our destinies, we the crippled, blinded, "psycho" warriors? Will we even have a place in which we fit in postwar America? The most hopeful veteran (played by the then-unknown Mark Stevens) says he has the answer: he is going to become a lawyer, so that he can become a political leader.*

Among the soldiers who were lucky enough to come home, who could want anything less than their old job back? Most wanted more—such as Air Force Captain Dana Andrews in *The Best Years of Our Lives*, who had to go back, bitterly, to

---

*This outburst in *Pride of the Marines* is initiated and led by Dane Clark, playing the bravest soldier in the platoon, a "Jew Boy." In a similar scene in an earlier war film, *Action in the North Atlantic* (1943), Clark also leads a group of merchant mariners on Raymond Massey and Humphrey Bogart's ship in wondering what they are dying for—medals? *Action in the North Atlantic* was written mainly by John Howard Lawson; *Pride of the Marines*, by Albert Maltz. Both would be blighted by HUAC's postwar incursion into Hollywood's "Communists."

soda-jerking. Yet the women war workers also deserve our sympathy. I have been harsh on the contemporary feminists who overvalue the ground that was broken for women's rights by the career-girl pictures. But of all distortions of the forties, this one hurts the most, even more than the myth that all the Chris and Jo Joneses were schlocks. The craze in the mirror seems so obvious: all those vinewrapped happy endings I clung to now look so clearly like boa constrictors. It seems clear now that the "strong women" movies really taught young women and men in the forties to pity and laugh along with Jimmy Cagney and Rita Hayworth at suffragette Olivia de Havilland in *The Strawberry Blonde* (1941), and to recognize that a happy ending is on the way when, dating Cagney, de Havilland immediately drops all those silly notions, like initiating a kiss.

The message is equally clear in the wartime propaganda films set in the home front. In the movies like *Tender Comrade*, the woman's career is to manage the home while her husband and/or sons win the war. The women did this admirably—with a stiff upper lip, a quick step, and a smiling eye. Some, such as Jo Jones, and Claudette Colbert in David O. Selznick's tribute to the "unconquerable Fortress—The American Home (1943)," *Since You Went Away* (1944), even insisted on a war plant job in addition to their housework. But with Rosie the Riveter, as with Mrs. Miniver, there was a point at which our model failed: the women belonged on the job only as long as the men were on the firing line.

The Good-Bad Girl, the Devil-Mom, the Mean Best Friend, and Other of My "Womanly Models"

Hollywood formulated its postwar "woman, go home" message as it had its wartime propaganda, and earlier, its anti-Depression hype,[31] around the stereotype of that icon of icons of my childhood, the American Mom. What dizzy dumbbells remained after the coming of Ma Joad, the wartime movies transformed into staunch matriarchs as vital to the war effort as the nurses of Corregidor. In my childhood, we saw the Claudette Colberts running things, and we also saw women working and living together and liking it. In *Tender Comrade,* Ginger Rogers, Ruth Hussey, Kim Hunter, and Patricia Collinge, war wives working at Douglas Aircraft in Los Angeles, decide to live together, and to housekeep for them, they bring in Mady Christians, a war wife who cannot get a defense job because she is a German native. In *The Very Thought of You* (1943), Eleanor Parker and Fay Emerson work together making parachutes in Pasadena, California, support each other emotionally, while their men, Dennis Morgan and Dane Clark, fight, are reported missing, and recover from their wounds. *Music for Millions* (1944) feature José Iturbi's almost all-girl symphony orchestra, brought about by the male musicians being at war. That was the gimmick; but the plot was essentially that of *Tender Comrade:* mutual support among The Girls, June Allyson, Marsha Hunt, Marie Wilson, et al.

Such sisterhood was everywhere in the movies of the war years. It was not entirely new, at least among show girls; and, in part, it was created by Washington to make American women feel good about their hard, habitual, and manless lives. But for whatever ironic reasons, and however short lived it was, strong, sisterly women were common, realistic heroines in my childhood. In the war years *The Women* (1939) of Claire Boothe Luce became courageous, uncomplaining, cheerful, and, above all, loving but not sexual. Erotic stimulation of the audience would have undermined, not enhanced the war effort. *Variety* reminded Hollywood of this repeatedly, encouraging the Mrs. Minivers. But as a stranger to *Variety*, and a nice girl, I took the sexless stalwarts as the heroines they were formalized as.

In *Since You Went Away*, I now look at Claudette Colbert's unbending cheerfulness in the face of such adversity as a husband missing in action and a daughter's sweetheart killed, and I see her unbending, cheerful, total resistance to the dashing family friend who loves her (Joseph Cotten), and I guess that Selznick's epic of the "unconquerable Fortress" must have plunged wartime American women a light year deeper into guilt. In *Music for Millions*, June Allyson—even June Allyson—breaks down from worrying over her missing husband, Joe, and when her sister Mike (Margaret O'Brien) begs her to pray for him, says bitterly, "I'm so lost and lonely. . . . What does God know about a woman's aloneness when her husband's gone and her baby's coming. . .?" Yes, she does pray, and Joe does come back, and the baby is a boy. But in this moment of bitterness, she must have expressed the guilt feelings repressed in thousands of American war sweethearts, and that must have given them release. But not Claudette Colbert's perfect Mrs. Hilton, the model of a grown-up girl.

Of Mrs. Miniver, Anne Hilton, et al., Marjorie Rosen says,

> They learn to live *without* their men. Their survival, not as hysterical, embittered martyrs, but as womanly, capable models of human adaptability, was a Hollywood screen first.[32]

But the forties I remember seem better caught by a critic of the time. In his *New York Times* review of the British Navy epic *In Which We Serve* (1942), Bosley Crowther wrote:

> Celia Johnson, Kay Walsh and Joyce Carey play the wives of the three men [Noel Coward, John Mills and Bernard Miles] as such should be—plain in appearance, unpretentious, but as real and dependable as home.[33]

Whether the women liked it or not, the propaganda juggernaut that worked during the Depression to associate them with home and family did it again in the forties, even during the war years, when it also had to juggle images of Anne Hilton as Swing Shift Maisie. They succeeded, but looking back now, it strikes me that the propagandists must have wondered if they were going to pull it off. The deep, inchoate fears stirred, especially in faraway fighting men, by masses of independent, working women, may have something to do with the antiwomanism that I can see suffusing these "real and dependable" women, an ugly blotch just under the Camay bride's skin. Anne Hilton is hopeful, industrious, ingenious, chaste, and cruelly better than thou. It now seems appropriate that Philip Wylie's broadside against American "Momism," *Generation of Vipers*, appeared in 1942.

Wylie's "Mom" was the "end product of She," and "*She* is Cinderella," in the forties, the "magazine-movie-novel-radio" image of the fairy tale heroine:

> The shiny-haired, the starry-eyed, the ruby-lipped virgo artemis, of which there is presumably one, and only one, or a one-and-only for each male, whose dream is fixed upon her deflowerment and subsequent perpetual possession.

Mom, who lives off her man and eats up her sons, is an "elaboration . . . [of] Cinderella."[34]

Or, as Leslie Fiedler put it in 1960, about the mother he saw dominating the fiction of our century, she was not

> a traditional Bad Mother—descendant of the stepmothers in Grimm— . . . but a *Good* Mother, whose very goodness is revealed as a threat, a loving mother, whose love serves only to unman her son.[35]

If I had read Wylie in the forties, or James Agee's diatribe against Mrs. Hilton, Jo Jones, and The Power Girl ("a mass of women, frightening to conceive of"; one of the "archetypical national diseases"), I would not have understood. Even in 1960, newly married and a brotherless child, I underestimated Fiedler. Now, all over the field of forties film, as over the fields of fiction and life, I can see the dominant mothers, models of perverted sexuality; and I can see how these viragoes grew, twisted and stunted by romantic dreams, from *me*: Cinderella.

Reviewing *The Very Thought of You*, I am startled to find a Mom I do not remember as so awful, and until recently, would not have expected to find in a 1944 movie about the All-American family. Played by Beulah Bondi, this Mom of crow-eyes, pinched-back hair and thin, graphite lips is so mean to her kids that I must wonder how Agee missed her. (He reviewed the film cursorily, merely noting that it had some "pretty good family quarrels."[36]) Bondi's Mom embodies Agee's national disease of nagging. Not only is she suspicious of daughter Eleanor Parker's beau, even though he is Dennis Morgan, she is immediately inhospitable when Janet brings Dave home, and later, she is terrified that Dave has "made love" to her daughter (that is, kissed her). She objects to their marriage, whining that she only wants her daughters to "profit by [her] mistake" and Marry Well.

She is particularly given to putting down Pa, a character who now seems as interesting as Ma. An unusually explicit strong, gentle man, Pa (Henry Travers) is a self-proclaimed failure: "I know I'm not worth much," he says. "I was on W.P.A., and now I'm just a clerk, but. . . ." What is interesting is that the film establishes the "but." It anchors Pa in the role of his daughter Janet's counselor, and in matters of conscience and compassion, places him at the heart of his All-American family.* At the end, when the missing-and-found wounded Dave is returning, the movie quickly and unconvincingly humanizes Mom (she will allow Dennis Morgan a kiss). But it does this through Pa's leading the family in joshing at, not with, her. Would Dave be shocked if she kissed him? Ma asks. "Well, Ma," says Pa, "He's been through a lot. . . ."

If Agee was so keen to omnivorous mothers that he could sniff them in Powers Girls and charming Claudette Colbert matriarchs, how could he miss the wicked Beulah Bondi witch? After reviewing many more films like *The Very*

---

*The screenwriter of *The Very Thought of You* was Alvah Bessie, another HUAC victim.

Thought of You, I can only guess that Agee missed Bondi because she was so common. (Only when disguised as a glamour girl, or the heroine of a David O. Selznick epic, might she need exposing.) Wolfenstein and Leites link the forties Strong Mother exacting harsh tribute from her son, to the moviemakers themselves, the middle-aged and older male studio heads whose notions largely controlled what we saw on the screen.[37] This may seem airy, Freudian speculation; it did to me until I looked again at the movies of my childhood, and particularly David O. Selznick's *Gone with the Wind*, which deserves and gets a chapter to itself.

But Wolfenstein's and Leites' point is also made by numerous run-of-the-studio films—it could not be made without their number—which, apparently unconsciously, turn on the psychology of men's relationships to their mothers or mother surrogates. For not all the Strong Mothers are actually mothers. Some are motherly wives or girl friends, such as Bacall's Irene Jansen, who harbors the convict-on-the-run Bogart in *Dark Passage* (1947). Some others—usually played by Judith Anderson or Agnes Moorehead—are governesses, mentor-executives, or old friends of the family. But they are all shadows of Citizen Kane's mother—played by Agnes Moorehead—who sent child Kane away from her, or they are shadows of the more accessible mother of Philip Raven in *This Gun for Hire*. Based on Graham Greene's novel, this tough-compassionate view of a killer was a popular 1941 movie. At the end, finally trusting someone (Veronica Lake is the Irene Jansen here), Raven (Alan Ladd) talks to his past: a mother who died when he was a child, and to boot, an aunt who took him in only to beat him.

The decade ended with another antihero movie that explicated the Freudianism of it all: *White Heat*, in which the gangster Cody Jarrett (Cagney), has a psychotically close relationship with his mother (Margaret Wycherly). In between *This Gun for Hire and White Heat* are *Kiss of Death* (1947) the giggling gangster Tommy Udo (Richard Widmark) pushing the mother of a stooly down a flight of stairs, and a number of other films that range from the Bs or failures—such as *My Name is Julia Ross* (1945), with Dame May Whitty spurring on a murdering, maniacal son (George Macready); *Moss Rose* (1947), with Ethel Barrymore as the Bad Mother; and the textbookish *Sign of the Ram* (1948), with Susan Peters as a crippled, psychotically possessive wife and stepmother,—to *Notorious, Dark Passage,* and *All Through the Night* (1942), a Bogart programmer that seems to have gotten caught up by the war and turned from comedy melodrama to patriotic propaganda, and thus to historical document (it was released a month and three weeks after Pearl Harbor). In *All Through the Night*, Jane Darwell, the Ma of *The Grapes of Wrath,* joins the super virago of the era, Judith Anderson. Darwell plays gambler Bogart's sweet and crusty old Ma, to whom he is, of course, devoted; and Anderson is an American Nazi who wears severe black dresses, hairdos, and pillbox hats, and whose name is merely "Madame." Madame seethes with silent dedication to chief Nazi spy Conrad Veidt, hisses at ingenue Kaaren Verne because Veidt likes her, and generally exudes icy, butch hatred. Because of Ma's intuitions and spurrings-on, Bogart eventually turns the New York gangs to patriotism. They round up the Nazis, and Madame is vanquished by Ma.

In Bogart's postwar melodrama *Dark Passage,* Agnes Moorehead, the other super "Devil-Mom" (In Leslie Fiedler's terminology), exhibits her motiveless discontent. (Unless it is overacting and carelessness with the plot that is being exhibited; with forties programmers, this must always be considered.) As *Dark Passage* begins, Moorehead's Maggie Rapf seems to have beaten down the love of one of those decent sorts (Bruce Bennett, who had the same kind of role opposite Joan Crawford in *Mildred Pierce*); and in the course of *Dark Passage,* she seems to be revealed as the murderer of Bogart's wife, her best friend. In *Since You Went Away,* Moorehead only knifed her best friend Claudette Colbert with barbs about Colbert's handsome friend, Joseph Cotten, and her daughter Jennifer Jones' degrading herself by working in a hospital. In *Dark Passage*, she becomes Bogart's nemesis, for he has gone to prison as his wife's murderer, and after he escapes and pins it on her, she falls from a window to her death, taking with her his vindication and the conventional ending. (This movie ends with Bogart's lamming it to Peru and Bacall's joining him there for happiness ever after in an unusual exile from both America and the Law.) Moorehead falls from the window simply, and very strangely. Backing away from Bogart's charges, like a nemesis, she wraps herself behind a billowing drape; then we hear her falling scream. Did she jump or merely fall? The movie is as ambiguous about her suicide or accident as it is about her motives. We are never let inside to understand the witch. We have only a musing from Irene (Bacall) that Maggie seems to destroy for no other reason than plain meanness. Thus, Maggie appears starkly a figure of Evil, irredeemable and unvanquishable even if she has to die to thwart justice and the lovers.

Bacall's Irene Jansen is no Maggie Rapf. She is the Good Woman who hides Bogart and cares for him while he recovers from the plastic surgery to give him a new face. But because of this nurse role viz-á-viz Bogart, Bacall in *Dark Passage* appears a mother-lover. Something is going on here; something not on the formulaic surface is being suggested about mothers and mother surrogates in postwar America. (We return to *Dark Passage* in Chapter 4.)

Bacall's Irene is the Strong Mother who is not mother but sweetheart. But I can see now that she also represents the "recurrent theme" in American movies noted by Wolfenstein and Leites: the plot in which the hero is loved unconditionally while he withholds his love "pending investigation of her merits." This is the theme of *Casablanca, To Have and Have Not, The Big Sleep, Gilda, Notorious*, and more; and as Wolfenstein and Leites say, it is a theme that reverses the "experience of American boys with their exacting mothers."[38]

I now also look at this theme from the woman's perspective: She who he does not trust is that popular type, the female who seems bad but turns out good. At the final instant when she cannot shoot him, Ilsa Lund recovers Rick's trust. Alicia Huberman is nearly dead, poisoned by her mother-in-law, before Dev (Cary Grant) decides she is not an alcoholic tramp. (Madame Constantine, playing the Nazi mother of Nazi Claude Rains, probably deserves the palm for Devil-Moms of the forties.) Bacall's roles in *To Have and Have Not, The Big Sleep,* and *Dark Passage*; Hayworth's Gilda, and Bergman's Cleo in *Saratoga Trunk* are other heroines of the forties who have to strive the length of the movie to prove their virtue to Bogart, Glenn Ford, and Gary Cooper. And they are among our classic forties heroines. In these forward women and standoffish men is a man's fantasy of the forbidden cake. The sophisticated lady is a trollop until the last reel, when she turns marriageable. Or, in Wolfenstein's and Leites' pithy caption for a still of Rita Hayworth as Gilda, "There's less here than meets the eye." [39]

In *The Lonely Crowd*, David Riesman says that forties children accustomed to the comics were disturbed when "in the movies" good looks did not necessarily indicate goodness. But in Riesman's late forties book, it is a late forties film he uses as example: Lana Turner's Lady de Winter in *The Three Musketeers* (1948); [40] and as we see in Chapter 4, bad heroines in postwar Hollywood films were not that unusual. In the war years, however, we had few surprises when we moved from the comic strips to the movies. The good-bad heroine who clarified as bad was sufficiently unusual that I wonder if we remembered those films—and perhaps overvalue them now—from surprise at the unconventionality.

For example, two of my memory's favorites are *The Fallen Sparrow* (1943) and *Hotel Berlin* (1945), in which Maureen O'Hara and Andrea King, respectively, appear at the end of each film to be the Nazis that John Garfield and Helmut Dantine hoped they were not when they fell in love. Garfield only deposits O'Hara with the Feds, but Dantine, a

Resistance leader, does Garfield one better and ritualistically executes King. Looked at closely, however, neither film clarifies the leading lady. Perhaps forties movies should not be looked at closely; the footage explicating motives may have wound up on the cutting room floor. Yet in *The Fallen Sparrow* and *Hotel Berlin*, the heroes become convinced that the heroines are bad, and there the movies end. But it is clear—at least it is now—that it could have gone either way. It is no more true to the plot of *The Fallen Sparrow* to have O'Hara turn out bad than it is true to what passes for a plot in *The Big Sleep* to have Bacall turn out good. At times in *Hotel Berlin* King assists Dantine and appears torn (she is loved by a Good German, the Prussian Nazi General Armin von Dahnwitz: Raymond Massey). In Vicki Baum's novel *Grand Hotel,* on which *Hotel Berlin* is based, the Andrea King character reforms at the end—perhaps in 1945 Hollywood, as "unconditional surrender" crested, she became a scapegoat. On the other hand, *Hotel Berlin's* whore, Tilli (Faye Emerson) is redeemed. (In Baum's novel, she goes to prison.) One movie reviewer charged that Faye Emerson was redeemed because, while she was shooting the picture, she married the President's son, Elliot Roosevelt.[41]

As a child, I did not dispute Garfield's and Dantine's final solutions, nor do I find the word *ambiguous* used in reviews of the time. But in both movies, the woman now seems no evil betrayer of America and men, particularly in *The Fallen Sparrow*. Suddenly convinced of O'Hara's perfidy (the movie rushes past how), Garfield bumps her from "the Clipper" and flies off to Europe to fight Fascism, leaving her with the cops. Not for him, her explanation that she had to work for the Nazis in New York because they had control of her daughter in Europe (this time they are led not by Conrad Veidt but by Walter Slezak, with a quintessential booted limp which his daughter tells me he used to amuse the children and expatriates, in forties Hollywood). But the movie ends with O'Hara gazing after the departing Clipper;

and as anyone who knows the forties knows, Hollywood movies about Nazi spies rarely closed on close-ups of the spy's tear-starred, beautiful face.

The Bs utilized the twist of the heroine, usually Faye Emerson, who turned out bad. Why not? It was dramatic. And there were a few fatal heroines in the war years who were not Nazis: Linda Darnell's greedy sexpot in *Summer Storm* and Susan Hayworth's decadent socialite in *The Hairy Ape* (both 1944). But both of these films were unusually "serious"—they were based on a Chekhov story and Eugene O'Neill play, respectively—and neither was a hit at the box office. The only popular wartime film with a thoroughgoing villain as heroine was *Double Indemnity* (1944), with Barbara Stanwyck, which now looks like a forerunner. One example from many films in the postwar era is Bogart's *Dead Reckoning* (1947), in which Lizabeth Scott played the Bacall role ("Coral Chandler").* But rather than saving Bogart at the end, Scott nearly killed him with a doublecross like Mary Astor's in *The Maltese Falcon* (1941), the forties prototype of these Surprise, She's Bad movies. But the Dragon Ladies were not common, and generally they were not popular, until the postwar era. Usually, the bad girls of my childhood could be enjoyed in all their low-cut, slinky innuendo, their hearts of gold comfortingly predictable.

"Rick, You Will Have to Think for Both of Us"
Themes of Nostalgia and Loss

The woman's analog to the Gilda dream of the good slut is the Rhett Butler fantasy of ecstatic rape. But before we get to

*Scott got the part because Warner Brothers would not lend Bacall, and Columbia's offerings, Marguerite Chapman and Evelyn Keyes, dissatisfied Bogart. (*Variety*, June 5, 1946, p. 2) It is interesting to speculate on how the Bogart-Bacall image would have been affected had she played this good-bad girl who turns out bad. But if Coral Chandler had been Bacall, it is more likely that she would not have turned out bad. In the forties, plots were like that.

GWTW, a summary of forties men-women relationships seems enlightening. Wolfenstein and Leites classify the vamp who turns out good; the woman superior in talent to her man, who "benevolently" arranges his success; the woman who Gives In to Love, but not to respect; and the psychotically possessive woman who draws her man from His Work.[42]

The vamp who turns out good is Gilda, Ilsa, "Slim," and Cleo, and for my generation, Elizabeth Taylor's Carol in *A Date with Judy* (1948), who took Robert Stack, but left Oogie Pringle (Scotty Beckett) for Judy (Jane Powell). Boss-lady movies exemplify the second and third classes: women superior in talent to their men, who nevertheless give them the whip. Scarlett is also in that third class of the woman who "loves" and scorns. And the last class, the possessive woman, is seen in Milly's and Preston Drake's relationship in *Old Acquaintance*, and among others, in Gene Tierney's Fatal Lady in *Leave Her to Heaven* (1945) and Joan Crawford's *Humoresque* (1946) and *Possessed* (1947). The little lady fixit characters epitomized by "Blondie" (Penny Singleton), and by June Allyson's parts in the forties, are a variety of the second, "superior" class; and I think cover what remains of heroines in forties films.

If Wolfenstein's and Leites' categories are comprehensive, and I see nothing to refute them except the few good-bad heroines who end up bad, mainly the villainous vamps of the postwar era, then we may say that there is not a single "recurrent theme" in forties movies that represents a relationship of equal, open, loving sexuality between men and women. And this is the dream factory that shaped us so deeply. What could the few loving independents, such as Bergman, Bogart, and Bacall do against the weight of all the buttoned-down Cary Grants, and the Jeanne Crain ingenues with baby blue or pink hair ribbons? In Molly Haskell's words, " 'exceptional' women" threaten " 'ordinary' women . . . whose options have been foreclosed by marriage or income, by children or age." To the " 'ordinary' women," let us add, "men."

One of the most exceptional women of the forties was Scarlett O'Hara, even then a mythic figure. Scarlett's romances with Ashley and Rhett embody the definition of "romantic love":

> Romantic love . . . is Oedipal love. It looks backwards, hence its preoccupation with themes of nostalgia and loss. It is fundamentally incestuous, hence its emphasis on obstacles and nonfulfillment, on tragedy and trespass.[44]

Here, Philip Slater defines romantic love precisely as I now define the conventions of the romantic movies on which my generation grew up. Others begin to do the same; even *Time* and *People* notice. But in the forties, who among us knew Oedipus? Who knew in this way Cathy and Heathcliff, Scarlett and Rhett, Ilsa and Rick, Jane Eyre and Lord Edward, Gilda and Johnny, Gable and Turner? "I *am* Heathcliff," Cathy cried, and now we are trying for Denis de Rougemont's "We are not '*One*': We are two in contentment."[45]

Yet it comes to me only now, a child of the forties turned forty, wise to Oedipus, that we still need to deal with the *liveness* of those dream loves, and even more with the romantic conventions: the formulaic tragedies and trespasses which, far more than Bergman, Bogart, and Bacall, created the Ilsa and Ricks who smother us still, with amazing vitality, and despite Liberation and all good sense.

Notes

1. *In Popcorn Venus: Women, Movies and the American Dream* (New York: Avon, 1974 [1973], pp. 234-35, Marjorie Rosen cites this same passage from *Lady in the Dark,* although her wording is slightly off from the dialogue in the movie, and she gives as the date of the movie, the date of the original Moss Hart-Kurt Weill play (1941). But the more subtle, important error is buried in her judgment that Rogers' "breakthrough" with her psychoanalyst "must have set psychiatry, as well as female autonomy, back a few light years." Those two setbacks, and even their

dimensions, may be true, but Rosen's implication that there was something unusual about *Lady in the Dark* is not. The career women films she praises as steps toward liberation were as macho as *Lady*, often more.

2. Helen Dorsey, "I'm Louise Fletcher; I'm Somebody," Chicago *Daily News,* January 31-February 1, 1976, Sec. 2, pp. 19-20. Fletcher has since left her husband for the son, much younger, of forties romantic hero James Mason.

3. Charles Higham and Joel Greenberg, *Hollywood in the Forties* (New York: Paperback Library, 1970), p. 157.

4. Cited in Dr. Albert Ellis, *The Folklore of Sex,* Rev. Ed. (New York: Grove Press Black Cat Books, 1961 [1951]), p. 73.

5. Ted Sennett, *Lunatics and Lovers: A Tribute to the Giddy and Glittering Era of the Screen's "Screwball" and Romantic Comedies* (New Rochelle, N.Y.: Arlington House, 1973), pp. 197-98.

6. Marjorie Rosen, *Popcorn Venus,* p. 207.

7. *Variety,* June 3, 1942, p. 8, col. 5.

8. Molly Haskell, *From Reverence to Rape: The Treatment of Women in the Movies* (Baltimore: Penguin Books, 1974), pp. 128-29.

9. Mike Steen, interviewer (New York: G.P. Putnam's Sons, 1974), pp. 79-80.

10. Rosen, *Popcorn Venus,* pp. 194-95. See also Parker Tyler, *Magic and Myth of the Movies* (New York: Henry Holt, 1947), on how Bergman in *Spellbound* "decides the destiny of the man she loves by her skill in psychoanalysis." (pp. 258-59).

11. Pauline Kael, "The Man from Dream City," *New Yorker,* July 14, 1975, pp. 40-41; 65.

12. Martha Wolfenstein and Nathan Leites, *Movies: A Psychological Study* (Glencoe, Ill.: The Free Press, 1950?, p. 41.

13. Ralph Gleason, in Howard Koch, *Casablanca: Script and Legend* (Woodstock, N.Y.: The Overlook Press, 1973), pp. xii; xi.

14. Kael, "The Man from Dream City," p. 42 (on Dunne); pp. 64-65 (on Crawford, Hepburn, Loy, Bergman and Garbo).

15. Rosen, *Popcorn Venus,* pp. 243-45 and picture page following p. 224.

16. Kael, *New Yorker,* October 27, 1975, p. 25

17. Stuart Hall and Paddy Whannel, *The Popular Arts: A Critical Guide to the Mass Media* (Boston: Beacon Press, 1964), p. 207.

18. Perhaps, like Bergman, there was something about Bacall, the good-tough girl, that got through. (New York: Pantheon Books, 1977), p. 156.

19. Haskell, *From Reverence to Rape,* pp. 212-13.

20. In Richard Schickel's television documentary, *"You Must Remember This". Hollywood in the Forties.*

21. Leigh Brackett, "From 'The Big Sleep' to 'The Long Goodbye,' and More or Less How we Got There," *Take One,* January 1974, issue of September-October 1972, p. 27. Director Howard Hawks remembers Chandler wiring the name of a character and he, Hawks, replying that " 'he couldn't have [done it?; he was down at the beach at the time.' " Michael Goodwin and Naomi Wise, "An Interview with Howard Hawks," *Take One,* March 1973, issue of November-December 1971, p. 22.

22. *Variety,* August 14, 1946, p. 10.

23. Frank D. McConnell, *The Spoken Seen: Film and the Romantic Imagination* (Baltimore: The Johns Hopkins Press, 1975), p. 185.

24. David Hinshaw, *The Home Front.* (new York: G.P. Putnam's Sons, 1943), p. 43.

25. *Variety,* March 11, 1942, p. 1, col. 5.

26. See Rosen's *Popcorn Venus,* Chapter 12, "The Rise and Fall of Rosie the Riveter," pp. 201-20, for information on how women were perceived from war years' issues of *Business Week, Nation's Business, Time,* and other popular journals.

27. Richard Lingeman, *Don't You Know There's a War On? The American Home Front 1941-1945* (New York: G.P. Putnam's Sons, 1970), pp. 156-57.

28. *Nation's Business,* June 1942, quoted in *Popcorn Venus,* p. 202.

29. Ibid.

30. Lingeman, *Don't You Know. . .?* pp. 158-59.

31. In the words of historian Warren Susman, "all the devices of the media, the energies of psychology and social science were enlisted in a major effort to revitalize and reassert the primary importance of the family." "Introduction," *Culture and Commitment: 1929-1945* (New York: George Braziller, 1973), p. 16. See also Robert Sklar, *Movie-Made America: A Social History of American Movies* (New York: Random House, 1975), Chapter 11, "The Golden Age of Turbulence and The Golden Age of Order," pp. 175-94; and Erich Von Stroheim, "Movies and Morals," *Decision,* March 1941, pp. 49-56, for an argument that sexual liberalism, at least, was reviving as the Great Depression waned.

32. Rosen, *Popcorn Venus,* p. 205.

33. Bosley Crowther, December 24, 1942; in Goerge Amberg, ed. *The New York Times Film Reviews, 1913-1970: A One-Volume Selection* (New York: Arno Press, in cooperation with Quadrangle Books, 1971), p. 205.

34. Philip Wylie, *Generation of Vipers,* (New York: Farrar & Rinehard, 1942), pp. 44-45; 184. See Wylie's Chapter V, "A Specimen American Myth,,)" on *Cinderella,* pp. 44-51; and Chapter XI, *"Common Women,"* pp. 184-204.

35. Leslie Fiedler, *Love and Death in the American Novel* (New York: Criterion Books, 1960), pp. 320-21.

36. James Agee, *Agee on Film* (Boston: Beacon Press, 1964), p. 130. John McManus, of New York's *PM,* caught Ma and said of hero Dave's entrance into the Wheeler family: "What he meets shouldn't happen to a deserter." In *New York Motion Picture Critics Reviews,* I (New York: Critics Theatre Reviews, 1944), 178.

37. Wolfenstein and Leites, *Movies: A Psychological Study,* pp. 110-40.

38. Ibid., pp. 166-67; 306.

39. Ibid., between pp. 32 and 33.

40. David Riesman, with Nathan Glazer and Reuel Denney, *The Lonely Crowd: A Study of the Changing American Character.* Abridged ed. (New Haven: Yale University Press, 1973), p. 100.

41. Eileen Creelman, *New York Sun,* March 3, 1945, in *New York Motion Critics Reviews,* I, 446-47.

42. *Movies: A Psychological Study,* pp. 59-75.

43. Haskell, *From Reverence to Rape,* pp. 160-61.

44. Philip Slater, *The Pursuit of Loneliness: American Culture at the Breaking Point* (Boston: Beacon Press, 1971 [1970]), p. 87.

45. Denis de Rougemont, *Passion and Society,* trans. Montgomery Belgion (London: Faber & Faber, 1940 [1939]), p. 335. Published in America as *Love in the Western World.*

2

My Own True Love

From my scrapbook, a late forties movie magazine essay by Chris Brent, entitled "The King," on the "key to [Clark Gable's] potent power":

It's masculinity. Rugged animal masculinity that comes across on the screen and seeps into the auditorium and takes hold of every woman's imagination and boils it. . . . Masculinity of this sort. . . . comes from living, from *being* a man, from learning about women, living with them, loving them and never having them forget you.

The delicate structure of desire that is inbred in every woman is rich in a sensitivity that will sense these things innately. They cannot be fooled by a camouflage or caricature. It must be the real thing. Gable has the real thing. Women know it—and they belong to Clark Gable as long as he wants them.

. . . Real women, contrary to most published opinion, care not so much for a pretty face as for strong arms that have fought for and taken what they wanted. . . .

From a letter by Robert Anderson, author of *Tea and Sympathy*, to its movie director, Vincente Minnelli, 1965:
"I attack the often movie-fostered notion that a man is only a man if he can carry Vivien Leigh up a winding staircase."
—quoted in *I Remember It Well*, p. 312.

Nearly all the complications to which [the] plots [of popular novels and films] resort do not amount to more than a monotonous arrangement of the contrivances of an enfeebled passion in quest of *secret* obstructions. . . . Unable to take the other as he or she is, because that would mean being first of all content with oneself, a man or woman now sees on every side nothing but things to be coveted. . . .For to be faithful is to have decided to accept another being for his or her own sake, in his or her own limitations and reality. . . . The contemporary mind recoils from nothing so much as from the notion of a limitation deliberately accepted. . . . I have tried simply to expound the nature of the situation; but I realize that this . . . may not be very well received. We are too fond of our illusions to suffer gladly any attempt even to name them.

—Denis de Rougemont, *Passion and Society [Love in the Western World]*, 1939, pp. 297-98.

. . . Since the movies have an impressive atmosphere of reality and their version of non-love is presented to adolescents at the formative period of their lives, they may themselves be contributing to the unhappiness in marriage of the American people. Certainly half a century of upholding the sanctity of the marriage bond has not diminished the number of divorces on the grounds of adultery, and if we are approaching a single standard for men and women it is the standard of accepted promiscuity. Perhaps this is the inevitable result of presenting love as trivial, marriage as sexless and cohabitation as an act to be delayed as long as possible.

—Gilbert Seldes, *The Great Audience*, 1950, pp. 76-77

If we had had the benefit of psychiatry, then we would have seen how all that stuff about *nice girls don't* could really screw a person up, particularly if you think that nice girls don't and then you find out that your mother *does it*. It's all very confusing.

—Joseph Cotten, in *The First Time*, 1975, p. 57

I'm writing a memo to David O. Selznick. Even though he's dead, I'm writing a memo to him. "Dear David. Go fuck yourself. . . ."

—Sandra Hochman, *Happiness Is Too Much Trouble*, p. 41 (paper)

"I got so hung up on the stories, I forgot about the sex."

—a radical woman in the TV movie *Loose Change*, Part 2

(CBS, February 27, 1978), talking about her post-sixties consciousness-raising group reading Frank Harris, *Fanny HIll*, et al.

I shall never cease to marvel at the way we beg for love and tyranny.
—Francine du Plessix Gray, *Lovers and Tyrants,* 1976, p. 14

Like Liza in *Lady in the Dark*, and all the other boss ladies, the heroine of *Gone with the Wind* tries domination and is satisifed only when a real man overwhelms her in the genteel rape of the movies, beyond which lies happiness ever after. Not, however, in *Gone with the Wind*. Scarlett does not get to keep Rhett; and for all these years, we have blamed her. She was not virtuous enough. But like Cary Grant's sexiness and Bette Davis' independence, suddenly now, as in illusion drawing, insight reverses: It is Bergman who is sensual, Miriam Hopkins who is heroic, and Rhett Butler who is a poor fool.

Unbelievable. Rhett Gable? Incredible. And very liberating.

Up a Winding Staircase

My sister Dorothy and I saw *GWTW* [in 1942]. We had "Gone With the Wind" dresses and of course wanted to be like Scarlett (loved by every man, desirable, wanted). She was—now that I think of it—the prototype of the ideal of the 40s: popular. Nobody quite knew what "popular" meant—or maybe we did, it meant dancing every dance, having a date every other night, being constantly surrounded by a group of admiring friends of both sexes.

. . . We *knew* Rhett would come back to her eventually. . . . I sympathized greatly with the Scarlett-Ashley relationship because I always had a crush on some unattainable person (Dorothy and I both had a terrific crush on_____, as did most of his other female students; I finally married him when I

was 29 and he was 39. But I fell in love with him when I was 10
and he came to _____ to teach. . .)
                              —a girl of the forties, born 1924

Gone with the Wind, my favorite of childhood movies, seems
now the romance or romances, a paradigm of romantic fantasy illuminating the strains in forties love stories, and in
ours. *"GWTW"*—the novel and the movie—epitomizes
American notions of sexuality, notions that are being looked
at and amended only now, and only perhaps. At the heart of
Gone with the Wind lies the assumption at the heart of these
notions, an assumption that its extraordinary popularity
must have strengthened, and one that may yet do us in: the
fearsome, still largely unacknowledged belief that love and
sex are opposites, that love is associated with power and
possession, and sex with loss of power.[1] This split—clear now
—lies at the heart of our contradictions, perpetuating the
good-bad girls, the Devil Moms, the savage, raping saviors.
Like Scarlett and Rhett, we fear losing our power over the
sexual force, but we also fantasize the South Seas lover, the
Belle Watling, and the "ecstasy of surrender"[2] The morning
after Rhett sweeps her up the dark stairs—Scarlett feels someone with "arms that were too strong, lips too bruising. . . .
someone she could neither bully nor break, someone who was
bullying and breaking her," carrying them both "up, up into
the darkness again, a darkness that was soft and swirling and
all enveloping."[3]

In a midseventies study of "Pornography for Women,"
Lois Gould reported that the sweep up the stairs in *Gone with
the Wind* was the love scene most frequently cited by women,
even women in their twenties, as the "most erotic"
stimulant.[4] If that is not sufficiently disquieting to
"equalists,"consider the other aspects of love in this novel-
movie so many of us love so much, for now they too, seem
composed of destructive oppositions. Scarlett's love for gentle Ashley Wilkes (Leslie Howard) is, as Molly Haskell said,
the love of a "tigress for a kitten," because Ashley is

ultimately as unattainable as a "celibate clergyman" or " 'confirmed bachelor.' " This makes him, complexly, both "a challenge to a woman and a relief from the sexually aggressive male":

> [Ashley's] resistance and general effeteness assure us that even if he were to succumb she would have the upper hand. She is a diabolically strong woman—deceptively so, in the manner of the southern belle—and she fears the loss of her strength and self-hood that a total, "animal" relationship with Rhett would entail. [5]

True, and false; for Molly Haskell implies only Scarlett's sexual failure, and not the similar, perhaps even larger failings in Rhett. The dark at the top of the stairs in the movie *GWTW* fades to a sunlit morning shot of Scarlett waking, stretching, entirely relaxed, lithe as an animal, then remembering the night before, but accepting it, blushing and giggling. Then Rhett enters, embarrassed, drawn into the sardonic, unable to accept his wife as his whore.

What is illuminating about Haskell's view is that it is characteristic: to her, Scarlett is diabolic and deceptive; to the psychiatrist Harvey R. Greenberg, Scarlett is "bullheaded, scheming"; to Leslie Fiedler, she is "bitch-lady. . . . bitch-killer"; to Marjorie Rosen, "Rhett-Gable" is a "fortress of strength, charm and romance fighting [Scarlett's] infantilism." [6] And I, just as typically, saw *GWTW* seven times, read the novel—or at least its love scenes—even more times, and never noticed until my midseventies' viewing that ultimately, Rhett Butler is impotent. The old assumption that blames the woman endures.

And endures it does. In the summer of 1976, after the producers of *Jaws*, Richard Zanuck and David Brown, announced a sequel to *GWTW,* the *New York Times* printed the responses of fifteen "prominent authors" to the *Times* query for a plot outline of *GWTW*-II. Only one, Lois Gould, saw Scarlett as a woman of good, or at least complex strength:

The character of Scarlett is so different, much more textured, than the spoiled Southern belle created in the popular image. Seeing the movie again, one becomes more aware of her strength, love of the land, and self-reliance. I see her rebuilding Tara and growing into an abrasive and quite formidable woman. Rhett becomes a roving hero, of the 1970s movie type, a rogue leading a wild, independent life. On the decline, or feeling himself to be, he decides to have one last fling at a reconciliation with Scarlett, but she has become a different person. I don't see them working the farm side by side. They touch again and finally part.[7]

Lois Gould was also the only respondent who seemed to take the query seriously, perhaps because she had looked at the movie with seventies eyes. For the others, including the number "surprising" to the *Times* who did not respond because they had not read the book or seen the movie, it was still the same old Tara, a prison unrecognized because it was seen as Selznick saw it as "just a facade," and only a movie.

It is likely that my generation was more receptive to *Gone with the Wind* because we waited so long to see it (the almost instant classic, the immediate myth), and perhaps we were even more receptive because its postwar rerelease in 1948 coincided with our sexual awakening. We had heard so much about the book and the movie (in that era, whispered), and finally we could see it, just at the time many of us were feeling responses to love scenes different from boredom. *My* first response to a love scene was to a Clark Gable-Lana Turner movie, *Homecoming* (1948). I went home from it and wrote the "good parts" into a play, enacted in someone's garage with me as Lana—"Snapshot"—and Florence as Gable, and our less developed girl friends as the dull others, such as Gable's wife. Thus, when at last I could see *Gone with the Wind*, I went as a pilgrim to Gable, barely able to believe in the dream come true.

We wended quite a way to the holy site, my friend Florence and I, for the movie was playing in a shabby theater on the edges of a shabby city. Defying our mothers, we snuck to the theater on a summer afternoon, so happy the air of Newark,

New Jersey, seemed a shimmering halo. The Good God protected us from the crumbling plaster and codgers who, with us, were the only ones come then to worship at the small screen that film already larger than mind, already myth.

When I saw *Gone with the Wind* in 1975, I had not seen it since the late fifties (when I went to it for three consecutive nights, and on the third night, evidently at last satiated, fell asleep). In 1975, I could watch it in a modern movie palace, with the 70 mm screen and the stereophonic sound; and I was startled and unexpectedly moved by the faded print. The greens that meant so much to this movie were gone. The green of Tara and Vivien Leigh's eyes, the sprigs in her first ballgown, the bonnet that Rhett brings her from Paris, the portieres of Tara from which she fashions a costume to woo Rhett for the taxes. Who knew to value the greens before they faded? Everything now had a reddish cast, and outlines were hazy; the whole film seemed to reflect Atlanta burning. Now it seemed less a movie than an old painting. Like its world of the Old South, like our childhoods, it itself now became memory.

Well, its fade is appropriate, for as much as slavery, the sexual ideals implied in *Gone with the Wind* are not to be mourned.

It Isn't Bogart, It's Her Husband: The Romantic Conventions

The forms for these ideals—the romantic conventions in *Gone with the Wind*—draw the man, Rhett, into a focus in which the woman, Scarlett, now stands alone, the focus of sexual fear. To see how this matters to us now, we have to start with the conventions, because on these bare bones were hung all our different "favorite love stories" of the forties, the fifties, the thirties, the seventies. . . . The structure of romantic art, film or other, grows from preoccupation with conflict: from barriers and "trespass." The fundamental romantic theme is that what is desired is forbidden, nearly (but not wholly) unattainable, an almost impossible dream. The theme takes a number of forms, but there is a pattern, and conventions, in them all.

In the romantic love story, one of the lovers is commonly an outsider in the world in which the other lives, as cynical Rhett Butler from cosmopolitan Charleston is an outsider in the war-fevered Deep South; or as the cynic Rick is detached from the fevered idealism or fear of the anti-Nazis clustering in Casablanca. But typically, the beloved is also an outsider at home, like Scarlett the aggressive belle, or Ilsa, detached enough in Paris and in Casablanca to fall for Rick. It is this "differentness" that first attracts the lovers to each other and first signals their relationship to the audience.

The lover may also be an outsider because the beloved, fighting his or her own outsiderness, does not recognize an own true love. Ilsa fights, until she tries to, but cannot, shoot Rick. Lovers like this live in figuratively separate worlds until the blind one awakens, almost always at the end, as Scarlett does, or the "executive" Liza in *Lady in the Dark* or Tracy Lord (Katharine Hepburn) in *The Philadelphia Story.* Scarlett's sudden awakening is also typical: Ilsa suddenly lowers the gun, and never fights again; and after Melanie's death, Scarlett realizes—literally blinking her eyes in close-up—that Ashley really has loved his wife, and that her belief that he loved her has been her illusion, and his.

The barrier between Ilsa and Rick and Scarlett and Ashley—a spouse—is a classic romantic obstacle, traditionally unshakable. Until recently, Hollywood built most of its lovers' stumbling blocks as walls of virtue, often by borrowing that hoary plot device, mistaken identity. That is, until the awakening, the person who is loved mistakes the lover as immoral. So Scarlett perceives Rhett; and so in *Casablanca*, before Rick learns that the real barrier between Ilsa and himself is the immovable one, a husband, he first holds the two of them apart by mistaking her for Victor Laszlo's mistress and scoring her as a light woman. *Notorious* erects a similar barrier between Grant and Bergman from his mistaken belief that she is a loose woman. Difficult to believe about Bergman, it is easier in other, less "classy" cases. In *The Hucksters* (1947), who questions Deborah Kerr that Clark Gable is no better than he ought to be, especially with Ava Gardner hanging around? The plot of *The Hucksters* is another romantic formula, also used as one of the subplots of *GWTW*, with Kerr in the role of the good woman denying her bed to the man she mistakes as coarse (as Scarlett denies Rhett), and Gardner's Jean as another Belle Watling. (It was a typical Gardner part. In *Mogambo* (1953), her "Belle"-broad gets the guy—and this was Gable's first postwar "boffo.")

Gable and Bergman frequently endured mistaken identity—and Gilda and Bacall also in *To Have and Have Not*, among others. And it was also varied by the forties favored device, amnesia. Greer Garson and Ronald Colman could not get together for good in *Random Harvest* (1942), so long as his amnesia kept him from remembering that they were already man and wife. Gregory Peck could not give in to his and Bergman's passion in *Spellbound*, while his amnesia kept him from knowing who he really was (not a murderer). As these two instances suggest, amnesia, like mistaken identity and like death, was usually a circumstantial romantic barrier: a device picked from the plot box to delay the happy ending, and through tension, whet our desire for it. In one forties romance, however, *Love Letters* (1945), the heroine's amnesia was at least hinted as a metaphor for the romantic barriers inside us.

In *Love Letters,* Jennifer Jones falls in love with Joseph Cotten through his wartime love letters to her. But Cotten has written these letters for a soldier buddy, who she marries. Understandably, the marriage fails, she disappointed and he guilty at the lie he lives. When she thinks she has killed him (right after he tells her the truth), she becomes amnesiac; and in her new life, with a new name she gives herself (the masculine name "Singleton"), Victoria Morland innocently

falls in love and marries the letter writer, Alan Quinten. But
her psychiatrist tells Alan that if Singleton learns who he is, it
may tip her into madness. Finally, the real killer confesses,
Singleton again becomes Victoria, and deduces happily that
Alan is the "Roger" she first loved and married. It is a com-
plicated story to summarize, but important, it seems now,
because more than in most Hollywood romances (and thanks
perhaps to the screenwriter, Ayn Rand), the barriers between
these two lovers seem metaphors of personality; specifically,
images of the split in us between desiring and fearing really
knowing, and really being known by our lovers. Perhaps this
explains why this movie is one of the haunting, better-
remembered love stories for many children of the forties.

Generally, though, like the mistaken tramps, the amnesiacs
in romances merely represent a conventional hurdle. Equally
circumstantial is that ultimate barrier, death. The death that
ends the forties love stories of men at war (and a few women),
is not romantic. Nor is death from disease, such as Bette
Davis' in *Dark Victory* (1939), Maureen O'Hara's in *Sentimental Journey* (1946), or Margaret Sullavan's in *No Sad
Songs for Me* (1950), in which Sullavan spends her final days
finding her husband a new wife. In such films there is neither
conflict between the lovers nor tension in the audience,
because a happy ending is out of our hands. *Flight for
Freedom*, with Rosalind Russell and Fred MacMurray, is a
romance not because her Amelia Earhart character is killed at
the end but because throughout the movie there have been
obstacles between them, obstacles that they resolve only the
night before her last flight. The film ends with her plane falling into the sea, but the romance is over the night before,
when she and MacMurray finally clinch.

There are, though, a few forties films in which death is at
the center of a romantic plot. *Portrait of Jennie* (1948),
another favorite in memory for many, is about the love of an
artist, Joseph Cotten, for a ghost girl, Jennifer Jones (and
again, it is a Selznick production: no one understood, and
manipulated, the romantic conventions as he did—except

Hitchcock). There is also *The Ghost and Mrs. Muir* (1947), more complex than *Jennie* because it mixes comedy with the romance. Mrs. Muir (Gene Tierney) moves into the house and life of a most virile dead man, Rex Harrison; safe in this plot and the comedy, forties Hollywood indulged in licenses such as an invisible Harrison watching Tierney undress, and at the granny gowned end of the process, commenting on her "figger"; and later, as she sleeps, kissing her, a most corporeal Harrison.

More common in the forties, as always, was the traditional barrier of age, the Older Man. I know only one forties film romance in which the woman is the older lover: *Old Acquaintance*, and there Bette Davis' affair with Gig Young does not show up until the last third of the movie, could not be depicted with less passion, and ends with her giving him to Miriam Hopkins' appropriately young daughter (Dolores Moran). Whether it was Robert Stack's older man in his twenties and teenage Elizabeth Taylor in *A Date with Judy* (1948), or worldly Rhett Butler and the belle Scarlett, the pattern and the image were the same as in the eighteenth-century romantic novel, in Pamela's Mr. B and Clarissa Harlowe's Lovelace: Older, he was wise, mysteriously experienced, and thus, exciting. There are few films like *Tea and Sympathy* (1956) and *Forty Carats* (1973) overall, perhaps because filmmakers fear that older women in the audience will see all women lovers over forty as pitiful Mrs. Robinsons. But they can be sure that Rhett Butler's evident experience and worldly wisdom, apparently so much greater than that of the women he calls "child," will charm the audience as it does her—though it is part of the structure of barriers in *GWTW* that foolish Scarlett not recognize this as we do.

In *The Constant Nymph* (1943), another well-remembered forties romance, Joan Fontaine must convince the worldly composer Charles Boyer, who she adores, that she has grown up from the barefoot country child, Tessa, who he loved as a nymphet. When at long last Fontaine accomplishes this, she dies, fulfilling the film's implication that she belongs to another, more delicate world. Because she and Boyer do not consumate their love, and because she has to surmount such time-honored obstacles as his indifference because she is too young, and a beautiful wife-who-does-not-understand (Alexis Smith), Tessa's death, unlike Bette Davis' death in *Dark Victory* et al, is part of á romance. (Yet, looking back at this film as an adult, I see that, like *Spellbound*, it is more complex. For after Boyer at last recognizes their love, he tells Tessa that it is not only her age and his marriage that keeps them apart. It is also his lifelong, unworldly calling to his art, and he implies that that will always separate them.)

In *Jane Eyre* (1944), Fontaine slowly wins another classic type of older man: the one haunted by the past, made stern and forbidding by agonizing memories. In *The Seventh Veil* (1947), James Mason plays a role similar to Orson Welles' Rochester. In this film, which seems one of the more memorable romances of the forties, Ann Todd, a Grace Kelly-ish British ingenue, portrays a disturbed child-woman, cut off as by veils from what she really wants, who she really is. Mason is her sadistic guardian, who underneath it all really loves her, and who eventually she recognizes as her in-escapable soul-mate. Molly Haskell ascribes Todd's choosing "misogynous" Mason to his "English" manner: "the type most irresistible to the puritan woman . . . [because he] makes no sexual demands."[8] Haskell is right; there is no warm gleam in a crinkled, challenging eye when Mason looks at Todd, as there is when John Wayne looks at fiery Susan Hayward in *The Fighting Seabees* (1944) or cool Claudette Colbert in *Without Reservations* (1946). When at the end of *The Seventh Veil*, Francesca (Todd) chooses Nicholas (Mason) over her other two loves, it appears less roman-tically right than the appropriate conclusion to a psychology text on masochistic women. Still, the power of the romantic conventions shows never more strongly than when the lovers manipulated by them are not particularly sexual. Thus, Mason appeals as well to the unpuritan woman, because of the irrational pull of the romantic barriers. Our heads may know that Nicholas is as repressed as Ashley Wilkes, but by the end of *The Seventh Veil,* all we want is release from two hours of tension between a man and a woman fighting sex. Our sexual tension in experiencing the film does not admit the question, what kind of a husband will he make? (What would Rick and Ilsa be like, married? Or Rochester and Jane . . .?)

Since You Went Away (1944) now seems one of the clearest illuminations of how we grew, fed by the romantic formula. This film, which is David O. Selznick's *GWTW* of the war years, is an epic of the world of boarders, hoarders, margarine, intense encounters, telegrams, and tears. It is a panegyric to the resilient American war wife, but it may also be the epitomal conventional romance. More consciously, it seems, than in *Gone with the Wind*—more routinely—Selznick, who took over the script of *Since You Went Away,* played the whole bagful of romantic devices. An example, the more indicative because it is minor in the movie: Mammy in *GWTW,* Hattie McDaniel, dislikes Rhett Butler (too sexual) until he wins her with a sexual token, a red petticoat. Similarly, in *SYWA,* the All-American family's maid, Fidelia (Hattie McDaniel again) dislikes the family's debonair best friend Joseph Cotten until he gives her a sketch he as made of her—as an uptown matron svelte in a satin gown. How sensitive that indirect focus shows how. How wise he appears, obliquely. How commanding.

There are five main lines in the epic plot of *Since You Went Away:* the Hilton family's concern over their head (played by Neil Hamilton only in family photographs), who has "joined up," and who in time is reported missing; the estrangement between their wartime boarder, crochety Colonel Smollett (Monty Woolley) and his grandson Bill (Robert Walker), because the Colonel thinks that Bill is not a fighting man (Bill redeems himself by getting killed at Salerno); the crush that the elder Hilton daugther, Jane, has on an older man (Jennifer Jones and Cotten); the young love between Bill and

Jane; and Cotten's love for the family's matriarch Claudette Colbert. Of these five plots, two are traditionally romantic: the lovely, emerging woman's crush on an older man, and the dominant plot in the picture, Tony Willett's hopeless "verbal passes" (as he puts it) at the faithful wife. (Jane and Bill's love is pretty, and when he dies, it is sad, but it is not romantic because there are no barriers between them.)

With the admiration I have developed for David Selznick's Pavlovian gifts, I am reluctant to say that the Jones-Cotten relationship may be more erotic than was intended in this family epic. Jones seems now a singularly erotic sweet young thing—but this may come from the hindsight of her romances with Cotten in *Love Letters* and *Portrait of Jennie*, and from her real life divorce from her young husband, Robert Walker, and marriage to the powerful older man, David O. Selznick.

In any case, for whatever reasons, the conventions of the Older Man crush are all in *Since You Went Away*, and working well even today when I see them clearly. There is the dance she longed for, at last won, over his protests that he's too old, and danced at a romantic soldier's ball, in a vaulting airplane-hanger that is all shadows, playing spotlights, and dreaming music. There is his closeness when she plays the piano, he supporting himself naturally by resting his arm behind her as he leans over, smiling. And when she comes down with a humiliating disease—mumps—his arm curves around her bed pillow as he bends down to comfort and, at last, kiss her—alas, on the forehead.

In the relationship between Tony Willett and Anne Hilton, the conventions are even more fascinating (the snake and the mongoose again). Here, Selznick, used a full battery of devices, and then he intensified them. Not only do Tony and Anne also dance in a romantic atmosphere—that soldiers' dance to which he goes reluctantly because he is older and an officer, and at which he thus appears, romantically, as the distinguished outsider. Then also they dance to hers and her husband's song, "Together" ("We strolled the lane, together/Laughed at the rain, together. . ."). Then they take a moonlight ride in a convertible along a sea cliff. She deflates his would-be pass with unwavering smiles. He visits at sentimental, vulnerable times, such as Christmas. Invariably, they are in close physical contact. He takes her arm, lays his arm across her chairback, and leans down toward her (she goes on smiling), moves closer to her in the convertible and covers her hand in her lap. Always, it is contact within the conventions of friendship, but just within. The romantic tension in *Since You Went Away* may be more intense than in any movie I know, because nothing happens. In the scenes between Jennifer Jones and Joseph Cotten, we may sense sexuality, especially in her. But it is not acknowledged, not even hinted. Colbert is staunchly devoted to her nonexistent husband, and ultimately it is Cotten's Tony who hammers the last nail into Xanadu's coffin when, after she twits him, he admits that if she did respond to one of his verbal passes, he would lose his ideal. Like all of us romantics experiencing his epics—and perhaps equally unwittingly—Selznick seems to have wanted both the cake and the eating, both the sexy, romantic tension and the other love.

So it is with *Gone with the Wind*. In our preoccupation with romance as Rhett Butler defines it, we may not remember that from Scarlett's point of view, throughout all but the last few minutes of the movie, her love is for Ashley and is analogous to Anne Hilton's love for her husband Tim, as Joseph Cotten's Tony Willett is brother to Rhett Butler. From this perspective, Scarlett's biggest barrier is Ashley's wife. In *GWTW*, as in many romances, the spouse is a relative or close friend of the rival. Scarlett makes Melanie her sister-in-law by marrying Melanie's brother the day after Ashley marries Melanie, and Melanie cherishes Scarlett as her dearest friend after Scarlett delivers hers and Ashley's son and saves them from burning Atlanta. Rick Blaine has never met Victor Laszlo before Laszlo appears at Rick's bar. But morality creates fraternity in the movie second (if that) only to *Gone with the Wind* among favorite film romances. Admiring Laszlo's underground work, Rick returns Ilsa to the husband who needs her to inspire him in the fight against fascism. John Wayne, Susan Hayward, and Dennis O'Keefe enact a similar triangle in *The Fighting Seabees*; and it is important to note that even today, reviewing this typical Hollywood "programmer," Wayne and Hayward are no less engrossing than the iconic Ilsa and Rick as, over and over, they rush toward and retreat from their attraction to each other.

There seems a pattern: the sexier the "wrong" person, the more moral is the "spouse." It even seems masochistic now. Paul Henreid and Dennis O'Keefe play roles that are as unexciting as the plot could devise; they grovel and even offer to give their women up. But Ilsa is Victor's wife, and Hayward is O'Keefe's "intended." After we learn to love Gable and Turner as lovers fighting in *Homecoming*, the movie kills Turner off, making it easy for Gable to return to his wife (Anne Baxter), a lady as perfectly nice as Melanie Wilkes. Note: it is not that the actors are unexciting; it is the conventions. Henreid and O'Keefe and Anne Baxter also all played romantic leads, as well as these perfect, dull spouses.

In some romances, perhaps the most sadomasochistic of all, the "spouse" is not a wife but a noble career (Gary Cooper's as a Frank Lloyd Wright figure in *The Fountainhead*, or a noble cause (the Spanish Civil War, which comes ahead of Bergman for Cooper in *For Whom the Bell Tolls*). *Her* career is the obstacle in the plots of the boss-lady comedies, but because love's ultimate triumph in New Jersey was equally conventional to this type of film, there is erotic tension only when there is enough difference in the actors' personalities to break the conventions: laconic but interested Tracy versus thorny but maybe a little fascinated Hepburn; Marine Wayne and Lady Writer Colbert in *Without Reservations*. Looking back, it seems only Bogart, with Bacall, who could meld other, higher priorities, and an ultimate joining up that did not diminish her.

In *To Have and Have Not, Dark Passage* and *Key Largo*, with Bacall's integral help, Bogart implied that his being a loner was thoughtful and well-intentioned, and hence sympathetic, no matter how wrongheaded. But at the end, he came around. He came for his reasons, under his own power, but also clearly humanized by her. This may go a long way to explaining why he moves us so now. As I noted in the previous chapter, Bogart had a unique ability to suggest that he had power to spare; and that, besides, power was a delusion, and domination was not only obscene, but an obscene joke. But it seems that also, alone among the romantic heroes of the forties, Bogart went to the ultimate barrier and handled it: the question, why join up in love when there are so many irrefutable reasons not to? He implied philosophical reasons, political reasons, and the complex personal reasons of a decent, *used* human being. He never spelled these reasons out; when the scripts gave him the words, he threw them away. And when he joined up, he never really said why; he just celebrated the joining, intelligent, skeptical, but also moral, and hence implicitly hopeful. This may be why it is Bogart, and not Gable who in the seventies is the romantic hero of the forties. To see why this is so, despite Gable's having the most romantic man's role of all, only requires looking at that role with clear eyes. Sometimes it takes seven viewings, and almost thirty years.

". . . her eyes fell on a stranger, standing alone. . . ."
—from the novel *Gone with the Wind*, describing Scarlett's
first sight of Rhett (p. 96)

"Rhett Gable": At First Sight

Essentially, Rhett Butler is an outsider. In his first scene in *Gone with the Wind*, at the barbecue at the Wilkes' plantation Twelve Oaks, he appears amid the swarm of Scarlett's young beaux: older, broader-shouldered, darker, with that mustache above those white teeth and that grin. From the beginning in 1939, he has appeared inescapably as Clark Gable, at once overcoming any tow-haired, chinless juveniles. At a Chicago showing of GWTW in 1975, the au-

dience applauded Gable's first appearance, ironically one in
which he looks up, rather than down on the youths. He
stands at the foot of Twelve Oaks' swirling staircase,
smiling sardonically, admiringly, at Scarlett on the landing,
raking in the swarming beaux. Does a contemporary audience
cheer the icon Gable? Or do they cheer themselves because,
like Gable, they are not callow? It does not matter; the cheers
are really for those romantic conventions that enable Rhett to
convey without speaking a word that he is different, older,
stronger, wiser, and hence freer.

For the outsider to appear the hero, we must believe that,
against the mob, he is right. Gable's second scene in *GWTW*
is in the library at Twelve Oaks where the men talk war while
the ladies, upstairs, nap or fan themselves. As in his first appearance, Rhett Butler stands among but apart from the bab-
ble. He is silent, observing, smiling his crooked Clark Gable
smile, his eyes Gable-crinkled, the cynic. He says nothing until he is asked for his opinion, and then, at a stroke, cuts
through the hyperbole of the hot-blooded southern bucks.
(Here he is stronger, and hence more romantic, than in the
novel, where he only offers his opinion.[9]) Has anyone realized that the South has no cannon factories?, he responds. No
iron foundaries? No navy? Telling the truth earns Rhett an
invitation to a pistol duel. He declines elegantly and leaves
the room, thus allowing Ashley to tell the hothead, and us,
that his life has been spared by one of the most accomplished
shots in the South.

The southerners' hot baiting, Rhett's cool removal of
himself, and Ashley's revelation all add to Gable's appeal,
and are not in the novel. Like the change from his offering to
his being asked his opinion, these additions make Rhett-
Gable seem still more remote, mysterious, expert, and powerful. Only two appearances fix him firmly as a romantic hero.
An outsider in every way from his saturnine looks through his
cynical values, he is not only handsomer and smarter; he is
superior by *their* standards, which he disdains. The romantic
hero must appear expert at whatever he scorns; he cannot

seem to fear or to have failed at anything he dismisses, but rather, from his greater knowledge, he must seem to have chosen against it. So Gable appears; he seems cool, like Bogart. Ultimately—in the last scenes of a seventh viewing—this impression clarifies as its opposite, and unlike Bogart, Rhett Butler appears not as a model, but rather as the antihero in our romance. But throughout most of the movie, like Bogart in his films, Rhett Butler is self-assured, detached from whatever is foolish, unrealistic or indecent, our surrogate in the story, and its major distancing device. No wonder the real southern gentleman who unmasks at the end of the movie remains so well hidden.

In nothing is Rhett Butler's detachment clearer than in his language. As his manners, in Margaret Mitchell's words, "burlesqued" southerners' by "contempt overlaid with an air of courtesy,"[10] so in his mouth southern rhetoric usually satirizes Brittanic gentlemen. The perfect example is Rhett's proposal to Scarlett, in which he sweeps to his knees and simply because it is *he* using them, mocks the grandiloquent phrases we have heard in her earlier proposals. At other times, he fills the periodic and elaborately parallel forms of old world rhetoric with words that are realistic, caustic, and hence parodic. This is his language in the library at Twelve Oaks, and again when he is leaving Scarlett at the end of the movie, saying, "Never, at any crisis of your life, my dear, have I known you to have a handkerchief."

How deliberately this was done is indicated most clearly when, for the first time, Scarlett fools Rhett into believing that she cares for him. This occurs when she visits him in the Yankee prison in Atlanta. Trying to charm him out of money for Tara's taxes, she succeeds so well that at last, in a tone of real wonder, he asks, "Can it be, Scarlett, that you've grown a woman's heart?" That Rhett uses this cliché of the Old South sincerely in his first moment of surprised, real feeling, should be a clue that he is much more the southern gentlemen than he seems. Perhaps it would be, if we were not by that point so thoroughly taken in by the clichés of another stereotype, the romantic hero. Because Rhett sees so keenly through everyone else's facade, especially that of his beloved, and because he is so awfully attractive and assured, so epitomally the romantic hero, it tends not to occur to us to ask what Rhett Butler might be hiding.

This is another key to the romantic hero: he must imply not only sex-and-love but also invincibility. When Rhett finally meets Scarlett, directly after elegantly disdaining the duel with the whippersnapper, he establishes his omnipotence at once. He, and only he, has overheard Scarlett telling Ashley that she loves him; his revelation of her rejection is shattering to a southern belle. Then he announces romantically that only he understands her. They are alike in the "passion for living," which Ashley has just characterized in her. According to Rhett, it is a passion that the "elegant Mr. Wilkes" can discern but cannot feel. He and Scarlett are also alike, Rhett says, because they are both "no good." There is no chance we are going to believe this, but is is another indispensable part of a romance, rendering her, as well as him, an outsider.

But although it is necessary that we see Scarlett and Rhett as fated lovers, convention also requires that at least one of them resists the oneness. Scarlett resists (until the sweep up the staircase); and in another conventional pattern, her blindness takes the form of being a willful child to his "father." This relationship builds until their first tender moment, which occurs during the burning of Atlanta, and after Rhett discovers what we who have watched her tending the wounded and delivering Melanie's baby have already learned: that the belle Scarlett has become a take-charge midwife, and so is due respectful tenderness when, after all the horror, she falls in his arms sobbing, begging to be taken home to her mother. Rhett draws Scarlett's head against his chest, enveloping her in his strong arms, hushing her wild weeping, a father-protector. This above all is the problem, is what we all want, is what is required of a hero by Scarlett O'Hara, by Heathcliff's Cathy, Jane Eyre, Ilsa (to Rick: "You will have to think for both of us"), and the rest of us.

It Isn't Bogart; It's His White Tuxedo

At this point, we need to drop a level deeper into the details of the romantic formula. The conventions are richly textured, elegantly complex. The hero's physical largeness, for example is a constant. When he is a Gable or an Orson Welles, the broad shoulders and chests are emphasized. For slighter lovers, such as Bogart, the camera makes up the difference. In *Love Letters,* the embrace that Joseph Cotten holds back, from fear of driving Jennifer Jones mad, finally happens on the driver's seat of a cart, shot from below to emphasize his encompassing arms and shoulders. Bogart spends most of *Casablanca* in a white dinner jacket and when, in his room over Rick's café, Ilsa gives up, telling him that he must think for both of them, she throws herself back into his encircling arm, against his broad white shoulder. In the early scenes in Paris, Rick has his arm around her in an open car, and then on her couch, and she turns from the window of *La Belle Aurore* and the announcement that the Germans will enter Paris tomorrow, to lean back on the sill, so that when he moves to embrace her he must reach down toward her and the camera behind and below her. And finally, a few minutes later in *La Belle Aurore*, in what is likely the forties most erotic love scene, she begs him to kiss her as if it were the last time, and he responds by raising his shoulder and lifting her face to receive his surprising, open mouth.

A related romantic gesture is the "pick-up": Gable bends down and in his strong arms tenderly lifts first Melanie, weak from childbirth, later Ashley, fainting from taking a shot while cleaning out "Shantytown," and finally Scarlett, who not so tenderly (but with the memory of his tender totings), he sweeps up the dark stairs. How deeply this gesture is embedded in our image of romance I can now see in two stories about Gable that were national news, and, like the movie magazine story about his "potent power," were cut and pasted into my scrapbook.

A 1939 picture in *Life* magazine of the milling crowd outside Loew's Grand in Atlanta, spotlit for the premier of *GWTW*, states in its caption that Margaret Mitchell, a petite lady 4 feet 11 inches short, was "wedged in a crowd and rescued by Clark Gable, who swept her to safety." In August 1949, A. P. bulletins reported that Loretta Young collapsed on the set of *Key to the City* with a threatened miscarriage and "was carried to her dressing room by co-star Clark Gable." The follow-up bulletin of August 26, 1949, announcing the loss of Ms. Young's baby, repeated the story of Gable's carrying her to her dressing room two weeks earlier.

Now I know that what I was really cutting and pasting was (besides an insider's story), King Kong. That the hero's sweeping the woman up in his arms is an archetypical romantic gesture, related to the primal ape man metamorphosized from brute abductor to savior: Tarzan and King Kong.[11] Looking back at forties romances, the mixture of sexual threat and attraction is striking. Obvious in such favorites as *GWTW, Jane Eyre, The Seventh Veil,* and *The Fountainhead*, it is now clear in less openly sadomasochistic pairings: all those comic spankings and totings, with her squealing and beating her fists on his back, all the passionate kisses that could not be, but nonetheless, finally were.

Joseph Cotten is no rapist in *Love Letters*. He knows that Jennifer Jones may go mad if her memory returns, and her memory is of a past in which she loved him through his letters. Yet, ultimately, he gives in to his feelings and kisses her passionately, thrillingly, and, it turns out, sanely. This happens directly upon another romantic convention. Cotten picks Jones up and carries her to the cart because the heel of her shoe breaks. From this typically accidental, and romantically unromantic beginning, the lovers' forbidden coupling follows, as Scarlett and Rhett's first embrace follows their fleeing burning Atlanta with a newborn baby, a newly delivered mother, and a keening Prissy. Thus, it looks the more as if the lovers were overwhelmed by passion.

Even Rhett's "rape" of Scarlett—the sweep up the staircase—is romantically irrationalized by his being drunk; but not, of course, too drunk to be attractive. Let's call this the "stray lock of hair on the forehead" convention. There is nothing accidental, however, in the overture to the rape in *The Fountainhead* (1949). Ayn Rand's first novel, and its film for which she wrote the screenplay, is undoubtedly best known for her philosophy of individualism; but the film may have been equally influential as a romance, and perhaps may still be. The rape scene ranked high among erotica in Lois Gould's survey. In *Against Our Will: Men, Women and Rape*, Susan Brownmiller reported that for over twenty years she kept in her memory a "vivid picture" of the scene in the novel *The Fountainhead* in which Howard Roark rapes the rich man's secretly-raging-for-it wife, Dominique Françon. When Brownmiller checked the novel out of the library in the seventies, it fell open to the rape scene; and, she says that it is still as she remembered it, "torrid" (a good forties word). In Dominique's thoughts, quoted by Brownmiller, " 'the act of a master taking shameful, contemptuous possession of her was the kind of rapture she had wanted' "; and this, according to Brownmiller, "heated my virgin blood . . . and may still be performing that service for schoolgirls today."[12] Characteristically, Brownmiller offers no schoolgirls today who have read or seen *The Fountainhead*. But there is Lois Gould's survey.

Ironically, though, the "rape" in the movie *The Fountainhead* has little to do with Ayn Rand, and everything to do with the romantic conventions. This is not only the product of the Production Code but also of the movie star who played Howard Roark. Rand's Roark has nothing of the protective savage—the savior—about him; he is purely the "master" that her ironically named Dominique wants. But in the movie, though he tries for a face as stony as the quarry from which he has risen, toting his drill, Gary Cooper is undone by his sweet image. It makes his Howard Roark the conventional romantic hero, rather than Rand's brute. Ironically again, the movie's really erotic scene comes later, when in Roark's apartment, he and Dominique acknowledge their love, and thus even Ayn Rand has to allow him to give a little. In this scene, Cooper and Patricia Neal respond to each other with a movie passion that was perhaps not seen since *La Belle Aurore.* Another of the rare instances in forties films where mutually strong love and sexuality equalize the relationship between man and woman, it happened ironically, in a movie written by a woman who idealized Jehovan man and masochistic woman. This may have happened only because of the fluke that as they made *The Fountainhead*, Gary Cooper and Patricia Neal fell in love. As Bogart and Bacall innocently zapped Hemingway in *To Have and Have Not*, so Cooper and Neal transformed Ayn Rand's pathetic romantics, the master and his creature, into themselves, real people.

It is easy now to see real, mature sexual love in its few appearances in forties movies. But one relationship (Bogart and Bacall), some near misses, such as Bogart and Bergman in *Casablanca* and Tracy and Hepburn, and a scene here and there, as in *The Fountainhead*, insofar as they were noticed in the forties, were generally looked on as odd, the females appearing as "men's women." The romantic ideal was, as for many of us it still is, the rape in *The Fountainhead,* and the sweep up the stairs.

Another romantic convention, in tandem with the image of the man as protector, is the woman's resistance: would myth allow Jane to love Tarzan at first sight? Or Fay Wray to smile at the gorilla? After he shows himself as savior, the lovers' misunderstandings and other obstacles must continue, lockstepped with moments of intimacy and intimations of the passion that could be, until our tension and yearning for them to get together become almost unbearable. *The Fountainhead* follows this pattern almost exactly. Dominique and Roark move from rape to sexual love but not to marriage because she is already married, and even more because Roark doubts her mettle. Once she proves herself (by helping him dynamite a building he finds ugly), the romance is over, but the movie continues. Roark goes on trial for the dynamiting, with Cooper stumbling over the wordy Rand individualism that so appealed to late forties idealists like me, and it seems still does. But when the last obstacle between Roark and Dominique is removed, so is the romance.

Similarly, in *Jane Eyre*, the lovers, Lord Edward Rochester and his governess Jane Eyre, are separated initially by the assumptions they share: that they live in different social worlds and that because she is plain, she is unattractive. Jane is certain that she is no match for the British belle who wants Rochester. In the forties, comparing mousy brown Joan Fontaine and conventional blonde beauty Hillary Brooke, we agreed or would have had we not been so well versed in the conventions of both Hollywood and the romance, which of course told us that the hard-to-get star, not the all too accessible starlet, would eventually get the guy.

It takes more than half the movie for Jane and Rochester to get past the initial, internal barriers: for him to see her as attractive, and for her to believe it. But after they manage this, no small feat, they are separated, literally at the altar, by the revelation of his mad wife. Rochester gives into passion, but Jane refuses him (He: "Who would be hurt?" She: "We would be hurting each other"). In time, the wife removes herself by jumping from the parapet of the Rochester manor, which she has set afire. But now Rochester erects another traditional obstacle. Nobly trying to save his wife from the fire, he is blinded, and so tells Jane that, young and lovely as he now sees she is, she should not marry a "wasted" man. But, enough; the tension is at its limit (it feels so even now). After only a few minutes of fierce argument with Jane, Rochester's emotions seem almost literally to break through Orson Welles' body. He kisses her passionately, releasing us.[13]

Rhett: Closing the Door

Rochester's climactic kiss is the more thrilling because it is his and Jane's first. There are three kisses between Rhett and Scarlett (a statistic many forties girls will never have to research); but thanks to the conventions, there is no less tension. As *Gone with the Wind* draws to its close, the obstacles to Scarlett and Rhett's love become a barrage. They marry and grow close enough to have their Bonnie Blue baby girl. They draw apart when Rhett discovers Scarlett pining over Ashley's picture. After their night of ecstasy, Scarlett seems on the verge of becoming a new woman.[14] But, assuming that his passion has offended her, Rhett offers the first word in the morning, and it is a defensively sardonic apology which at once stiffens her. They go back and forth like this for the rest of the movie, coming close, then hurting each other and retreating. We see her happy smile when he returns from London, but he does not see it. We see his spontaneous grin when she reveals that she is pregant again, but she does not. When she is losing this baby, we hear her call for him and not be heard, and hear him ask if she wants him and he told, no. This goes on and on, emphasized in the movie more than in the 1,037 page novel, and ending only with Rhett's final closing of the door.

In this romance, there is no happy ending. Why? And why, now, does our hero of romantic heroes seem, unwittingly, a villain? Was Rhett not everything a romantic hero should be? Was he not so powerful that he could give a woman the strength to break any barrier between her and special him in his shining place? And was Scarlett not the woman as wily, strong, and sexual as Rhett? Why then does it all come to nothing?

No one is happy at the end of *Gone with the Wind*. Melanie is dead, Ashley is grieving, Scarlett is undeceived at last about him, Rhett is gone, and Scarlett is at last wanting him. Now, the end of this romance of romances overwhelms me with a sense of interminable loneliness, with tension and fear that no lovers will ever "connect." And I wonder if despite those final words of Scarlett's about tomorrow, did

Gone with the Wind teach us to view love and sex romantically—or bleakly?

As the movie concludes, Scarlett and Rhett discuss their misunderstandings. "I meant . . ."; "I thought . . ."; "I hoped . . ., but you . . . ." But this unraveling does not lead to the usual lovers' reconciliation. Instead, it ends with Rhett's judgment, "It seems we've been at cross-purposes, doesn't it?" With Bonnie's death, he tells Scarlett, his love for her died as well. "I liked to think that Bonnie was you, a little girl again, before the war and poverty had done things to you. . . . When she went, she took everything." And he tells her once again that she is only a child: "You think that by saying, 'I'm sorry' . . . ."

It seems that all these years most of us believed Rhett and agreed with his final judgment of Scarlett, when really he is as self-deceived about her as she was about Ashley. In reality she has not appeared childish since the siege of Atlanta, when she chose not to flee but rather to stay, to save and to bear life. And Rhett, who has scorned Ashley Wilkes throughout, at last reveals himself as Ashley's spiritual twin. When he met Scarlett at Twelve Oaks on the day the war came to Scarlett's and Ashley's world, Rhett told her that her beloved Ashley feared the "passion for living" which he, Rhett, saw as their lovers' bond. But at the end of *Gone with the Wind*, Rhett is announcing that he will return to his childhood home in Charleston, South Carolina, to look for "peace" and whatever might remain of the "charm and grace" of days gone by. How often did Ashley, too, mourn the southern past? Scarlett, on the other hand, ends the movie smiling through her tears, vowing that "tomorrow is another day." At the end, as always, she chooses the future, and life. Rhett seems suddenly no god but only a poor fool who knows nothing of love, much less a woman's sexuality. He could only get Scarlett to marry him through kisses when she was tipsy; and during their night of ecstasy he could not recognize her feelings. So she seemed to like it? Did she? And what does that matter in the morning? The morning in which a man must take a chance, as never he needs to with his whore, and believe it true that his wife enjoyed it.

Are Rhett Butler's feelings ever searched? Can he be looked at from the inside, instead of idolized? From a place inside him, with him, it seems to be he, not Scarlett, who finds sex indecent. After the "rape," sex and love finally begin to meld for Scarlett. Rhett does not even know that something happened. But this, the most profound misunderstanding in the *GWTW* myth, is less important as Rhett and Scarlett's misunderstanding than as ours. We are moved most by the kisses that imply the unknown, awesome rapture out there in the darkness beyond the happy ending. But for our lovers, particularly for the romantic hero of heroes, the kisses apparently mean nothing. No wonder that in 1975, the audience hesitated in applauding the line they had been waiting for, Gable's historic, "Frankly, my dear, I don't give a damn."* Once the godlike lover turned into Ashley retreating to the lost past, who could cheer his whistling in the dark walkout?[15]

". . .Such a Beating from Scarlett"

In *Memo From: David O. Selznick,* the creator of the movie may explain this Rhett Butler who in our childhoods broke our hearts by walking out on Scarlett forever, but taught us an unforgettable, unconscious lesson in men-women relationships by becoming our hero for doing so. In a September 1939 memo to his story editor Kay Brown, which, for some reason, he never sent, Selznick intimates that Margaret Mitchell wanted a more hopeful ending for the movie *Gone with the Wind:*

---

* It is interesting that the audience cheered the line in the snippet in *That's Entertainment II.* The people who had sat through all of *GWTW* in Chicago in 1975 tried to applaud, hesitated, and then petered out.

Please tell Miss Mitchell that I was terribly worried about the ending of the picture, as we found it impossible to get into script form even the hint that Scarlett might get Rhett back that is inferred in the book.

According to Selznick, the hopeful conclusion was dropped because Rhett

has taken such a beating from Scarlett that I think it would be the most puerile sort of ending to negate everything that has preceded it by bringing them together, and I did not succumb to this temptation, despite the coaxing of many Hollywooodites.[16]

This is how close Scarlett and Rhett came to at least the hope of true love. Later in the forties, Bogart and Bacall shot at the target. But *Gone with the Wind*, unique in its popularity, had the chance of setting us straight about the relationship between strength and love—not sex: love. And it did not happen mainly, it seems, because the moviemaker wanted to punish the woman. Was this in any way the result of the moviemaker's being married to the movie mogul's daughter? Selznick was married to Louis B. Mayer's daughter Irene until January 1949. According to Gavin Lambert in *GWTW: The Making of Gone with the Wind*, the marriage began to break up during the making of that movie, perhaps because in order to get money and Clark Gable, Selznick had to return to his father-in-law's studio. (He had left MGM in 1935 to form Selznick International Pictures and, as Lambert says, to escape from jokes that " 'the son-in-law also rises.' ") Thus, it may be that the ending of the movie *Gone with the Wind* was forecast in 1931, when Irene Mayer married the young man her father predicted would " 'end up a bum just like his old man.' "

Is this "Rona Barrett's Hollywood"? Can the failure of *GWTW* lie in the love story with a "B" plot of its thirty-seven-year-old producer? Well, the answers to important questions often are clichés. Rather than becoming Ashley

Wilkes, mooning for lost elegance, Rhett might have intimated a future in which his sexual power respected, rather than feared Scarlett's passion for living. But instead—nothing. And our conditioning is so strong that it comes hard even now to see that, at least as much as Scarlett, Rhett bears the fault for deceiving us about the nature of love.

Well before the end of *GWTW*, Scarlett no longer appears the child Rhett still calls her. She has not only endured and prevailed in the New South, she has grown in stature from the loss of children, parents, friends, and husbands. At the end, even the childish attitude expressed by "I'll think about that tomorrow" (and is it childish?), is refined to, "No, I must think about it now."[8] Thus, when she sinks to the stairs to think—the stairs up which Rhett once swept her—her thoughts seem not the illusions of a child but the solution of a resilient, spirited adult in at least some touch with her self and her strengths. She will go home to Tara, from which she draws the will to live, and she will try again, not putting off until tomorrow but investing in its promise. "Tomorrow is another day," and Scarlett's shining, final face to the camera: These words foretell not childish retreat but good, tough return. They seem the final expression of that passion for living which, as it turned out with *Gone with the Wind*, neither Ashley nor Rhett nor David Selznick could bear.

"Ilsa, I'm No Good. . .": Paradoxes

I wish that in "poor Scarlett," as Margaret Mitchell sometimes called her, strength had not been split from sex, and sex from love. I wish this were so because looking back at Scarlett, and at Liza in *Lady in the Dark*, Kit in *Old Acquaintance*, and Rusty in *Cover Girl*, I see me. But I also wish the same for Rhett. I wish that sex and love were not split in him; that they had both seen her strength as good, and had joined

their powers on these grounds. Now I understand that
"misfortune" of early adolescence, as the psychiatrist Harry
Stack Sullivan put it (in the 1940s, note): the misfortune of
the young person's "separation of lust and intimacy," intimacy focusing on the good man or woman—the one like my
father or his mother—and lust deviating to the bad one:
Rhett, who could rape; Scarlett, the "bitch-killer."[19] Now I
understand, but with rue (some "misfortune," that). For
then, of course, I did not see, though it was all there: the ex-
planations from the psychologists and their evidence in the
stories we read, the movies we saw, the songs we dreamed to.
Later, Leslie Fiedler would write that American literature, as
he might have written of the movies, is characterized by the
"breach between consciousness and unconsciousness, . . .
society and nature," the good love and marriage and the
"temporary alliance with a savage maiden whose language one
cannot understand": "Is there not, our writers ask over and
over, a sentimental relationshiop at once erotic and im-
maculate. . .?"[20] It seems—now—the question that Rhett did
not know he was asking. Nor did I.

Had I read Dr. Albert Ellis' *The Folklore of Sex,* for example, I could have seen that all my entertainments reflected and
were reinforcing the split between good love and bad (good!)
sex. Ellis, like Dr. Alfred Kinsey, one of the pioneer
popularizing sexologists—again, in the late forties—surveyed
the sexual references in popular media available in New York
City on January 1, 1950. Ellis studied best-selling novels,
magazines, plays, popular songs, radio programs, and
movies, adding a study of sexual attitudes to the Kinsey
research into sexual behavior. Whatever media Ellis studied
and whatever outlet—fornication, adultry, "petting,"
whatever—he found sex and love split, good love espoused
and bad sex decried as—delightful. And, he concluded, if sex
without love is proscribed but enjoyed, either in fact or in
fantasy, "the result is inevitable; namely, a piling up of an
enormous burden of guilt and regret that will tend to inhibit
or destroy . . . ."[21]

Ah, but who read these studies? Who understood them? I remember sneaking into the pages of *The Kinsey Report* with my girl friends, and I also recall our disappointment. Who understood what we were reading? Certainly not we nice children who floated, dreaming, into this mixed-up world of monogamous statements and libertine shadows. I find among my childhood memorabilia a scrapbook I made when I was eleven, and titled "A Girl's Life." It begins with "Baby Days": a dozen or so pictures of babies cut from magazines, captioned with my neatly printed, newspaper-style copy about the birth of "Patricia Lynn Kirby," six pounds and seven ounces and "auburn" haired, born in the "Apple Cove, Massachusetts General Hospital." The next section is "Home": a New England clapboard cottage, and pictures of interiors with bay windows, tieback curtains, ladder-back chairs, and chintz couches. "Childhood" is little girls with smooth, shining curls and starched dresses (I had straight hair and pigtails I hated to have brushed out); the little girls in the pictures are helping mother in the kitchen, playing with their dolls, hugging father when he came home from work, and laughing under the Christmas tree with brother, mother, and father.

"Teenage" is girls in pairs at football games, in prom gowns, and finally alone with a boy and ice cream cones in a convertible. This chapter ends with a *Good Housekeeping* picture of a graduation procession, dated June 1946. The next section is "Career": a model who looks like Veronica Lake and who I labeled, "age 20 years." Next comes "Romance," a montage of boys and girls kissing or cheek-to-cheek and smiling. "On June 16, 1947, in Apple Cove Congregational Church" came the "Wedding" to "Robert James Scott," attended by similarly Anglo-Hollywood names: "Sherry Baxter," "Guy Dexter," "Craig Graham". . . .The "Honeymoon" was in Cuba (*Holiday* magazine photograph of turquoise water, white beach, and striped cabana); and it is followed by "our first home" in "Seaford, Maine": a cottage set off by a white picket fence covered with roses. The scrapbook ends with pictures of its chintz couches, white tie-backs blowing in a sunny breeze, and finally, a pink and white nursery. I do not remember intending the symmetry of it all. I made the scrapbook, I realize now, at about the time that Florence and I discovered Tommy at dancing school, closeted ourselves to listen to "Temptation," and fought with our mothers for our "too tight" sweaters. In a month or so, I now know, we would sneak off to see *Gone with the Wind*.

Love was romance, white chiffon, *Stardust* and
soft summer breezes. Sex was sordid, torn
black blouses, the blues and sultry nights.[22]

This is Lucy Freeman, not a child in the 1940s, but a pretty dark-haired, dark-eyed college graduate beginning a glamorous "career" as a *New York Times* reporter; and in 1951 publishing *Fight Against Fears*, about what she learned during the psychoanalysis that began when the prettiness and glamour turned frightening. One thing that Lucy Freeman learned was that she had been shaped by movies, ballads, and "romance" magazines, and that she had used them to safely project her shameful sexual feelings: "I could revel in abandon, yet not feel too wicked."[23] Of course not. We nice girls would never do what the girls did in *True Romances*; not in real life. Lucy Freeman learned, through a long, hard time, but it took most of us longer. The answers were relatively easy; it was finding the questions in the verities that was so hard.

In the seventies, I read with irony Helen Deutsch's pioneer *Psychology of Women*, another publication of the forties. In the eyes of today's feminists, Deutsch is usually seen as a villain. Yet it seems now that she had many of the answers. And there is another irony: Deutsch could have learned from the movies and ballads and romance magazines. In the first volume of the *Psychology*, "Girlhood," she defined the " 'active woman with a masculinity complex' " through

Brunhild. But would Deutsch not have been more meaningful to more readers had she used Scarlett instead?

> These women vainly seek a Siegfried who could make them feminine, for they avoid active men, and the passive ones can hardly develop into Siegfrieds. . . .Their relationships with active men always end in conflicts, in which both partners are filled with hate and aggression.[24]

Deutsch takes her licks from today's feminists, but, read carefully, she is not prescribing rape, female masochism, penis envy, or other bad things. She is a describer, and one whose critics would do better to look into why her insights are not more dated than they are.[25]

In any case, in *The Psychology of Women* (1944-45), we could have read what was in store for us if we were "active" women. But would we have learned? Even if the conflicts *had* been imaged by Scarlett and her "passive" Ashley, and by her relationship with Rhett "filled with hate and aggression," could we have learned? Could we have learned when everything in our stardusted, schizophrenic world suggested that transcendently beautiful Scarlett, loved by the greatest lover of all, was ultimately a bitch-killer, and that dull old Melanie was the true model for nice girls like us?

We could have learned that Deutsch did prescribe that women break the "vicious circle" of their innate passivity by seeing passivity *her* way: as willed, active identification with a cause, "life process," or a man in whom the woman believes. Ideally, Deutsch's woman chooses to activate, add, and meld her synthesized erotic and intellectual gifts: her "greater intuition and greater subjectivity in assimilating and appreciating the life process." Ideally, then, there is a balance and a seamless joining between sexuality and "ambition and talent," between eroticism and "motherhood," between sex and love.[26]

Deutsch does not say that the ideal is often realized. How could she in 1944? As much as *Gone with the Wind* and

Casablanca, The Psychology of Women reveals how pervasive, encompassing, and vexing was—and is—the split between sex and love. In that time of our "misfortune," adolescence, Deutsch, like Harry Stack Sullivan, tells us that "sexuality and erotic longing for a love ideal" often "split," because conventional adolescent girls—we nice ones—sublimate our sexual desires, transforming them into fantasies. And (bleak truth): "There are many such women who all their lives long for erotic love and the experience of the *grande passion*. . . ."[27]

> There are. . .women are know only *being in love* but not *love*; they can experience love only as an. . .ecstasy of feeling. . . . As soon as the ecstasy has passed, the love disappears.[28]

Our answers were all there.

Ideally, said Deutsch, women's *doppelgänger* masks of identity, the narcissistic and the masochistic, are resolved. (And are they women's alone?) But here, as in the sex-love split, synthesis is rare. Deutsch told us that women's sense of identity is so precarious (only women's?), and the narcissism that succors it so strong, as to create a world of us who cannot love because we cannot leave ourselves, can only love our lovers' love of us. And the masochism—the self-destruction—that grows from degraded feelings is too easily thrilled by power, too responsive to rape. Up the stairs. Into the dark. Looking for Mr. Goodbar, or "Mr.President.". . . Yet it almost enlightened the strong person, Scarlett. If only the conventions had not done in Rhett, for whom it was only Belle Watling, not his wife Scarlett, who was supposed to enjoy it.

But in the forties, few of us read Deutsch, and only a few (certainly not we children) analyzed "the movies." Who, for example, saw herself and himself in the ad for *The Loves of Carmen* (1949), which featured a picture of Rita Hayworth cowering under Glenn Ford, his arm raised to smack her, and the copy, "The world is full of Carmens. They may not know it except in their most secret day dreams." Now we may see the rape at the heart of Scarlett and Rhett's romance, and reject our old hero Rhett Gable. But with whom do we replace him? A gentle man who is strong, like Bogart's images? Or one who asks little because, like Ashley Wilkes, he fears "passion for living"? A lot of the gentle, sensitive contemporary heroes remind me of Ashley; few recall Bogart's Harry Morgan in *To Have and Have Not*, who is strong and secure and, as Molly Haskell says, "heroi[c]" at the end because he joins up with a woman.

John Updike, whose fictional heroes are frustrated romantics, wondered in a recent essay whether the novel would survive the removal of the sexual prohibitions that provide its tension.[29] It is, of course, not really the novel but the romance on whose extinction Updike muses. As John Cawelti says in his recent text *Adventure, Mystery, and Romance: Formula Stories as Art and Popular Culture*, "the coming age of women's liberation will invent significantly new formulas for romance, if it does not lead to a total rejection of the moral fantasy of love triumphant."[30] At this time, however, we might ask about *our* survival when sexual prohibitions are repealed: How many of us can deal with a relationship after all the conventional barriers are removed and only the real ones remain? I wonder if many of us, or many younger men and women, will find much sexual love, or other than token sexual equality, until, as in a Bogart-Bacall film, we go to the personal arena, take a chance with ourselves, and try to meld gentleness and strength. If we try and it works, we have the freely given, mutually enjoyed sexuality that changes both the rape and the reverence when it anneals them. It will not be ideal, but it will be a good relationship. It seems not widely, or easily achieved. For that, *Gone with the Wind*, that favorite of favorite romances, the dream of dreams, must answer.

As must *Casablanca*, the favorite movie of many of us,

including our romantic President John Kennedy. It would be striking, I think, to know how many Americans could recite these lines:

Ilsa, I'm no good at being noble, but it doesn't take much to see that the problems of three little people don't amount to a hill of beans in this crazy world.

It would be striking because in the seventies, Vichy, the Nazis, the refugees, the hope of America, the moral decay of Europe, moralism itself, and The War itself, have all faded, and this crazy world and those three romantic people remain, still enthralling us. Rick would have appreciated the irony.

Notes

1. See Molly Haskell, *From Reverence to Rape: The Treatment of Women in the Movies* (Baltimore: Penguin Books, 1974), p. 166.

2. Margaret Mitchell, *Gone with the Wind* (New York: The Macmillan Co., 1936), p. 941.

3. Ibid., p. 940.

4. *New York Times Magazine*, March 2, 1975, pp. 60-62.

5. Haskell, *From Reverence to Rape*, pp. 166-67.

6. Harvey R. Greenberg, *The Movies on Your Mind* (New York: Saturday Review Press, E. P. Dutton & Co., 1975), pp. 13-14; Leslie Fiedler, *Love and Death in the American Novel* (New York: Criterion Books, 1960), p. 319; Marjorie Rosen, *Popcorn Venus: Women, Movies and the American Dream* (New York: Avon Books, 1974 [1973]), p. 180.

7. In Ralph Tyler, "Literary Figures Offer Plots and Quips," *New York Times*, August 1, 1976, Section D, p. 13.

8. Haskell, *From Reverence to Rape*, pp. 164-65.

9. Mitchell, *Gone with the Wind*, p. 110.

10. Ibid.

11. In a rare use of popular culture by a forties scientist, Helene Deutsch cites King Kong as the prevalent hero of "a girl's dreams": rapist and rescuer merged in a single "mighty hairy human-animal." *The Psychology of Women: A Psychoanalytic Interpretation* (New York: Bantam Books, 1973 [1944]), 1, "Girlhood," 227.

12. Susan Brownmiller, *Against Our Will: Men, Women, and Rape* (New York: Simon and Schuster, 1975), pp. 314-15.

13. The reviewer for the Los Angeles *Evening Herald Express* (Feb. 11, 1944)

wrote, "The back breaking kiss given the heroine by the hero along with a blast of trumpets or something, at the finale, brought the type of yell from the audience lately developed by the manifestation of Frank Sinatra." Sumiko Higashi quotes this in *"Jane Eyre:* Charlotte Bronte Vs. The Hollywood Myth of Romance," *Journal of Popular Film* 6:1 (1977), 23. Higashi's point is that "male-dominated" Hollywood could not help betraying even the relatively mild woman's view of Charlotte Bronte's nineteenth-century novel because of the prevailing " 'true romance'. . . .ideology." (She might have said the same of Charlotte's sister Emily's *Wuthering Heights*, made in Hollywood by David Selznick.

14. In the novel, Scarlett's reaction is more complex. She is sexually thrilled, but thrilled at being "used. . . brutally"; and she plans to use her new knowledge that Rhett loves her to make him "jump through. . .hoops." (pp. 940-41)

15. For Joan Mellen, in *Big Bad Wolves: Masculinity in the American Film*, the Rhett who cries over Scarlett's miscarriage (and as Mellen notes, Gable protested against this crying because of his "image") is Margaret Mitchell's dream man (and Mellen also points how he is even more unconventionally un-macho in the novel). Mellen sees his behavior at the end as, in effect, his giving up: after the death of Bonnie and Scarlett's accusing him of being her murderer, Rhett, says Mellen, "is returned to that fantasy male persona for whom weakness or distress is unthinkable." For her, this final failing is unimportant: "Clark Gable as Rhett Butler" is "the image of male perfection," to which "depth is added by his gentleness. . . ." (New York: Pantheon Books, 1977), pp. 123-24.

16. Selected and edited by Rudy Behlmer (New York: Avon Books, 1973 [1972]), pp. 258-59.

17. Gavin Lambert, *GWTW: The Making of Gone with the Wind*, (Boston: Atlantic Monthly Press, Little, Brown & Co., 1973), pp. 31-34; 74; the quotations are from pp. 9; 12.

18. I am grateful to Kary K. Wolfe for pointing out the relationship of this line, "No, I must think about it now," to the impression that by the end of *GWTW*, Scarlett is not the child she appears to Rhett or to most interpreters of the novel and movie.

19. Harry Stack Sullivan, *The Interpersonal Theory of Psychiatry*. Edited by Helen Swick Perry and Mary Ladd Gawel (New York: W. W. Norton & Co., 1953), pp. 274-76. This text is taken from 1946-47 Sullivan lectures, posthumously collected. "Bitch-killer" is Leslie Fiedler's term (see note 6).

20. Fiedler, *Love and Death in the American Novel*, pp. 331-32.

21. Albert Ellis, *The Folklore of Sex*, Rev. Ed. (New York: Grove Press Black Cat Books, 1961), pp. 211-13; the quotation is from p. 213. This study was originally published in 1951 and reissued in 1961 with additional material from 1960.

22. Lucy Freeman, *Fight Against Fears* (New York: Crown Publications, 1951), pp. 122-23.

23. Ibid., pp. 139-40.

24. Deutsch, *The Psychology of Women*, I, "Girlhood," 302. Deutsch uses popular art only twice in this volume. There is the King Kong example, previously cited; and a reference to Sally Benson's 1941 novel *Junior Miss* (also a Broadway play and a 1945 movie), illustrating the propensity for "identification" in the "prepuberty" phase. (I, II)

25. Susan Brownmiller, for example, believes Deutsch "has caused real—and incalculable—damage to the female sex." (*Against Our Will*, p. 316) See also Juliet Mitchell, *Psychoanalysis and Feminism: Freud, Reich, Laing and Women* (New York: Vintage Books, 1975 [1974]); and, of course, Karen Horney's classic charge in *New Ways in Psychoanalysis* (New York: W. W. Norton & Co., 1938), and Deutsch's defense, that female masochism is a reality, born of unnecessary, but nonetheless real feelings of insecurity, and needing to be "steer[ed]. . .into the right paths." (*The Psychology of Women*, I, 285, fn. 13) Susan Brownmiller's *Against Our Will*, among other information, suggests that it is still a reality.

26. Deutsch, *The Psychology of Women*, I, 131; 133; 135; 142-43; 151-52.

27. Deutsch, I, 190.

28. Deutsch, I, 220.

29. John Updike, "The Future of the Novel," *Picked-Up Pieces* (New York: Alfred A. Knopf, 1975), pp. 17-23.

30. John Cawelti, *Adventure, Mystery, and Romance: Formula Stories as Art and Popular Culture.* (Chicago: The University of Chicago Press, 1976), p. 42.

3

My Favorite Brownette: An Iconography of Hollywood Beauty in the Forties

...The main thing [about the glamour girl of the thirties-forties] was that she should resemble as closely as possible the archetypal model represented by the leading movie actresses and the girls who posed for fashion ads. . . . .A great part of the resources of the industrial era was devoted to making her as lovely as possible. Her carefully waved hair swept to her shoulders; her evening gowns, based on simple classic models, swept to the floor. Her demeanor was natural, friendly and, on the whole, placid. Technological advance and the ubiquity of the movies and picture magazines spread her influences through every level of U.S. society to the point where glamour girls could be found on any street corner or behind any department-story counter. Never before had so many women been so beautiful.
—Winthrop Sargeant, "Fifty Years of American Women,"
Life, January 2, 1950, p. 67.

What obsesses [men] far more than a mother image is "standardized beauty.". . . .A man who falls passionately in love with a woman whom he *alone* finds beautiful is supposed to be a prey to nerves.
—Denis de Rougemont, *Passion and Society [Love in the Western World]*, 1939, p. 294.

I will tell you all about my standards of beauty in the forties because they were—and still are—an enormous influence on my life and values, alas.

I recall the perfection in appearance of women in films. There was never a flaw in their features, even when they were not pretty. Nor was there a flaw in their complexions. I never had a very bad case of acne, but I had a little—and every pimple made me into an obviously inferior person. The stars, of course, were the standard; whatever feature fell short of Hollywood's perfection was not just a physical defect; it was a token of some personality or character deficiency. In fact, it was downright immoral (I am not exaggerating) to have defects: didn't Hollywood tell us that perfection was possible? And if one was not perfect, one wasn't good either; one had let some part of oneself go. God hated me for being so ugly to begin with: he gave me red hair to punish me. He also knew that I was a bad person because my head was full of wicked thoughts— especially about sex—almost all the time. So my turpitude was visible to everyone in my looks: it was clear I was no movie star and would never be one.

—a child of the 1940s

Ingrid Bergman, who now seems the only complete woman in forties movies, was not by forties standards beautiful. "How could anyone be glamorous without fire-red lipstick?": The scorn of us children, as always the most rigid standard-bearers, was matched by the indifference of most adults. How could it be otherwise? *Life* and the movie magazines did not see Bergman as a glamour girl; and how could *that* be otherwise? She was so aberrant from the model.

Her hair was rarely coiffed; usually, it looked hazy and flyaway, as in *Gaslight*, or casually tucked behind her ears, as in *Casablanca*. Its dark blonde color was also undefined, and her features, too, were soft. In the forties, who thought of Bergman in Technicolor? She had no contrasts, except those magically white teeth which, it seems, she showed only when she really felt warm and good. It seems now that only Bergman really smiled in forties films. But at the time she just looked "different," and different was not beautiful.

Of Bergman's first American film, *Intermezzo* (1939), Pauline Kael recently wrote that "the film's only real claim on anyone's attention was Bergman, whose natural look (full eyebrows, and even a shine on her nose) seemed revolutionary."[1] But Kael should say "seems," not "seemed," for in the forties Bergman's looks, like her sensuality, caused no revolution. She was not a glamour girl; and hence, as hard as it is to believe today, the forties generally found her as one man says of his memories, "big and bovine."

Vivien Leigh, on the other hand, fit the forties standards of transcendent beauty precisely. Then, as Winthrop Sargeant's midcentury piece for *Life* affirms, beauty was defined by the Cover Girl, a model with regular and harmonious features and coloring. Transcendent beauty, such as Leigh's, was the model plus drama, but a drama of contrast, not exaggeration. If exaggeration had been thought beautiful, Hepburn would have been a model because of her cheek-bones (she was a model, before the forties), and Bette Davis because of her eyes. But contrast co-existing with regularity *contains* difference, makes the unusual safe, and removes threat. The contrasts of Vivien Leigh's black hair, alabaster skin, and green eyes framed by black lashes were beautiful in my childhood because each unusually lovely element was delimited by a conventional frame. The greener than green eyes were conventionally shaped, not too round, too oval, too small, or too bulging. The lashes were clearly defined, but neither too meager nor too obtrusive. The raven hair was luxuriant, but not wild. The red lips were neither spinsterish-skinny (though they tended that way), nor were they slashing, like Joan Crawford's. The cheekbones were not cadaverous, but Yeatsian. In other words, Leigh's was a face reflected throughout the forties, in Hedy Lamarr, Merle Oberon, Paulette Goddard, Maureen O'Hara, Jennifer Jones, Jeanne Crain, Jean Simmons, and, ultimately, Elizabeth Taylor.

Our focus now is the "looks" of the forties woman in its

model form, the movie star, and even more, the starlet, the movie version of the nearly anonymous fashion model. It is a subject that begins—neatly, it seems now—with the transcendent beauty of Vivien Leigh in the grand romances of the early forties, *Gone with the Wind* and *Waterloo Bridge* (1940), and ends with the ineffable, and it seems indescribable beauty of the young Elizabeth Taylor.* It is a subject that does not include Ingrid Bergman, but does encompass the starlet Dolores Moran and the Cover Girl Francine Counihan, who are not often in the coffee-table art books of beautiful faces.

"God Hated Me for Being So Ugly. . ."

We grew up in the forties believing that to be beautiful was very heaven. It was the key to the Right Man and the Home Beautiful—if, of course, we were also virgins. Marjorie Rosen attributes our deification of beauty to the Depression, which removed women from the job market and made "concern with appearance" an "acceptable time filler, even an obsession"; and she attributes the spread of the obsession to the wartime emergence of teenagers as an affluent consumer group.[2] But whereas it is probably defensible to see the Depression intensifying an escapist cult of beauty (though one largely limited to the affluent), and whereas it is evident that in the war years "bobby-soxers" became more visible in the economy, and hence in the culture, our belief in the power of beauty still depended on neither disaster. This goddess is ages old, and its worship by adolescents is part of the rite of passage. From age to age and among societies, only the standards change, only the models.

---

* Whom family friends wanted to test for the role of the child Bonnie, in *Gone with the Wind*, because she looked so much like Vivien Leigh. James Robert Parish and Ronald Bowers, *The MGM Stock Company: The Golden Era* (New Rochelle, N. Y.: Arlington House, 1973), p. 696.

In the forties, the models were—models: the Powers Girl of John Robert Powers; the Cover Girl of Harry Conover, et al. This, of course, is a tautology; in whatever cultures she exists, the professional model embodies the standards of beauty. But in the forties, particularly in the war years, these conventions were especially rigid: The model was classic in her regular features and solid form (by 1960s-70s standards, American beauties of the forties all look bovine). Her hair was the long, glamour girl bob, varied by sausage rolls or "upsweeps" of small, tight curls. (Make little of this psychologically; the repressed curls came from the primitive "permanents" and "dryers," to which each curl was plugged by its own ganglion. Getting a "perm" was a protracted torture; I gave up my pigtails for my first permanent in 1945, and still smell foul chemicals and electrical ganglia. Though we didn't know her then we all felt lucky when we did not come out looking like Elsa Lancaster's *Bride of Frankenstein* [1935]).

Back in the forties, the model's eyes were round, not too near but not too far from the nose. The nose was straight and slim but not skinny. (Mine had a bump, which all by itself, made me switch my dream from "actress" to "radio actress.") The model's lips were not too thin, not too full. (A male child of the forties remembers being fascinated by "the way the lipstick didn't match the shape of the lips.") Looked at now, all the models or movie starlets of the forties vary, one from the other, in some way (though sometimes one has to look hard). But then, so prone were we to see them as alike, that they did look alike. In the fifties, no one missed Marilyn Monroe's difference, but in the late forties, she was another indistinguishable Blonde Beauty in the chorus line. So was Shelley Winters, a bit named "Bubbles" in Rita Hayworth's chorus in *Tonight and Every Night* (1945). As in the stories, so in forties "looks," it was the form, much more than the content, that mattered.

Thus, our models were also not the superstars. In their looks as in their roles, Garson, Hepburn, Davis, Dunne, et al.

seemed to live in another world. In some way, each was exaggerated: Hepburn in her cheekbones and mouth, Davis in her eyes, Garson in the color of her hair, and Dunne in her thirties-style thin lips and eyebrowns and prominent nose. But it was not so much their looks as their images that set them apart. In her thirties films, a blonde Bette Davis is virtually indistinguishable from the other girls. But in the forties, in their roles, their ages, and their images, the superstars belonged to our mothers. (That is, the women did. The older men, such as Gable, also belonged to us for crushes.) When I went back to one of my mother's favorite movies from the early forties, *Old Acquaintance*, I carried only the dimmest memory of the stars, Bette Davis, Miriam Hopkins, and John Loder. *I* remembered the ingenues, Gig Young and Dolores Moran; and now I am surprised to discover that they do not even appear until the movie is two-thirds over. Now I can guess that the sophisticated atmosphere of *Old Acquaintance* imprinted itself on my dreams, and now I can wonder if Bette Davis taught me that the most romantic love is forbidden sex. But until I reviewed *Old Acquaintance*, I did not know it was about the split between sex and love, and I remembered the elegance only hazily, as a dreamlike backdrop for the dark-haired, handsome Young and the pretty blonde Moran. In a survey from the time, a "young salesgirl" is quoted: "I used to like Star X very much when he was playing in important supporting roles. Now that he is playing leads he is not as attractive to me as he used to be. . . .' "[3] I was another young salesgirl, and so, my interviews tell me, were many other children of the forties—and beyond. In our pasts, we all have a Veda Ann Borg or a Dolores Moran, or an Yvette Mimieux or Katharine Ross, perhaps because unlike the Bette Davises, the starlets could belong to us.

The fluid jersey gowns and the furs that Davis wears in *Old Acquaintance* look attractive now; but I know that I ignored them then, and why shouldn't I? What had they to do with me? The superstars did not go to proms or to state fairs. They talked, usually seriously, sadly, angrily, lengthily, intensely, instructively, confusingly. Their movie lives and persons were too expensive or important for us to aspire to; as we say today, they were inacccessible. Now, forties superstar Ginger Rogers looks startlingly like forties dependable B-lead and "best friend" support Lucille Ball. But I never noticed this at the time. Little seen and heard, as Molly Haskell notes,[4] children, especially we girls, tended to identify with the stars' best friends: Geraldine Fitzgerald in Bette Davis' *Dark Victory*, Jane Wyman, Eve Arden, Faye Emerson, Ruth Hussey, et al.; and even more with the starlets. Along with the movies, everything from fairy tales through "Ivory Baby" ads and popular songs, conspired unwittingly to teach us subservience and to inculcate a reverence of beauty. It occurs to me only now that the ugly duckling never was acceptable as an ugly duckling.

Beauty Was Not . . .

Being beautiful in the forties seems now to have meant two negatives: not looking different and not looking sexy. Avoiding uniqueness is an unvarying adolescent intention, but how did we charm the right man without looking sexy? Writing about a typical ingenue of the time, Joan Caulfield, James Robert Parish gives our answer: "Joan represented the ideal woman of the 1940s. Her sexual appeal never burst into overtness and she seemed the type of female happy to be a woman in a man's world."[5]

Winthrop Sargeant of *Life,* said such the same in hymning the glamour girl's "blooming health and . . . air of virginal innocence which was somehow never compromised by her good-natured friendliness toward the male." And the movie magazine *Hollywood*, June 1941, in a story titled "Saga of the Sirens," defined Rita Hayworth, Jane Russell, Ann Sheridan, et al. as "typically American in appearance, retaining all the appealing wholesomeness of the school girl with a more mature feminine allure.'' Of Russell, the *Hollywood* story said:

> Healthy, full-figured, hard-working, athletic—this is the girl who is today setting the standards of beauty for America's young women. Hers is . . . a beauty that every woman, in gazing upon her, feels is as much her own as the property of an alluring screen star.

As this implies, even the pinups, the sex symbols of the forties, were played down as sex figures and played up as model wives. We can see now that these standards were based on fear: Harlows and Dietrichs threatened the family, and after Pearl Harbor, they threatened the morale of the girls the men who went to war left behind. But at the time we children knew only the wholesome glamour girls of the forties, and thus, a basic standard was not to "burst into overtness": not to suggest that you had "done it," or even worse, enjoyed doing it. (The more forties movies I see now, the more anomalous and amazing Bergman in *Casablanca* and *Notorious* appears.) Thus, we dogged after the happy ending, modeling ourselves upon Joan Caulfield rather than Gilda. But the culture that hid sex could not help but make the romantic chase look move inviting than the sanctioned, but scarily unknown "bliss" that always came after the final fade.[6]

A girl could avoid bursting with sexiness by modeling herself upon an ingenue. But what could she do to avoid looking different? Here enter the merchandiser, who in the thirties could make Bette Davis look like everyone else in the chorus line, and in the forties fan magazine portraits, make Katharine Hepburn a glamour girl with enlarged crimson lips, coiffed hair, and even spikey lashes. Judy Garland was ecstatic when for *Meet Me in St. Louis*, she was at last given the rounded eyes, arched eyebrows, and fuller mouth of the glamour girl.[7] The studios did groom some different looking actresses—the specialties, such as Carmen Miranda. Among ingenues, June Allyson is a unique example until the postwar years. But even if we loved Junie, we placed her outside the range of beauty because, according to the standards of the forties, looking beautiful did not mean looking like either Allyson or the forties Bette Davis. It meant looking like Dolores Moran.

The Intricate Rules of Wonderland

Dolores Moran had butter-blonde hair that curled away from a center part to fall down her back. Her face had cheekbones, but was pleasantly rounded. Her eyes were large and round under perfect arcs of eyebrow. Her nose and mouth were also modeled on the circular, lush but not bulbous. Her features were regular and in proportion. She was a model because she looked like the professional models, who, in turn, looked like her. She is only an example; I could substitute any of the "sultry brunettes" from my Typology—Sheila Ryan, Marguerite Chapman, Ramsay Ames, et al.—or other "blonde beauties," such as Martha O'Driscoll or Lee and Lynn Wilde. The Wilde twins are the perfect symbol of the forties model. Not only were their features perfect according to the standards of the time but each was so far from looking different as to duplicate the other.

I can see now why I liked a 1944 programmer I used to think was only one of those inexplicable favorites that everyone has. *Nine Girls* included Jinx Falkenburg, a professional model *cum* starlet, and eight others, such as look-alike, look-like-Dolores-Moran blondes Leslie Brooks, Lynn Merrick, and Anita Louise. Nine from whom to pick a favorite: the challenge was their similarity. It was a "Miss America" contest for the pretelevision forties; as were *The Powers Girl* (1942; Anne Shirley, George Murphy, and Carole Landis), its spin-off *Cover Girl*, the Danny Kaye-Samuel Goldwyn pictures featuring the handpicked "Goldwyn Girls," and *Du*

Barry Was a Lady (1943), starring Lucille Ball and twelve "Du Barry Girls," derived from Varga.[8]

The models looked like mirror images in form, but intense opposites in coloration. (I see that the game was complex, as are the classic children's games.) In form and even in hairstyle, the blonde Dolores Morans and dark Acquanettas were near duplicates. But in hair color was realized Flo Ziegfeld's dream of glorifying the American girl: "blonde, brunette, redhead" (as William Powell's Flo put it in *The Great Ziegfeld,* 1939). The demarcation of hair color, and the emphasis on it, were important; it is clear now that Bob Hope's *Favorite Blonde* (1942) (Madeleine Carroll) and *Favorite Brunette* (1947) (Dorothy Lamour), are symbolic. *Ziegfeld Girl* (1941) starred Hedy Lamarr, Judy Garland, and Lana Turner, and the ad-makers emphasized " 'The Three B's of Beauty, i.e., Brunette, Bronzette and Blonde.' "[9] It may sound silly now, but hair color was solidly rooted in the psychology of the early forties.

In that time, hair color was as intense as those rich-red, full lips. Turner and Grable were strongly blonde (compare them to the anomaly, Allyson). Lamarr, Lamour, Montez, Darnell, et al. were Dark Ladies; and Hayworth, Garson, Maureen O'Hara, and Lucille Ball, each in her shade, was distinctly a redhead. This intense and demarcated coloration must in some way be related to the exciting developments in Technicolor in the early forties. But I wonder now if it did not reflect real life as well as nourish it; for despite today's nostalgic thesis that the forties were a happy time, even for children, real life then was pervasively, deeply, and dreadfully preoccupied with the World War. Perhaps at some deep level the clear-cut categories of women's looks bespeak our time's need for clear and simple signals. As a sign of how the seventies differ from the forties, with the exception of Hepburn and Crawford, the movie actresses of the forties who have been elevated to superstardom in the seventies are all among the minority who had indeterminately colored hair: Bergman, Bacall, Davis, Stanwyck, Garland, Sheridan, and Lupino.

Looked at today as a memory of perfection, Dolores Moran looks imperfect—of course. Moran or Acquanetta: now they all look as distinctive as June Allyson. Specifically, in profile Moran looks like Liza Minnelli, who no one has ever accused of looking like a Cover Girl. Even more my model than Moran and Sheila Ryan, probably because she was even more obscure, was Francine Counihan, a Harry Conover Cover Girl brought to Hollywood for the grandest of its forties genre of model movies. When I saw *Cover Girl* originally, Counihan won my vote; and needless to say, when I looked back from the seventies, she no longer looked perfect. The first time I reviewed *Cover Girl*, I could not even find her (which must make my point about the anonymity we wanted in our models). On a second re-viewing, I found her posing as the *American Home* cover.[10] On first sight (which is all you have, since each model is on close-up for only a few seconds), she looked like Jinx Falkenburg's clone. But then, did I see it? Was her nose a little long and skinny? Think on this: a young model in New York, Betty Bacall, had to choose between a sure thing, the role of the *Harper's Bazaar* cover in *Cover Girl,* or a chancy look-see by Howard Hawks, searching for someone to play with Bogart in *To Have and Have Not.*[11]

Even Lee Wilde looks different now from Lynn (I think). And yet how different were Lee-Lynn's looks from Lana Turner's? How distinct was Hedy Lamarr from Acquanetta? Not very—now. Turner and Lamarr, or Gable and Darnell, are clearly types of the Blonde Beauty and the Sultry Brunette. But although they were young enough not to be as inaccessible as the superstars, Turner and Lamarr, et al., had enough image to discourage our identifying. In the cocoon of the movie hosue, a young girl might inhabit a little known Dolores Moran, but not a star like Lana Turner.[12]

When Evelyn Keyes, Rhonda Fleming, Yvonne de Carlo, Ava Gardner, Susan Hayward, Dorothy Malone (Maloney), or Jane Greer (Bettejane Greer) were starlets listed late in the credits as "Girl," they could be our models. But as their roles grew, they began to look less typical and more distinctive. As with everyone, the more we saw them, the more individual they became. This simple fact of perception explains why the forties movie actresses who I cherish as models or beauty in a special, inarticulate corner of my memory, are not the supernally beautiful icons Elizabeth Taylor and Ava Gardner, but the nearly anonymous starlets who were almost ignored even by the movie magazines. (Pictures of Dolores Morgan were treasures, not to mention pictures of Lenore Aubert. . . .) The number of these women was comforting, and everyone else's indifference was delicious. The "girl bits" belonged to us; but each of us thought she belonged to *me*. From *Nine Girls* I remembered Jinx Falkenburg and the look-alike blondes. But until I looked it up, I had forgotten that there was a star among the nine: Evelyn Keyes. I had even forgotten that Evelyn Keyes was in *Nine Girls*.

The Avis Girl and the Shiny Sedan

The movie moguls of the forties searched among starlets and models for young women who looked enough like the popular types to appear pleasingly familiar, but different enough to stand out and become stars. When they found a Rita Hayworth named Marguerita Carmen Cansino, they changed her name, her hair color from dark to auburn to make her look different, and her hairline, to make her look "normal."[13] We girls also looked for the pleasingly novel, but like the moguls, within limits that now seem as rigid as they were then unquestioned. One could not have an abnormally low forehead or bumps on the nose and be beautiful. The point at which a girl bit became too well known was similarly exact—and unconscious. Susan Peters, for example, survived the rise to ingenue stardom with me because she did not rise too far (perhaps for a tragic reason: in a 1945 hunting accident, she was crippled). My other midforties favorite, Jeanne Crain, also survived stardom until, in the late forties, she was everywhere in all the movie magazines, at which time I lost interest in her. It may have been something else. As she began having children (three sons born between April 1947 and August 1950), Jeanne Crain began to look more matronly; and as there was also more of me, I, perhaps for this reason, began to lose track of the Francine Counihans and Dolores Morans, and for the glamour girl of my dreams, to move all the way to Elizabeth Taylor.

But it is clear now that we also had models who were not by any standards glamour girls. It also seems clear that we accepted these variations from the model-starlet norm because they filled a need for another kind of model. The conventional beauties were physical models, guides to getting Mr. Right. But few of us believed that we would ever look like a Cover Girl. Thus, we needed realistic surrogates: the "cute kid," as well as the glamour girl.

The ingenue who was not modeled on the Cover Girl was cute. Rather than Ziegfeld's blonde, brunette, or redhead, her hair was usually brown or blonde-brown—"American Blonde," it was democratically called, and sometimes, "muddy blonde." Sometimes she wore it short, instead of in the glamour girl bob. She might even wear pigtails (Jeanne Crain in *Home in Indiana*, 1944). Her nose could vary from the straight, thin norm, as June Allyson's and Jane Powell's did. Her eyes could be unconventionally small (Allyson) or prominent (Powell); her lips, less full, and pink rather than crimson (Allyson; Diana Lynn). The cute girls were imperfect—the Avis girls who had to try harder—as most of us in the audience did.

The split between the two types of ingenues is illustrated by a casting phenomenon of the forties. In this period of clear demarcations, contrasts, and pairings, Hollywood developed a gimmick it seems never to have had before or since. It paired two ingenues, one the conventional Cover Girl type and the other a little different looking, and ballyhooed them as a contrasting pair. Because they were newcomers, the fillip for the audience was to rate them and predict which one would become the star. (Boys had their favorite rookies, new car models. . . .)

Jane Powell and Elizabeth Taylor are the model for these movie pairs, although they were not the first; in fact, they came late in the spree. They made only one picture, *A Date with Judy* (1948), although the movie magazines extended their pairing by having them double dating and bridesmaiding for each other. They were also atypical in being relatively well-known at the time they were paired. But in their looks and images, they epitomize the principle of balanced antithesis that seems largely to underlie Hollywood's handling of men and women in the forties. And like the other pairs, they were among our favorite and best remembered ingenues.

Jane Powell was the "little lady with the big voice," L.B. Mayer's new Jeanette Macdonald.* Powell had short, curly dark blonde hair, a flatbridged nose, and slightly too large eyes and a too full mouth. But the eyes were an unusually sparkling blue, and since she had a pleasantly true light operatic voice, she was cast to sparkle exuberantly. In 1948, Elizabeth Taylor had long, "raven" waves, center parted, making her look at once classic and Madonna-like. Her eyes were contrastively light, violet blue, and perfectly oval in form; her dark brows were almost, but not too luxuriant. The cheekbones were there, but they were not obtrusive; and like the rest of us who were her peers, she probably gave no thought at all to the settling of the jowls. Her nose was

---

*Powell actually played Macdonald's daughter in *Three Daring Daughters* (1948). The pairing of established, aging stars and newcomers in mother-daughter roles is not unique to the forties, but it is another example of the principle of balanced antithesis. Jennifer Jones and Shirley Temple played Claudette Colbert's daughters in *Since You Went Away*, and June Allyson was Colbert's stepdaughter in *The Secret Heart* (1946). Elizabeth Taylor was Garson's and Pidgeon's daughter in *Julia Misbehaves* (1948) and Joan Bennett's in *Father of the Bride* and *Father's Little Dividend* (1950; 1951). And in *Secret Ceremony* (1968) Mia Farrow played Taylor's surrogate daughter. In the fifties, Sandra Dee played Lana Turner's daughter in *Imitation of Life* (1959) and *Portrait in Black* (1960), and in *A Summer Place* (1959), Dee's mother was the forties perfect young wife, Claudia—Dorothy McGuire. . . .

perfect, as was her mouth; and who would try to describe the way Elizabeth Taylor looked when she was seventeen? In 1948, Elizabeth Taylor may have been so perfect as to wipe out the conventions of beauty; it is an idea I return to at the conclusion of this chapter. Yet despite this awesome beauty, Taylor illustrates conventional good looks in the ingenue pairs of the forties because her beauty in *A Date With Judy* was a surprise, a first-blooming. She was not then a superstar, and was, in fact, billed third, after Jane Powell and Wallace Beery.

Like the other paired beauties, Taylor, because she was an ingenue in *A Date with Judy*, was as good a girl as her cute partner. But because beauty implied allure, even a beautiful maiden suggested sex, she was the young good-bad girl from whom extraordinary sex emanated subtly. Similarly, her personality was usually quieter than that of her opposite. She was more serious, even regal, as befitted a beauty queen. The cute one, compensating as most of us were, was sassier. And—what a surprise this is now—in all but one of the ingenue pairs of the forties, the cute one was the star. In all but the Gail Russell-Diana Lynn pairing in the *Our Hearts Were Young and Gay/Growing Up* movies, our surrogate got top billing—and the man. If the story called for her and the beauty to compete for the same man, she even got him. At the time, it did not occur to me that the moviemakers were psychologists enough to play to our reality of flat-bridged noses, as well as our impossible dreams of looking like Elizabeth Taylor.

The usual combination was two newcomers whom the studios decided to pit for the run to ingenue lead. All three of the major pairs were launched in 1944. From MGM, June Allyson was the cute one and Gloria DeHaven was the professional model type, interchangeable with a hundred other starlets whose real names were "which one is she?" or "I get her mixed up with. . . ." We all know now who won that race, but in 1944, when Metro Goldwyn Mayer co-starred

Allyson and DeHaven in *Two Girls and a Sailor,* it was a "toss-up," as James Robert Parish and Ronald L. Bowers say in *The MGM Stock Company,* as to which of the two would emerge the star.[14] It was and it wasn't a toss-up. The script gave Allyson the sailor, played by the wartime heart-throb Van Johnson. It looks as if the dice were loaded in Allyson's favor. Sure enough, after *Two Girls,* June became MGM's All-American Girl star, and Gloria, as Parish and Bowers quote her, was relegated to roles of " 'the immature, snotty glamour-girl type.' "[15]

Among the male ingenues of the forties, *my* favorite was not Van Johnson, but a curly-haired blond and blue-eyed Apollo named Guy Madison. More than his movies, it was the movie magazine pictures of his romance with dark-haired Gail Russell that made him my favorite. Russell was the beauty in Paramount's 1944 pair of ingenues, with Diana Lynn the cutie. Gail Russell was made in the Vivien Leigh-Elizabeth Taylor mold, with olive skin, thick dark hair, and large blue eyes. Now her nose looks imperfect: flat-bridged and the tip splayed. (Alas, Madison's nose, it is now clear, was the old "ski-jump.") But then we saw Russell as beautiful; at least partly because we compared her with her partner, Diana Lynn, who had a high forehead, an unusual short bob for her blonde-brown hair, a wide mouth, thin lips, and sloe eyes. Today, Lynn looks interesting; then we saw her as intentionally cute, but rather plain.

Like Allyson and DeHaven, who came from Arthur Freed's MGM musical stable, Lynn and Russell played together before Paramount co-starred them in a feature. In *Henry Aldrich Gets Glamour* (1943), they vied for Henry (Jimmy Lydon), and Lynn, playing his faithful girl friend—soul sister of Ann Rutherford's Polly in the Andy Hardy series—retrieved Henry from glamorous Gail. Of this B-movie, Parish writes in *The Paramount Pretties:*

Russell, in her screen debut, was radiant if stilted, and at

19 years of age was already too mature for the adolescent nonsense of the Henry Aldrich mystique. She and Diana [Lynn] would appear in four films together, each depicting contrasting elements of wholesome, maturing womanhood, ideals precious to audiences of the time.[16]

The phrase, ''she [Russell] and Diana'' indicates their relative status in the forties. Yet, it is ironic because it comes from a chapter on Lynn. In the seventies, Russell is not one of Parish's choices from the Paramount pretties.

Our Hearts Were Young and Gay (1944) was forties nostalgia for the twenties, based on the memoirs of Cornelia Otis Skinner. Russell starred, but perhaps only because she played Skinner. Lynn was Skinner's friend Emily Kimbrough, and they did not compete for a man. Each had her own: a handsome blond for Lynn (Bill Edwards), and a dark-haired counterpart for Russell (James Brown). And *that* was what I remembered through the years from that movie: two handsome men, one dark, one light, paired with one dark beauty and one cute ''American blonde.'' Contrast and balance. The neatness was comforting, like the coupling of handsome blond Guy Madison and beautiful dark Gail Russell in real life. I knew that even then, just as I knew that movie magazine life was movie life, not *real* real life.

Our Hearts Were Young and Gay was popular enough to generate a sequel, *Our Hearts Were Growing Up* (1946), and to raise both Lynn and Russell to about equal, mediocre careers. Like Gloria DeHaven, neither Lynn nor Russell rose above the pack and the programmer. James Robert Parish, who rates Lynn as underrated (I agree), notes that she was cast as Amy in David O. Selznick's 1946 epic, *Little Women,* with Jennifer Jones as Jo. (I would have reversed that casting.) Wardrobe and set tests began, according to Parish; but then, beset by the postwar hard times, Selznick sold the property to MGM.[17] When Louis B. Mayer's *Little Women* came out in 1949, Amy was Elizabeth Taylor in a ''dramatically different'' blonde wig. In 1949, Diana Lynn was again playing second fiddle in a pair, this time supporting

Marie Wilson's title role in *My Friend Irma*. Both women
were overshadowed by the movie debut of a superstar pair of
the fifties, Martin and Lewis. In 1971, Diana Lynn died of a
stroke as she was preparing for a comeback in *Play It As It
Lays* (in the role played by Tammy Grimes). Russell, an ar-
tistic and apparently a reserved person, who grew up in the
aesthetic community of Hyde Park, Chicago, died in 1961,
troubled by drink. And Guy Madison—who to my great
relief finally married Russell in the last year of the forties (for
a while)—disappeared into obscurity by way of foreign-made
westerns. And yes, it all matters to me; for in the forties, they
were as real as real people, and much more real than most of
them.

Like Russell and Lynn, the third pair of newcomers launch-
ed in 1944 was presented as more or less equal partners;
and again, both rose to about equal stardom, although
Jeanne Crain and June Haver both rose higher than Gail
Russell and Diana Lynn. Of all forties pairs, the two from
Twentieth-Century Fox were the most similar. Crain and
Haver debuted in the same movie, as bits in one of Busby
Berkeley's banana musicals, *The Gang's All Here* (1943).
Haver was the epitome of the American showgirl blonde, and
Crain was a hazel-eyed, brown-haired ingenue who could be
classically beautiful, or in pigtails for *Home in Indiana,* a
" 'nice hoyden,' " as New York *Herald Tribune* reviewer Howard Barnes wrote in 1944.[18] In *Home in Indiana*, the movie in
which Fox paired Haver and Crain as good girl rivals for the
All-American boy, Lon McAllister, Jeanne Crain was billed
over June Haver, and like the other cute one, June Allyson,
she got the hero. But Crain could as easily have been the
beauty; in fact, in every other movie she made as an ingenue,
she was. Better than any other forties pair, Crain and Haver
illuminate how fine the line was between the beauty and the
cute girl, and how much our perception, and hence their images, were determined by the comparison, the pairing. Alone
as a leading lady, Jeanne Crain could be the cute beauty.
When, in 1954, she left Twentieth-Century Fox, a matron at

the age of twenty-nine, she said, " 'I've been cute long enough. . . .' "[19] Similarly, it is clear in retrospect that the blonde beauty June Haver could have passed for cute as well as Jeanne Crain did in *Home in Indiana*. In *Scudda-Hoo! Scudda-Hay!* (1948), a picture as bucolic as its title, Haver did just that, and even with Lon McAllister as the boy. All it took was short curls instead of long waves, or upswept curls, a little less eye makeup and lipstick, and peasant blouses and dirndl skirts instead of sequined gowns.

Generally, though, Haver was cast as a showgirl and the leading lady, and when she was joined by a relatively cute ingenue, such as brownette and pigtailed Vera-Ellen in *Three Little Girls in Blue* (1946),* or Debbie Reynolds in *The Daughter of Rosie O'Grady* (1950), she looked even more like a conventional blonde beauty. Reviewing *I Wonder Who's Kissing Her Now* (1947), Otis L. Guernsey, Jr., said that Haver was " 'so colorless as to be virtually indistinguishable from the members of the chorus.' "[20] And when Haver played Marilyn Miller in *Look for the Silver Lining* (1949), her sisters were played by the identical Wilde twins, Lee and Lynn. It may be this anonymity in spite of stardom that explains her popularity with us young people. With the general public, she never fulfilled Fox's hope for another Grable, to replace the one who wanted to have babies, who had replaced Alice Faye when Faye wanted to have babies. At the end of the forties, Fox lent Haver to Warner Brothers, but in 1948, in *Romance on the High Seas*, Warner's introduced Doris Day. In 1954, after a romantic second marriage to a tall, dark, older movie star, Fred MacMurray, June Haver retired and became a crinkly-eyed, plumpish matron with short reddish-brown curls.

It is, of course, screen presence—a more exact term than talent—that finally determines who wins and who loses. Probably nothing better would have happened for the losers had

---

*The third little girl, a showgirl type, was Vivian Blaine.

they not been paired. June Allyson got the guy in *Two Girls and a Sailor* because in their earlier bits, she looked more like a potential star than did Gloria DeHaven. Allyson was brought to Hollywood from Broadway to repeat her songs and dances from *Best Foot Forward* (1943), and she was championed thereafter by the movie's producer, Arthur Freed, a power with Louis Mayer at MGM.[21] DeHaven, the daughter of a show business family, had debuted in 1936 at the age of eleven, as one of Paulette Goddard's sisters in Charlie Chaplin's *Modern Times*. In 1944, after seven bits, including *Best Foot Forward* and a song with Allyson and Virginia O'Brien in *As Thousands Cheer* (1943), DeHaven starred in Freed's *Broadway Rhythm*—not one of his hits. Whether you like June Allyson or not—and my interviews suggest that she was *too* successful a compensator for many of us to like her[22] —Allyson stands out, and stands up as a star among forties ingenues. I am surprised now at what her just slightly gritty presence does for weepers such as *Music for Millions* (1944). Still, like the conventions of the romantic movie that made us respond to Orson Welles as we did to Clark Gable, the formula for physical pairing also made us see things not necessarily as they were. In the forties, it was formula more than personality, the conventions more than the individual, that shaped us. I wonder now if that may not have set a pattern.

Favorites

In the early forties, Jeanne Crain was one of my three "favorites," one of those special stars who rated her own scrapbook, and who now seem to shed light on our forties childhood. In the early forties, before men were favorites, mine were Crain, Susan Peters, and Maureen O'Hara. Crain and O'Hara are frequently cited by other forties girls, and all three seem representative of other favorites who are repeatedly named: Deanna Durbin, Esther Williams, June Haver,

June Allyson, Rita Hayworth (the Rita of the war, not the postwar years), Susan Hayward, and Doris Day. They were all young, and in their real lives, living our dreams; dating and then getting married and having babies. Moreover, they were neither superstars nor pinups. Sufficiently well-known to discuss and debate, they were not inaccessible, like Lana Turner, much less Loretta Young, Bette Davis, et al. They were not our comfortingly unknown and uniformly pretty starlet favorites; they were our favorite *stars*.

In Technicolor, Maureen O'Hara in the midforties seemed to many of us to be the most beautiful face imaginable. In the pirate movies *The Black Swan* (1942), *The Spanish Main* (1945), and *Sinbad the Sailor* (1947), and in the color portraits in the movie magazines, her long dark red curls, deep-set green eyes, defined cheekbones, and perfect red mouth appear now the crown of forties dramatic coloration normalized by classic features. But she had no screen personality. In the fifties she developed one, a hot-blooded Irish shrew and John Wayne's woman, but in the forties she was empty. Even I who drank in her beauty and was a dumb kid knew that Maureen O'Hara could not act. Now, as with June Haver, I wonder if it was not just that emptiness which, along with her extraordinary beauty in the exciting new Technicolor, made her a favorite. Susan Peters and Jeanne Crain were perhaps even more accessible. Less dramatically beautiful than O'Hara, they were also better cast to spur the dreams of nice girls.

Susan Peters had dark brown hair and eyes, contrasting pale skin, and delicate bones. She began with bits such as Jefferson Davis' daughter and Ronald Reagan's love in *Sante Fe* (1942), under her own name, Suzanne Carnahan. She was the ingenue in Bogart's last doomed-gangster-named-Duke movie, *The Big Shot* (1942), and in *Tish* (1942), one of the first movies I remember. An MGM B-movie about small-town America during the war, I read now with surprise that *Tish* starred Marjorie Main, Zasu Pitts, and Aline MacMahon: three old ladies. *I* remember Lee Bowman and

Virginia Grey, the young lovers separated by his war service. Virginia Grey was such a stereotypical blonde beauty that through all the years until I looked back, I remembered her in *Tish* as Martha O'Driscoll. Bowman, who was my wartime dream-man second only to Guy Madison, was a dark-haired, mustached, slighter Clark Gable, whom I, like everyone else, forgot as soon as the real one came home. But mainly I remember a scene in *Tish* in which Susan Peters, as Richard Quine's secret war bride, faints in the post office. Even at the age of seven, I recognized that the swoon meant that she was "expectant"—the end of all our rainbows. In 1943, Peters and Quine were married, as my scrapbook records, he in his Coast Guard uniform, she in the gown of the time, stiff white satin with a sweetheart neckline. Movie art and movie magazine life melded comfortably, as, in fact, they still and always do.

As an MGM contract player in the forties, Susan Peters could be the leading lady in features, as she was in two films in 1943, *Assignment in Brittany,* in which she played a Bretonne maid, and *Song of Russia*, in which the maiden was Russian. Or, she could be third, ingenue lead under Lana Turner and Laraine Day in a tribute-to-the-WACS called *Keep Your Powder Dry* (1945). But, except for me who remembers her in *Tish*, Peters is generally remembered most for *Random Harvest* because this 1942 movie was one of the most popular films of the war years. She was nominated for a Supporting Actress Oscar for nobly releasing Ronald Colman from their engagement when she intuited that "something was wrong."[23] What was wrong was Greer Garson, wife to "Smitty" (Colman) when, before his engagement to Peters, he became one of the numerous Hollywood amnesiacs of the forties. Though I did not know it then, it was because of the rigid character system that I sympathized with Peters: could it even cross my mind that Greer Garson would lose the leading man? Yet, now, it is not the stars who seem important but the starlets and ingenues such as Susan Peters, with whom we identified. Peters now seems to symbolize young American womanhood in the years of World War II: delicate but true, sensitive but staunch, virginal, but in the depths of her brown eyes, warm.

This might also be said of my third favorite, Jeanne Crain. In movie and movie magazine image, she was the Susan Peters type, with one variation. Crain could be a pinup, and in the magazines, often was, in bathing dress and pose as genteel as a Miss American runner-up of 1941 ought to be. Appropriately, a television documentary on Twentieth-Century Fox musicals represented forties beauty with Jeanne Crain in *State Fair* (1945), a dreamy girl at a bedroom window, framed first by softly blowing brown hair waves and then by white tiebacks, and singing "It Might As Well Be Spring" (dubbed).

But as with all our favorites, it was the movie magazines as much as her roles that made Crain a model. Perhaps it was more the magazines, which came out every month; even in the factory-forties, the new movies did not come that frequently. Helpfully, Crain married young (1945) and immediately began to have babies, so that in the late forties, the movie magazines regularly featured classically beautiful Jeanne Crain and baby Paul Brinkman, then Michael, then Timothy. . . . A caption under a candid photograph of Crain and one of her sons is typical of others in my scrapbooks: "'Enjoy your children,' Jeanne Crain says, 'But don't neglect your husband.' "

In the forties, *Life* magazine showed Crain—and dozens of others—in a bubble bath, or Crain having her camisoled bust tape-measured in Wardrobe, or even Rita Hayworth in profile kneeling on a bed in tight black lace and white satin. (*Life Goes to the Movies* revealed that the bustiness in that iconic pinup was the result of "unexpected accenting shadows" caused by a flash bulb that failed to go off.) My scrapbook shows one photograph, a color portrait of Gene Tierney, which is a virtual duplicate of *Life*'s Hayworth shot. But such sex art was rare in the movie magazines. Generally, they showed Hayworth spooning baby food into Rebecca Welles, or Gene Tierney nuzzling newborn Christina Cassini. The magazines did not feature the Cassini's first child, Daria, because Daria was born affected by the German measles her mother had contracted while entertaining at an army base. In the movie magazine forties—that dream world from which I read every word and cut and pasted—leading ladies were not supposed to have any problems more serious than how to enjoy children without neglecting husbands.

When Jeanne Crain is mentioned at all in film histories, it is usually for *Margie* and *Centennial Summer* (1946), the nostalgia pieces in which she reflects the girl who married dear old dad. But we girls who grew up then remember better her contemporary roles. Perhaps the past is always boring to young people, and in visual media, costumes and sets intensify the difference in time. Jeanne Crain may have been a teenager in *Margie*, but *Margie* was set in the twenties, and Crain's war wife in *In the Meantime, Darling* (1944) was contemporary, and like her role in the movie magazines, a model for our dreams. Later, we could identify with her as a postwar veteran's wife in *Apartment for Peggy* (1948), or as the patient, beleaguered true love in *Leave Her to Heaven* (1945), one of my favorite childhood movies.

James Agee in his 1945 review of *Leave Her to Heaven* wrote: "In the rich glare of Technicolor, all its rental-library characteristics are doubly glaring."[24] Reviewing this film, I agree (except that, alas, the Technicolor has faded). *Leave Her to Heaven*, my favorite and number two at the box office in *Variety*'s 1946 figures,[25] now seems to epitomize the worst of forties movies: painful length, bathos, and unremittingly formulaic plot and characters. The prime reason for this may lie in the era's habit of treating best-selling novels reverentially. But because other films based on novels such as *Random Harvest*, survived, I now suspect bad acting for most of the faults of *Leave Her to Heaven*.

Ben Ames Williams' novel *Leave Her to Heaven* was an unrealized, poor man's Electra, made worse in the movie by leading lady Gene Tierney's wooden portrayal of the

murderously possessive wife, and even worse by Cornel
Wilde's petrified enactment of her unlucky choice of a husband. But as a key to the molding of the children of the forties, this film is an important favorite. I remembered one
scene with particular clarity through the years, in which
Wilde, playing a novelist, is typing under a white picket arbor
covered with red roses when he hears the sound of scissors.
He and the camera look up, and there, framed against an
ultramarine New Mexico sky, is Jeanne Crain, her brown
waves blowing lightly, red lips and white teeth glowing, smiling down at him as she gathers her roses. The point is to show
him so struck by her loveliness that although at the time he is
smitten by Tierney, we foresee his and Crain's final, true
love. Thirty years later, the ultramarine and the red lips and
roses look dusty, but as with *Gone with the Wind*, the fade is
appropriate for a perfect memory of how a girl should look
to a man, and the romance such looks should win her.

Reviewing *Leave Her to Heaven* for this remembered
scene, I now see what I could not have understood then,
other images of romance that it must have set. Its courtroom
scene, particularly, seems now a paradigm of romance. Ruth
(Crain) is tried for murdering her sister Ellen (Tierney), and
under the pressure of scurrilous, demeaning questions from
the "I've come for the rent" prosecutor, Vincent Price, Ruth
and Dick (Wilde) each reveal the love which, in their nobility,
they have kept secret not only from the world and each other,
but from themselves. Now I can recognize in this scene a
recurrent fancy (is it only feminine?): the sweet dream of
hearing a man profess his love for you publicly and at a cost,
and the matching dream that you do the same with equal
drama, but no danger. In that time, I now realize, it might
well have been called the "woman I love" fantasy, in witness
to the real romance of the late thirties, which it seems matched *Gone with the Wind* as erotica.[26]

At the end of her scene on the witness stand, Crain col-
lapses and Wilde rushes to cradle her in his arms. It is their
first embrace, and as releasing as when Orson Welles gives in

and grabs Joan Fontaine at the end of *Jane Eyre*. Today, one has to laugh at Crain's pathetic swoon; and in a society as educated to courtroom conventions as ours is, the trial, with all its "Do you love him?" questions from Vincent Price, is so ludicrous one has to hold hard to one's wits to see it for what I know it was, a powerful influence *because* it represented so banally the basic romantic message: the forbidden relationship is the most exciting, the most ecstatic and—the most pernicious message—ultimately the most rewarding. That is, the forbidden is finally not forbidden, if you are as virtuous and pretty as Jeanne Crain, or as noble and handsome as Cornel Wilde. You can have your cake and eat it too. That is the kind of message that can really mess you up, especially if you don't know you are receiving it. That is the idea that sends you out to Tucson, makes you discontented there, and then makes you think that it will all be O.K. if you can just get back to Monterey. Because Monterey, or Tara, is where it was true that if you were just a good girl long enough, and if you made yourself pretty, you could have whatever you dreamed of: Alice Faye's voice, Gene Tierney's husband, anything. Our *Leave Her to Heaven* was the mirror of Gatsby's dream. He would get his Daisy beyond the green light by doing. We would get our leading man by being. Being virtuous, being domestic (snip those roses), being patient, and primarily, being pretty.

Patterns

So it was in the war years of the forties: an absurdly orderly world at the edge, and yet at the dreaming heart of a disordered world. A world of pairs and hierarchies, symbolized not only by Eleanor and Franklin but also by Garson and Pidgeon; by F.D.R., Ike, and G.I. Joe; and also by *Keep Your Powder Dry*, with its Star, Lana Turner, its Dependable Lead, Laraine Day, and its ingenue, Susan Peters. It was a world of parallels and balanced antitheses: the blond beach boy Guy Madison and the ethereal/smoldering brunette beauty Gail Russell; delicate blonde Fontaine and tall, dark, and broad-shouldered Welles, Lawrence Olivier, Cary Grant, Tyrone Power (*This Above All,* 1942), Arturo de Cordova (*Frenchman's Creek,* 1944). . . . Except for Dick Haymes in *Billy Rose's Diamond Horseshoe* (1945), Betty Grable's leading men in the early forties were all dark: Tyrone Power, Victor Mature, John Payne, George Montgomery, and John Harvey (*Pin-Up Girl,* 1944). And when Betty did not have John Payne, blonde Anne Shirley or blonde Sonja Henie did. In *Moon Over Miami* (1941), Grable and blonde Carole Landis played sisters paired with Don Ameche and Robert Cummings. And sometimes Ameche was Alice Faye's hero, and sometimes John Payne was. It was Alice Faye and Linda Darnell in *The Fallen Angel* (1945), and guess which one was the fallen woman?

When Susan Peters was cast as leading lady Olivia de Havilland's friend in *Santa Fe,* she was given a blonde wig. When Lana Turner wanted Clark Gable in *Somewhere I'll Find You* (1942), so did a dark-haired starlet named Patricia Dane; and another Gable-type, Robert Sterling, also wanted Lana. But when All-American brownette Teresa Wright was Gary Cooper's true love in *Casanova Brown* (1944), she had blonde Anita Louise as a rival, as did Jennifer Jones in *Love Letters.* To win Lord Rochester in *Jane Eyre,* mousy blonde Joan Fontaine had to combat blonde beauty Hillary Brooke; in *The Constant Nymph,* Fontaine's rival was silver blonde Alexis Smith. Less seen than the leading lady, the rival always looked prettier to me, even when the pair were the equally conventional looking beauties Lana Turner and Pat Dane. Paradoxically, I found Anita Louise more beautiful than my surrogate, Teresa Wright, and Alexis Smith more satisfying than Joan Fontaine. But in *The Horn Blows at Midnight* (1945), in which Smith was Jack Benny's leading lady, the second female lead, Dolores Moran, was more interesting. It was a complex game.

There were also physical twins: June Allyson and Van

Johnson, Paulette Goddard and Susan Hayward (*The Forest Rangers and Reap the Wild Wind,* 1942), the Wilde Twins Grable and June Haver as *The Dolly Sisters* (who in real life were brunettes); and sometimes there were bonanzas of orderliness: *The Fallen Sparrow* (1943), with Maureen O'Hara, sleek brunette Patricia Morison, and saucy blonde Martha O'Driscoll; or *Without Love* (1945), with Katharine Hepburn, her best friend Lucille Ball, and her rival, Pat Morison. Of course, in the early forties, most movies were in black and white; O'Hara, for example, looked as dark as Morison, and Lucille Ball just looked blonde. But because of their color films and magazine portraits, in the black and white movies, our imaginations adjusted the color.

Anyone who knows the *corpus* of forties movies knows how this catalog could go on. Of course, to some degree, chance determined casts, and both the predominance of black and white films *and* the forties preoccupation with its new toy, Technicolor, lay behind the intense physical coloration. (The importance of hair color in the forties is indicated by the press coverage of croppings and color changes—Bergman's shearing for *For Whom the Bell Tolls*; Hayworth's cut and blonding for *The Lady from Shanghai*—and by this not unusual line from Kate Cameron's New York *Daily News* review of *Cover Girl:* " '. . . her gorgeous auburn hair gives [Hayworth] the perfect right to be called Rusty in the film.' "[27] Imagine that in a contemporary film review.) But however inchoate, the idea that beauty was either twinship or opposites in balance, underlay the forties, particularly the war years. And however the casts were assembled, what matters more is the effect of these "binary opposites." What we saw in the early forties were usually simple blacks and whites: redheads Jimmy Cagney and Rita Hayworth as the glamorous romantics in *The Strawberry Blonde* (1941), with brownette "Melanie," Olivia de Havilland, as the patient true love who gets Cagney, just as she gets Scarlett's Ashley.

In general in the forties, looks reflected character

stereotype, which like looks was also relative. In *Variety,*
February 3, 1943, Florence Forder, who for seventeen years
was in charge of Roseland Ballroom's hostesses, reported a
switch in preference from blondes to brunettes or brown-
haired girls. Miss Forder attributed this change to the fact
that the war was better complemented by "somber-hued
hair" than by the blonde, who was popular in the twenties as
an " 'unconscious physical answer to the buoyancy within the
flaxen qualities of blonde hair.' "[28] But despite Miss Forder
(an early structuralist), in Hollywood, whether an actress was
blonde, brunette, or redhead, if she was second female lead
and contrasted physically with the heroine, she was almost
always the rival. Somberhued Patricia Morison could be
staunch and intelligent as the heroine in the B movies, but in
features she was almost always darkly threatening (except to
us girls, to whom the Cover Girl types such as Morison and
Anita Louise were always beautiful as long as they were inaccessible "bits.")

The convention that dramatic looks represent dramatic
character is, or course, ages old. Leslie Fiedler's statement on
this is typical: Describing the seducer-savior in his "white-
hatted" aspect, Fiedler says he is sometimes

> permitted a genital past, symbolized by a previous con-
> nection with some dark, preferably Mexican prostitute, in
> which he has burned away all lust, purified himself for a
> blond Maiden.[29]

But Hollywood's maiden need not be Grace Kelly in *High
Noon.* She can be Vivien Leigh or Elizabeth Taylor, or even a
flamboyant redhead such as Maureen O'Hara or Rita
Hayworth. She can also be undramatically "American
blonde" such as Irene Dunne, Claudette Colbert, Judy
Garland, Jeanne Crain, Ida Lupino, Dorothy McGuire,
Esther Williams, Eleanor Parker, Anne Baxter, and as this
list implies, the greater number of forties heroines. Brownettes were rarely bad; if they were not heroines, they were

generally best friend supports, as Ann Richards was to Jennifer Jones in *Love Letters* or Marsha Hunt to June Allyson in *Music for Millions*. Bright blondes, burning redheads, or raven-haired beauties could be bad, good, or good-bad, like Gilda, but it was rare that they were neutral, like best friends. It was not only hair color; hair length and style also participated in the wartime stereotypes. For example, with the exceptions of Greer Garson and Lucille Ball, the redheads of this time were uniformly long-haired and temperamental: Hayworth and O'Hara, starlets Arleen Whelan and Cara Williams, and starlet *cum* star, Susan Hayward. In the war years, whether she was blonde or brunette, if her hair was long, wavy rather than curly, or worn in a bun—that is, if she was Lizabeth Scott or Ella Raines, Veronica Lake or Gail Patrick, Audrey Totter or Patricia Morison—then she was at least sultry, and perhaps bad. Long, short, or upswept, if her blonde hair was tightly curled, she was likely dumb, frizzy on the inside as well as the outside, on the model of Betty Hutton (Iris Adrian and Veda Ann Borg are examples). But if the blonde's hair was coiffed rather than buoyant, on the model of Madeleine Carroll, she would be the elegant, icy prototype of Princess Grace. In the forties, there were no blondes who were both elegant and dizzy, like Carole Lombard; and until the Britisher Ann Todd and Pat Neal in the postwar era, few elegant blondes of the forties were heroines. Like Alexis Smith in *The Constant Nymph*, Anita Louise in *Love Letters,* Hillary Brooke in *Jane Eyre,* and Louise Allbritton in John Wayne's and Marlene Dietrich's *Pittsburgh* (1942), they were usually the other women—whose inaccessible beauty I adored even as I rooted for the soap operaish heroine.

Blonde heroines of the forties were bouncy (Grable, Hutton), sultry (Veronica Lake, Lizabeth Scott), or both bouncy and sulty (Turner). Just as the elegant blonde dissolved into the sultry type, so the dizzy one was just a loosened curl different from the heroine who was friendly, common sensible, breezy, but true in values and sturdy of heart. Grable, Faye,

Henie, Haver, reddish Ginger Rogers, darker Ann Sheridan, Doris Day, and in most of her roles, Lana Turner, were followed by supports and B-heroines such as Marjorie Reynolds, Joan Caulfield, Peggy Knudsen of *The Big Sleep*, June Preisser, Mary Beth Hughes, Mona Freeman, Martha O'Driscoll, and the ubiquitous Wilde twins.

Turner was also the model for all the blondes who, with a change of hairdo and a contrasting other woman, could pass as either straight heroine or bad girl. Irene Manning, for example, was leading lady to Dennis Morgan in *The Desert Song* (1943)—and what could be straighter than Sigmund Romberg's operetta?—and gangster's moll opposite Humphrey Bogart in *The Big Shot* (1942). Contrast to Manning in *The Desert Song* was provided by Faye Emerson in a dark wig playing an Arab. But Emerson could be a breezy best friend, in subdued brown-blonde, in *The Very Thought of You*; or a bright blonde tramp in *Between Two Worlds* (1944), redeemed—and turned brown-haired—by God's "examiner" (Sydney Greenstreet, the Lord in the Greenstreet tropical white suit and fedora). In perhaps her richest role, in *Hotel Berlin* (1945), Emerson played a brassy blonde Nazi whore, supporting her Jewish fiance's mother. In the war era, Dolores Moran was bad-good in *Old Acquaintance* (before settling down with Gig Young, she had to be rescued by Bette Davis from almost flinging with playboy Philip Reed), a devoted War Resister's wife—an Ilsa Lund—in *To Have and Have Not*, and a tramp in *Too Young to Know* (1945) and *The Man I Love* (1946). An elegant blonde, such as Anita Louise, Louise Allbritton, or Hillary Brooke, was usually the heroine in the B-movie and the loser in the feature. In the later forties, Audrey Totter and Gloria Grahame could be groomed to fit either stereotype, but in that postwar era, as we see in the next chapter, the blondes like Totter, Grahame, and Lizabeth Scott could look the same in every film and be sometimes good, sometimes bad, and sometimes even ambiguous.

Just as with the blondes, there were all-purpose brunettes:

supports who starred in the Bs and provided contrast and conflict in feature romances, and also stars whose long dark manes could signal either the siren or the true and steady heroine. Hedy Lamarr, Jane Russell, Maria Montez, Linda Darnell, Gene Tierney, Merle Oberon, Jennifer Jones, and Gail Russell, et al. played both types of roles. Even Dorothy Lamour switched to bad woman roles in the late forties. The postwar coming of Christian Dior's "New Look" in fashion (long skirts) changed stereotypes by making the short curly bob the chicest hairstyle. From about 1948 on, until the long-haired sixties, short-haired Davis, Colbert, Bergman in *For Whom the Bell Tolls,* Turner in *The Postman Always Rings Twice* (1946) who were the forties exceptions, became the rule. Even Elizabeth Taylor cropped her madonna waves. But in the war years, short brown hair, dark or light, almost invariably indicated good sense and sympathetic staunchness in good friends or wives such as Myrna Loy, Jane Wyatt, Ruth Hussey, Marsha Hunt, Phyllis Thaxter, or Frances Rafferty. There was small difference in hair color between, say, Marsha Hunt and brownettes in glamour girl bobs, such as Jeanne Crain and Eleanor Parker, and there was small differences in their characters, almost always they were stalwart. smiling, and undramatic. But we never confused the two: the Crains and Parkers were Stars, the Hunts and Thaxters, our nearly anonymous, almost private good friends. Garson Kanin has written, " 'A tacky period, the early forties. . . — all those very fancy hairdos and broad shoulders.' "[30] But perhaps like most of us, Kanin misses what this standardization meant, and what it did to us to grow up with all those clear signals. That web of dependable leads and supports modeled on only a few types—the Cover Girls, the All-American ingenues, Clark Gable, and the others—were a certitude and stay against confusion, teaching us that if we too stayed within the lines, we could fit into the pattern. Thus were the conventions of beauty in the forties like the formulaic plots of love forbidden but if virtuous, consummated after The End and for ever, smiling through the roses.

It all seems an enlightening, depressing pattern: the castings, the characters, and even the plots manipulating us on unconscious aesthetic-psychological levels. In *Cover Girl,* I notice now a plot pattern of Friday evening visits to a Brooklyn oyster bar by the trio of stars, Hayworth, Kelly, and Phil Silvers. The point of the ritual is to search for the pearl in the oyster. But then Rusty becomes a Cover Girl, and subsequently a Broadway star. She is on the verge of ditching her Danny for a wealthy scion when she goes to Joe's bar alone to think. The scion, Lee Bowman, shows up with her benefactor, Otto Krueger, trying to talk her into marrige and stardom. But as soon as they sit, one on each side of her, on the bar stools in Joe's where Kelly and Silvers have regularly sat, the debate is over, won in our subconscious on purely structural grounds.

Other parallels and antithesis in *Cover Girl* include Hayworth's double role as Rusty and her showgirl grandmother, loved by a younger Otto Krueger (played by Jess Barker), who she spurns for a poor but true love, Danny McGuire's parallel. Gene Kelly's dance with his shadow-*doppelgänger* is a pair in itself; and at the center of the movie are the Cover Girls, fourteen different models shown in a snap-quick parade of faces, so that the different becomes un-differentiated and the individual appears to be duplicated (endlessly?) The principles of parallelism and balanced an-tithesis create a precise structural pattern that clarifies its con-tent immediately and unobtrusively, and hence manipulates on the most invincible rhetorical grounds. Whether or not we *want* Rusty to abandon her career for unsuccessful and ungenerous Danny McGuire, when we see the other man in his place in Joe's Bar, we are on Danny's side.

Cover Girl is only an example. Throughout the early for-ties, boy meets girl, and sometimes meets her again as an amnesiac (*Random Harvest*).[31] If girl meets boy, her sister or best friend meets his buddy. (When one of these movies, *Moon Over Miami*, was remade as *Three Little Girls in Blue*, there were three guys instead of *Miami's* two for Betty Grable and Carole Landis). Sometimes the star's best friend inherits his rival: as in *Without Love,* Lucille Ball gets a B Gable type Carl Esmond, and Tracy—could it be otherwise?—gets Hepburn. Or her rival finds his rival, as in *Easter Parade* (Astaire and Garland, Peter Lawford and Ann Miller), or *Lovely to Look At* (Howard Keel and Kathryn Grayson, Red Skelton and Ann Miller, who played this B-rival role a lot). Ingenue love paralleled glamorous romance; as in *Weekend at the Waldorf* (1945), the courtship of soldier Van Johnson and stenographer Lana Turner alternates with that of war correspondent Walter Pidgeon and movie star Ginger Rogers. Absorbing the devotion of Anne and (absent) Tim Hilton in *Since You Went Away,* could we even wonder whether daughter Jane would end up with her peer, or with an anomalous older man?

In the postwar years, the pattern broke. There were *Easter Parades,* as in the war years there had been some rivals who were ignored in the lovers' fade-out clinch, and even some pairs broken, usually by bombs. But in the late forties, the ambiguous heroine who turned out bad (probably)—Maureen O'Hara in *The Fallen Sparrow;* Andrea King in *Hotel Berlin*—turned up everywhere. Consider Rita Hayworth, who in the war years played in movies such as *Cover Girl* and *You Were Never Lovelier* (1942), in which she is one of Adolphe Menjou's four daughters, all with different color hair, but all paired by the end (Hayworth gets Fred Astaire, and brunette Catherine Craig, brownette Adele Mara, and blonde Leslie Brooks get their "Scarlett's beaux" types). After the war, Hayworth is Gilda, alone except for a Hitlerian husband, a mass of ravenous men, a true love who distrusts her until, in order to end the movie, a police commissioner tells him not to, and Steven Geray, the casino janitor, "Pop" the Night Watchman. And then, in *The Lady from Shanghai* (1948), Hayworth is a beautiful, glamorous woman who murders men.

Or consider *The Best Years of Our Lives* (1946), the postwar counterpart to *Since You Went Away.* Here again are parents (Frederic March and Myrna Loy), ingenue lovers (Harold Russell and Cathy O'Donnell), and in addition, slightly older "young marrieds." But the latter are not Lee Bowman and Virginia Grey in *Tish*; they are a triangle: the hero veteran, Dana Andrews, his greedy, promiscuous brass-blonde wife, Virginia Mayo, and his virtuous, patient brownette lady, Teresa Wright. Furthermore, the male ingenue, Harold Russell, was not your usual Van Johnson, but was instead, a real handless war veteran. His problem of learning to accept Cathy O'Donnell's help was a lot more complex than the problem of getting a date for the prom, and her problem—getting him—was similarly light years different from Jennifer Jones' strategems in *Since You Went Away* to get Robert Walker to overcome his shyness and propose to her. Finally, at the end of *BYOL*, when Harold Russell and Cathy O'Donnell are getting married and Dana Andrews and Teresa Wright are clinching, Myrna Loy is still worriedly nagging Frederic March about his drinking, and about the other signs that he has not "readjusted." A microcosm of all the differences between the American times reflected in *Since You Went Away* and *The Best Years of Our Lives* is the difference in their pairings.

Idea, Event, and the Forties Synthesis, Elizabeth Taylor

The forties conventions of beauty habituated us children of the era to want too much for our virtue, service, patience, and good looks. And it seems clear that the romances, such as *Gone with the Wind, Casablanca,* and *Leave Her to Heaven*, taught us to expect perfect, permanent love, plus a sweep up the stairs. It seems less clear that these romantic, powerful, and largely unrecognized expectations are as much, and perhaps more, the fault of Dolores Moran, as they are the fault of Bette Davis and Scarlett O'Hara. There were so many blonde beauties or sulty brunettes, and they all looked so safely the same. Surely they were eternal, and surely what they did fit unshakable patterns of behavior? In the postwar years, the conventions of beauty broke apart as much as those of character and plot, and people and life. But I doubt that many of us young people noticed.

Change was national after the war, slow change from values of sameness to values of difference. In addition, I grew older, and hence less anonymous. Yet, still I wonder if the model of the Cover Girl was not done in by one uniquely beautiful individual. It probably would have happened anyway, but looking back, it seems that that spell, in which all beautiful women were mirror images, was broken by the phenomenon of Elizabeth Taylor, grown up. The child actress we had watched mature in movies such as *National Velvet* (1944), and in the movie magazines, suddenly, in one movie, appeared so perfectly beautiful that, it seems now, she wiped out approximations. Without her or any of us knowing it, she freed us. (Until the next settling, and the next dialectic spiral.) Who could match her? Why try?

Elizabeth Taylor's beauty bloomed in *A Date with Judy* (1948), one of MGM's most formulaic programmers. There were the parents, Wallace Beery and Selena Royale (threatened only a little bit by comic vamp Carmen Miranda); there were the ingenues Jane Powell and Scotty Beckett ("A Date with Judy" was a popular radio sitcom); and there were the more mature young lovers, high school senior Elizabeth Taylor and her slightly older man, blond Robert Stack. *A Date with Judy* was not Taylor's first sexual role. That came in *Cynthia* (1947), in which Jimmy Lydon—"Henry Aldrich"—gave her her first screen kiss. But in *Cynthia*, Elizabeth Taylor's face was still slightly uncontoured, and her hair was a little lank. In her next movie, *A Date with Judy*, the camera captured what no one, perhaps not even she, knew had come, the moment of perfect beauty. It is all illustrated in the first *That's Entertainment,* which has scenes from *Cynthia* and *A Date with Judy*; and its history is

documented by MGM portrait photographer Clarence
Sinclair Bull, who in *The Faces of Hollywood*, recounts how
"sweet, simple, girlish" sixteen-year-old Elizabeth badgered
him to photograph her as a glamour girl. According to Bull,
he finally gave in and shot some "traditional vamp" poses: a
"leopard skin rug, a low-cut black satin evening gown. . . ."
Taylor took the finished prints to Louis B. Mayer, who called
Bull in to share a laugh about the " 'hell' " of " 'growing
up,' " and to say that he was now giving Taylor her first
grown-up part in *A Date with Judy*.[32]

"Grown-up" meant a high school senior who went to a lot
of parties and proms in yellow organdy, her hair a dark cloud
framing that face, or in powder blue tulle that matched those
eyes. Probably because it was not taken seriously and not
showcased, her beauty in this potboiler was the more startling, memorable, and indescribable. Nostalgia buffs go to *A
Date with Judy* for Carmen Miranda, but for those of us who
were Elizabeth Taylor's kid sisters, *Judy* means her beauty
and her romance with the handsome, blond, older man,
Robert Stack. At that end, she gets him; they will marry after
her graduation from high school, and that too was typical of
the forties.

But if she did not liberate our behavior, still Elizabeth Taylor
freed us. Marjorie Rosen says that the "concept of individual
attractiveness . . . vanished" in the Depression, replaced by
"conformity to popular image": "It was no coincidence that
Jean Parker, an MGM feature player, looked, sounded, and
even had a name similar to Jean Arthur. Or that Betty Grable
and Alice Faye were interchangeable. . . ."[33] The absence of
individualism spelled box office during the hard times of the
Depression and World War II because the adult public then
was generally as conservative as children always are.
Together, the generations promoted the pattern, the model,
rather than the distinctive one-of-a-kind who thrived again
after the war.

In the late forties, Marilyn Monroe was a standard blonde
starlet who was hardly distinguishable from Marilyn Maxwell

or Marie McDonald. In the fifties, she, Grace Kelly, Kim Novak, and Doris Day were all blonde superstars, but deliberately, each was different looking. From the sulty branch of forties ingenues, Elizabeth Taylor, Ava Gardner, Susan Hayward, Lauren Bacall, and Dorothy Malone grew to be fifties stars. But Leslie Caron, Audrey Hepburn, and Shirley MacLaine, who also became stars in the fifties, would likely not have shone in the forties, at least not looking as we know them. Roland Barthes correctly types Garbo's face as an "archetype," a "Platonic idea," the "Essence," and compares it to Audrey Hepburn's "individualized,"

almost unique specification . . . , which has nothing of the essence left in it, but is constituted by an infinite complexity of morphological functions. As a language, Garbo's singularity was of the order of the concept, that of Audrey Hepburn is of the order of the substance. The face of Garbo is an Idea, that of Hepburn, an Event.[34]

Among the starlets of the fifties, however, there seem as much similarity as I remember among the supporting players of the forties. Carol Lynley, Tuesday Weld, and Yvette Mimieux seem indistinguishable.[35] Yet male children of the fifties distinguish among these three clearly and adamantly. But whether the ingenues of the fifties were more individualized than those of the forties seems less important than whether it was the fact in the fifties as it was in the forties, that the more accessible starlets were more influential than the stars on "concepts of attractiveness," and on girls' notions of what to do with their good looks. In the fifties was Natalie Wood—a child in the movies of my forties childhood—related to Elizabeth Taylor as in the late forties Taylor was related to Greer Garson? Is fifties superstar Lana Turner—Sandra Dee's mother—analogous to my superstar mother image, Garson? What would a typology of feminine image in fifties movies look like, and tell us? These are questions for someone whose memories are ten years younger than mine.

Maureen O'Hara Snipped Her Locks,
and Jeanne Crain Lost Her Man. . . .

But first the postwar era must be factored into the forties, for in the years between the war and the Korean police action the roles and images of women changed profoundly. That is clear now. Jennifer Jones' erotic promise bloomed grotesquely in her *Duel in the Sun* sexpot. The Lizabeth Scott of *You Came Along* (1945) could no longer be counted on to be a sultry blonde who nonetheless was nice. In Bogart's *Dead Reckoning* (1947), as in most of her postwar roles, Scott was as bad as a sensuous body, a curtain of blonde hair, a lush pouting mouth, and smoky eyes could imply. Gilda barely escaped a bad end, but The Lady from Shanghai and Carmen got what they deserved. There was *Sinbad the Sailor* (1947); but in *Sitting Pretty* (1948), Maureen O'Hara, the gorgeous piratical fantasy, became a short-haired, aproned matron and straight man to Clifton Webb's comic hit, Mr. Belvidere. Our alluring heroines turned fatal (even Dorothy Lamour), our comforting ones became discomforting (in *Apartment for Peggy*, Jeanne Crain lost a baby), and like O'Hara, they all unsexed.

There were still romances that faded on the lovers' embrace after her high school graduation (Ann Blyth and Farley Granger in *Our Very Own*), but there were also young loves that failed because she was Negro. In *Pinky* (1949), Jeanne Crain is pretty, brown-haired, and "colored," and William Lundigan is blond and handsome, and the simple blacks and whites of forties movies take on new meaning. Largely unrecognized as an era, the postwar years in America bear attention as an unsettled, unsettling time. How could it be otherwise when millions of men's men came home, not to David O. Selznick's "facade," or to Winthrop Sargeant's "national, friendy and, on the whole, placid" glamour girls, but rather, to millions of independent women? "It isn't fair of you to bust in on us like this," Myrna Loy says lovingly, nervously, when Frederic March comes home from the war in *The Best Years of Our Lives*. It is an important line in American history.

Notes

1. Pauline Kael, "Intermezzo," *New Yorker,* November 3, 1975, p. 27.

2. Marjorie Rosen, *Popcorn Venus: Women, Movies and the American Dream* (New York: Avon Books, 1974 [1973]), pp. 193, 251.

3. Leo A. Handel, *Hollywood Looks at Its Audience: A Report of Film Audience Research* (Urbana: The University of Illinois Press, 1950), p. 141.

4. As Molly Haskell notes in *From Reverence to Rape: The Treatment of Women in Movies* (Baltimore: Penguin Books, 1974), pp. 4-5.

5. James Robert Parish, *The Paramount Pretties* (New Rochelle, N.Y.: Arlington House, 1972), p. 502.

6. In *The Hollywood Hallucination* (New York: Creative Age Press, 1944), pp. 45-47, *passim,* Parker Tyler explained all this—but who among forties children read Parker Tyler? Hollywood, said Tyler, not only reflected America's moral evasiveness about "the Great Act of Love." It also created the problem by investing supreme value in the first time "they did it," and stirred even more confusion with the convention that the first time follows The End.

7. Gerold Frank, *Judy* (New York: Dell Publishing, 1976 [1975]), pp. 229-31.

8. The best known Du Barry Girls are Marilyn Maxwell; Hazel Brooks, a late forties Sultry Brunette; Georgia Carroll (Mrs. Kay Kyser); and Kay Williams, the last Mrs. Clark Gable. See Hugh Fordin, *The World of Entertainment! Hollywood's Greatest Musicals* (Garden City: Doubleday & Co., 1975), p. 77 for a picture advertising the "Du Barry Girls." On *Cover Girl* as a spin-off of *The Powers Girl*, see "Inside Stuff," *Variety,* March 8, 1944, p. 25.

9. Quoted in *Judy*, p. 181.

10. Columbia made a mutually sweet deal with the popular American magazines to run contests or otherwise select their cover girls. (*Variety,* March 14, 1942, p. 16, col. 2). Besides Couninhan, the others were Jean Colleran (*American Magazine),* Betty Jane Hess (*Cosmopolitan*), and Peggy Lloyd (*Mademoiselle*), who were posed by *Life* as the "Three Graces" (*Life Goes to the Movies*, p. 93); Cecilia Meager (*Coronet*), Dusty Anderson (*Farm Journal*), Eileen McClory (*Glamour*), Cornelia B. Von Hessert (*Harper's Bazaar*), Karen X. Gaylord (*Liberty*), Cheryl Archer (*Look*), Betty Jane Graham (*McCall's*), Martha Outlaw (*Redbook), Susan Shaw (Vogue),* and Rose May Robson (*Woman's Home Companion*). This list is for other forties film buffs who picked a favorite from *Cover Girl.*

11. Joe Hyams, *Bogart and Bacall: A Love Story* (New York: Warner Books, 1976 [1975]), p. 62.

12. Edgar Morin, *The Stars,* Translated by Richard Howard (New York: Grove Press, 1961), p. 56.

13. Bob Thomas, *King Cohn: The Life and Times of Harry Cohn* (New York: G.P. Putnam's Sons, 1967), p. 176.

14. James Parish and Ronald L. Bowers, *The MGM Stock Company: The Golden Era* (New Rochelle, N.Y.: Arlington House, 1973), p. 176.

15. Ibid.

16. Ibid., p. 444.

17. Parish, *The Paramount Pretties,* p. 446. Parish attributes the casting information on Selznick's *Little Women* to Rudy Behlmer; but it is not in Behlmer's selections of *Memo From: David O. Selznick.*

18. Quoted in James Robert Parish, *The Fox Girls* (New York: Castle Books by arrangement with Arlington House, 1972), p. 564.

19. Quoted in *The Fox Girls,* p. 575.

20. Quoted in *The Fox Girls,* p. 540.

21. Fordin, *The World of Entertainment!,* p. 215.

22. If we could be objective, she was " 'sweet'—she reminded me of what a girl in my high school ought to look like. . . . [But] I wouldn't have gone out of my way to catch her latest movie." This was a woman, and all the forties boys I interviewed responded to Allyson in this admiring, but disassociated way. But more girls of the forties responded as one erupted: "No, I *didn't* think June Allyson was beautiful! I did not like her—I always thought of her as 'sickeningly sweet': She was just *too* good in the roles in which she was cast; i.e., too kind, generous, etc. etc. etc."

23. Slowness is a characteristic of many features from the war years. Two or two and a half hour long movies were common (Bette Davis' *Mr. Skeffington,* for example, is 146 minutes; *The Song of Bernadette,* 157 minutes; and *For Whom the Bell Tolls,* 166 minutes. *Gone with the Wind* is 217 minutes). James Agee noted that the "leisurely pace" was admirable when it was used to develop character and atmosphere. *Agee on Film* (Boston: Beacon Press, 1964), pp. 92; 138; 384-86. In *Random Harvest,* however, the leisurely pace does more—it develops characters and actually advances plot economically. In this scene in which Susan Peters recognizes that something is troubling Ronald Colman, subtle changes come over the amnesiac when, at their wedding rehearsal, the organist plays the wedding march. We watch Colman's sadness deepen from a perspective of knowing what neither he nor Peters knows: that an organ played the same music during his wedding to Greer Garson. In that earlier scene, the camera focused for what seemed an incomprehensibly long while on the organist, pumping away and filling our movie house with the music that Colman and we were to hear again and remember. Thus, when Peters gently calls off the wedding after watching Colman's face, we accept what might otherwise have seemed a precipitous decision or an artificial plot development motivated solely by the Breen office's desire that Colman not be a bigamist.

24. Agee, *Time,* January 7, 1946, in *Agee on Film,* p. 360.

25. *Variety,* January 8, 1947, p. 8.

26. Discussing women's narcissistic need for "great proofs of the partner's love and readiness for self-sacrifice," Helene Deutsch cited King Edward of Great Britain's broadcast abdicating his throne for Wallis Simpson as a "curious and unforgettable echo in the hearts of many women between 16 and 60 years of age." *The Psychology of Women* (New York: Bantam, 1973 [1944], v. I: "Girlhood," 203. These are unusually unscientific words from Deutsch; but from talking with women

who were old enough to reverberate to Edward and Wally, her response seems typical.

27. Quoted in Gene Ringgold, *The Films of Rita Hayworth: The Legend and Career of a Love Goddess* (Secaucus, N.J.: The Citadel Press, 1974), p. 150.

28. *Variety*, p. 1, col. 4; p. 43, col. 4.

29. Leslie Fiedler, *Love and Death in the American Novel* (New York: Criterion Books, 1960), p. 217.

30. Quoted in Gavin Lambert, *On Cukor* (New York: G.P. Putnam's Sons, 1960), p. 137.

31. Frederick Fearing in "The Screen Discovers Psychiatry," *Hollywood Quarterly*, I, 1945-1946, 154-59, says that "of all psychopathological phenomena," amnesia is probably the simplest to show in its "superficial aspects." Fearing then surmises that "this may account for its popularity in Hollywood films." (158, fn. 2) This assumes a desire on the part of filmmakers to explore psychopathological phenomena for *their* sake. Although true (perhaps especially in the forties), the simpler explanation may be that Hollywood used a popular cultural theme, amnesia, not so much from interest in psychology as from recognition of a grand dramatic device, a gimmick that gave both actors and audiences a bonus life to live vicariously.

32. Clarence Sinclair Bull, with Raymond Lee, *The Faces of Hollywood,* (South Brunswick, N.J. and New York: A.S. Barnes, 1968), pp. 79-81.

33. Rosen, *Popcorn Venus*, pp. 192-93.

34. Roland Barthes, "The Faces of Garbo," *Mythologies*. Trans. Annette Lavers (New York: Hill & Wang, 1972), pp. 56-57.

35. Marjorie Rosen agrees: *Popcorn Venus*, p. 314.

4

Then and Now:
The Dream Beside Me

There's a whole, wide, broken world to mend.

—Dr. Golden, psychiatrist in a Veterans Hospital, in *Since You Went Away* (1944)

. . . In fact, the interesting thing to me was not only how much trouble small children had accepting a father who had been away but how many fathers went through at least mild depressions when they came back out of the armed services. All the years and days they had been dreaming about coming out and when will this damn thing be over. And then they came home and had depressions. Somehow it didn't seem as marvelous as they'd dreamed.

—Dr. Benjamin Spock, in Roy Hoopes' *Americans Remember The Home Front: An Oral Narrative* (1977), p. 178.

Question is being raised about desirability of showing any US war pix with scenes of fighting between Americans and Germans with latter depicted unfavorably.

—*Variety*, December 19, 1945.

One should know better; one really does. But. Still. . . .

—Richard Schickel, "Growing Up in the Forties"

In 1944, in *The Psychology of Women,* which I was not reading then, Helene Deutsch described "prepuberty," roughly the ages between ten and twelve, as years of psychological struggle between a yearning to be recognized as an adult and a need for security, as a dialectic between the future, toward which we reached, and the comfort of childhood, into which we retreated. Girls, Deutsch said, most commonly want to be actresses, newspaper reporters, writers, or detectives.[1] I wanted to be all of these except Nancy Drew. And I see now that I retreated to the comfort of the movies.

But not the movies on the screen. At the ages of eleven and twelve, for me as for most of us, moviegoing became a peer social rite, and thus, at just the age when comfort was needed, going to the movies offered us the opposite. In the excruciating worry over whether "he" would sit next to you, and what he would "do," Saturday afternoon became the antithesis of the comfort of Friday night with Mother and Dad. But understanding that, I also understand now why those were the years in which my movie scrapbooks grew to their final oversize: hundreds, maybe a thousand sheets, on which I pasted pictures cut every month from a dozen or more movie magazines. I had thought that this insanity grew from the competition between my scrapbook and Florence's, but I see now that each of these monthly magazines was a bulwark holding off confusion, a retreat (like listening to the radio soaps when you were sick in bed), to the symbols of childhood comfort.

Another change that came with my passage in 1945-46 to what I now know to call prepuberty was that I became conscious of the effects that movies had on me. As my responses were intellectualized, I selected and rejected with greater control what I remembered from the films I saw. My memory of postwar Hollywood in the movie magazines is like my memory of wartime movies; an entity unified, if not complete. But, I have only spotty memories of the postwar films, and other men and women my age say the same. David Thompson also says he was not a "discerning or discriminating moviegoer until well into my teens." Earlier, he wanted "only bright spasms and the darkness"; but, he says, in "early adolescence," he discovered " 'kissing' " pictures as dreamy adventures:

> The movies were a secret garden that only I had discovered, because the flashing change of imagery was exactly suited to my own nervous apprehension. Every time I blinked in wonder the screen was transformed.[2]

The reason for the change in early adolescence seems clear now. We were beginning to analyze, evaluate, and classify, to accept some aspects of movies and reject others according to standards we were beginning consciously to form. Our standards can be generalized as "romanticism" and "idealism," and I can now see that the two were essentially one.

Deutsch could have told me this:

> What is true of erotic fantasies, in which the erotic longing in itself and not the beloved person is important, is also true of youthful enthusiasm for an "ideal." One often hears enthusiastic girls exclaim: "Ah, if I only had an aim in life, a great idea for which I could live and die . . . I would be ready to sacrifice anything."[3]

And David Thompson can see it now—an Englishman who named his son after John Wayne's chosen son, Mathew (Thompson's spelling) in *Red River*, and also probably wasn't reading Helene Deutsch in the forties. Thompson: "In mythic terms, the weepie [the romance] is not just a lamentation for unrequited love but intolerance of death, aging, the passing of time, and every mistake we make."[4]

Then I could not see changes in me any more clearly than; I now know, most Americans saw all the signs of postwar change. In historical perspective, shifts in attitudes and values are visible, and signs of them are clear in postwar movies. And similarly, examining my memories of forties films, now I can see a difference between the childhood and the adolescent memories.

I see that, like Thompson, I absorbed the childhood

movies in my undiscerning self, and that thus they shaped me far more than the movies I saw after I had grown old enough to intellectualize—old enough, that is, for the mind-feeling split. Now I sense an almost tangible gulf between the quality of my memories between 1941 and 1946, and those after. If I remember the movies I saw as a young child at all, I recall them virtually as wholes. They rise to the surface of consciousness wrapped in a hazy, glowing nimbus, like a hearth fire. This cocoonlike recollection is indistinct in detail, particularly in rational connections, but seems whole in itself, and thus live. That smoky red air in the opening scene in *Alice Doesn't Live Here Anymore* is a precise representation of my childhood memories.[5]

But when I call up the movies I saw in 1948 and after, I have fewer memories, and those memories I have are fairly clear outlines of particular plots and characters, accompanied, as it were, by a soundtrack on which I analyze why I remember *that*. I may recall only one or two scenes of childhood movies, such as the scene in *Tish* in which Susan Peters faints in the post office. But these memories will be metonymic, suggesting the whole movie and me at the time I experienced it, though not in precise, intellectual ways. (I have virtually no memories, of either the adult or childish type, of 1947 movies. I wonder at the coincidence that this was the year in which I discovered boys.)

My memories up to the ages of eleven and twelve, and those after, seem to differ as remembering differs from recognizing. Recognizing, psychologists tell us, is more abstracted and intellectual; remembering is more complex, involving wide-ranging associations, often images, and always emotion.[6] No one of about my age who I interviewed—that is, men and women who moved from childhood to adolescence during 1945-1948—showed any interest in late forties films; a number said they had "no memory" of movies from that period, even though they recognize that, as typical teenagers, they had seen many of them. Our childhood memories, implying unmonitored effect, seem pleasurably free, complete, and personal. Compare them to the abstract, fragmented, intellectual memories of adulthood; trace this kind of memory back as far as you can, and see if you too stop at the hazy point of "coming of age."

This difference between my childhood memories and those of my adolescence underlies my different approach to postwar films. This chapter is thus more intellectually analytical than earlier ones because its roots are in the conscious past—which is not to say that we saw then what we may see now. At the time, I knew that romance moved my feelings and idealism stirred my mind. But I did not see how closely the two are connected, and I did not see that I chose my ideals not so much in my head as in my fantasies. Now I also judge that in the years after the war, and because of it, the values represented by Rhett and Scarlett were reinforced; and that ideals such as equality among different kinds of people thus merged and collided impotently, because they unconsciously connected with exciting dreams of overcoming barriers and with fantasies of a strong man's power. But we who became conscious in this period are the last to be expected to see—then—sloughing beasts of which, it seems clear now, few of our parents were conscious, or if they were, could acknowledge.

Postwar America: A Red-Lit Era

In just this period in which I changed, so did almost everything else. When my generation moved from childhood to adolescence, our world passed through its own sea-change. This change made an epoch, the "postwar"—a short period lasting only until the "Eisenhower era," an era that has been little examined as a culture, perhaps at least in part because many of the most important changes passed underground, hidden from public record. These were "the best years," were they not?[7] Who would argue with values just fought and died for: David Selznick's "unconquerable Fortress: the American Home" and Claudette Colbert and Jennifer Jones at the hearth? How many wanted to admit that old refuges felt like prisons, much less explore why? Who saw Whittaker Chambers' Devil-Mom, grown old from Cinderella, and understood the pumpkin?[8] Who, after the holocaust, wanted to see Mom and Dad as the enemy, or consider that the root of evil might be "love," and the "final horrors . . . neither gods nor demons, but intimate aspects of our own minds"?[9]

But, however hidden then, it is clear now that the country was changing profoundly, and that the shift is reflected in the movies of the time. In some ways the postwar films are like earlier forties films, and in some other ways they forecast later fifties and sixties movies—and even current films. But most productively, they are distinct, more like each other than like movies before or after. Thus, they not only elucidate a "postwar era"; as a *corpus*, they attest to its reality, a time distinct from "the forties" or "the fifties."

Brian Donlevy at Stalingrad

After all wars the arts revive, and postwar American movies were no exception. They were still an "art" in which a documentary-style film about a real unsolved murder (*Boomerang*) could open on the same day, January 24, 1947, as a musical adventure, *Song of Scheherazade,* in which Yvonne de Carlo danced to the music of Rimsky-Korsakoff, Eve Arden played her mother, Jean-Pierre Aumont played Rimsky-Korsakoff, and Brian Donlevy was a Russian navy captain. Postwar Hollywood could still change a popular novel and play so that the leading character lived at the end, without changing the title, *The Late George Apley.*[10] But despite all the *Songs of Scheherazade*, from this historical perspective it is clear that the *Boomerangs* had a better chance than they had had, at least since the war-scare years of the very early forties.

Polls taken at the end of the war indicated a widespread desire for realistic movies with novel plots and educational-inspirational value.[11] Freshness also thrived when, as soon as the war ended, the government renewed its prewar effect to break the monopoly of movie producers, distributors, and exhibitors. Ultimately the powers found ways around the heart of these restrictions, as they did around the dollar freeze in Europe and Britain's 75 percent tax. But the fear seeded and grown while these matters wended their long ways from rumor to end runaround took a lot of fat out of Hollywood. More than anything though, it seems to have been declining moviegoing and rising costs that made movie makers give us more realistic films. We teenagers went to the movies primarily as a social event, not as an entertainment. But, moved by postwar inflation and by new interests ranging from having families and going to college to bowling, and eventually to watching television, Americans as a whole deserted the movies. Attendance at movies dropped over ten million from 80.5 million average weekly admissions in 1946, the peak year of the forties, to 69 million in 1948.[12] In the September 11, 1946, *Variety,* Twentieth-Century Fox chief Darryl Zanuck stated that *The Dolly Sisters* released the previous year, would now cost $511,000 more, mainly because of higher labor costs. Another Fox study in June 1947 showed production costs up 63 percent over 1946.[13]

Thus, the filmmakers' goal of making movies that were both invitingly novel and of wide appeal met and fed the normal postwar mood of restlessness mixed with idealism. Directly after the war, America's focus was on her fighting men. Hollywood, revitalized by the return of veteran stars, producers, writers, and directors, focused on the veteran's concerns. Unhappily, and perhaps largely unwittingly, these concerns were deeply antagonistic to women. Besides general creativity and freshness, the major, particular change in postwar American film seems to be a pervasive attitude of cynicism and underlying virulence toward women.

They Didn't Give the War, but Everyone Came

In most aspects of American life, hatred of the girl he left behind was *verboten* (although the serviceman was filled with German or Japanese propaganda about her making big money at his job, and doing it through the favors of his boss, who, in the case of the Germans, was a gross "Jew").[14] But in the postwar years there was one area in which antagonism toward women was socially sanctioned. In a time when politicians, the pulpit, and thus the popular media all represented G.I. Joe's cry that working women were both unfair and unfeminine, Hollywood movies, still dominated by the studios, cannot be expected to have sounded a different drum. Yet, looking back, it seems now that Hollywood was as unaware as the rest of America, including the warriors, of how deeply they feared and heated the self-sufficient women who were not the girls they left behind.[15] This was the war few admitted (or admit), but to which "everyone came."

Even in *The Best Years of Our Lives,* the national epic of the postwar period, and now a classic motion picture, the veterans' women are not presented as part of "readjustment," though they are *plotted* as problems. Closest to a link is the one reference in the film to its title. When he was a fly-boy full of ribbons, Dana Andrews was "gotten" by Virginia Mayo. But after the war, he cannot do better than his prewar job of drugstore soda-jerk. When Fred (Andrews) cannot give her the money or the fun she had gotten accustomed during the anything-goes war years, Mayo's Marie kisses him off with a bitter whine: "I gave you the best years of my life." In the mouth of the careless tramp attached to history like a barnacle, the cliché becomes ironic; the sweetheart no longer excited after the ball becomes a symbol of the veteran's postwar nightmare—Now.

It was a nightmare sprung from that Frankenstein's monster, the woman who had, in fact, replaced the man. (First the Depression, then the War. . . .) Besides the tramp, her other, masked aspects were represented in *The Best Years of Our Lives*: the home-front sweetheart whose sympathy and sufficiency can strike terror in the man safe-home and busting-in on Myrna Loy; and the starry brown-eyed American virgin, whose innocent, total love, and fearsome, fierce capability, can enrage a maimed man without a hand. The men in *The Best Years of Our Lives* also represent the veterans' problems: disablement, and hence dependence; degradation from hero to soda-jerk; Democracy's idealism replaced by "realism," as when Frederic March, who was a humble but happy sergeant, but is now once again a banker, has to reject for lack of collateral the application for a farm loan of a veteran who he knows in the war he would have trusted with his life.

Yet even this most sensitive exposure, *The Best Years of Our Lives* retreats from showing sweethearts as real, ultimate problems. Except for Virginia Mayo, the women are brownette models of understanding who end up with their men, with only the slight hint through Frederic March's drinking and Myrna Loy's nagging about it that readjustment was rarely tied down tight. Looking at *The Best Years of Our Lives* and similar postwar movies now, it is easy to see the abyss between the lovers come home from the rites of independence, idealism, and romance—and their women. But then the abyss was all too often veiled by the conventional happy ending—or at least it seems now that it was for conventional children like me. Now, more than any other forties movie, *The Best Years of Our Lives* is the one I wonder about. Can anyone who was a child then see it without pain? So quick is it with the dilemmas of our adult years, waiting and unrealized. . . .

Man's World

But besides a sanctioned attitude that "the boss was back," another simple reason why postwar movies were male-oriented was that America had men in it again. Audiences wanted to watch heroes handling the country, not Claudette Colbert; and Hollywood, too, had its men back. Some of the returning soldiers were actors the public was eager to see again, such as Gable, Jimmy Stewart, and Tyrone Power. Others, who returned, although less visible, were perhaps more influential ultimately, because they were the filmmakers who would contribute to postwar creativity by adapting to story the realistic style they had developed shooting combat documentaries. William Wyler, the director of *The Best Years of Our Lives,* was one of these; his best-known documentary is *The Memphis Belle*, shot in combat in a B-17 over Germany, and probably the best recalled scene from *The Best Years of Our Lives* is the "graveyard" scene in which Dana Andrews retreats to the glory days in a junkyard of scrapped bombers.

But probably the most influential parent of the documentary stylists was Louis de Rochemont, who, in the 1930s, was one of the creators of the *March of Time* series. De Rochemont returned from the war to make—"on location"—some of the favorite films of idealistic teenagers like me, such as *Boomerang* and *Lost Boundaries,* the latter one of 1949's four studies of racism, or as it was called then, "intolerance." It was a movie based on a true story of Negroes "passing," filmed in a twin to its real location, a small New Hampshire town.[16] By the end of the decade, the realistic ethos and techniques of the documentary influenced every genre, even the most escapist and conventional, the musical, as in *On the Town* (1949), shot on location in New York City.

On the Town also typifies the male bent in postwar movies. At the time, it was another of the numerous movies I avoided if I could—that is, if I didn't have a date—because it deemphasized the love story and didn't star my wartime familiars. such as June Haver and Jeanne Crain. A movie made by two buddies from early forties Broadway, Gene Kelly and Stanley Donen, who got their film breaks when the war emptied

Hollywood of men, *On the Town* starred a trio who was *not* Gene Kelly, Rita Hayworth, and Phil Silvers (*Cover Girl*, 1944: Kelly's big break picture), but rather Kelly, Frank Sinatra, and Jules Munshin, as sailors on twenty-four-hour leave in "New York, New York." The girls were second-lead song-and-dance staples of the time, Vera-Ellen, Ann Miller, and Betty Garrett. They were picked up, kissed, and dropped at the dock. *That* seems inventive and unconventional now; and it was popular then, even if it wasn't with me, the romantic adolescent.

All the genres popular in the postwar years were dominated by men: not only crime melodramas and John Ford or Howard Hawks' westerns but also comedies, "social problem" movies, and even "women's pictures." (As David Thompson points out now, this "offensive label" was created by a "male-dominated film industry, whether the box-office scorekeepers on *Variety* or the production bosses at the big studios."[17]) War buddies are the protagonists not only of musicals such as *On the Town* but of social studies such as *The Best Years of Our Lives* and its *semblable, Till the End of Time* (also 1946), and the antibigotry message movies, *Gentleman's Agreement* and *Crossfire* (both 1947) and *Home of the Brave* (1949). Arthur Kennedy, the murder suspect in *Boomerang*, there echoes *The Best Years of Our Lives* as a veteran who is bitter because there are no jobs. In jail, he tells the sympathetic prosecutor (Dana Andrews), "I put in five years. . . . I'm anxious. . . . You can't wait, mister." At his trial, Kennedy is hurt by the testimony of a waitress he had dated, spurned, and, in *his* bitterness, made bitter by saying that he did not serve in the army to work in a hash joint like she did. In *Dead Reckoning* (1947), Lizabeth Scott surprised the conventions by being a *femme fatale* who turns out bad, but she is less startling viewed in the postwar context of comradeship. The hero, Bogart, gets mixed up with her when he tries to unravel the murder of her fiancé and his war buddy (William Prince). Even when it was not much intended, postwar film, it is clear now, was permeated with the fears expressed by the "Jew-boy" Dane Clark in *The Pride of the Marines* (1945), that the home front was, at best, indifferent to his and his buddies' return.

Hollywood's postwar conservatism looks now like a lid on a bitter brew. This conservatism is apparent, for example, in the 1945-46 *Varietys,* which present "Bandaid" responses to the volatile times, as in the recurrent articles on the threat of "immoral" films such as *Scarlet Street* (1945), in which Edward G. Robinson is an unhappily married man who falls for *femme fatale* Joan Bennett. This mood can also be seen in *Variety* articles on the threat to the studios from independent producers, industry strikes, the government, the British, audience "squawks" about those patriotic shorts we never questioned during the war, and even the epidemic of fear caused by increased box-office holdups. Under "signs of the times," consider the *Variety* item that the Broadway comedy smash *Harvey* was nixed for USO Shows because it "makes a sucker out of a psychiatrist," and psychiatry, according to the US Army, was critical in treating "battle fatigue."[18]

One pervasive form for the unrest roiling these "best years" was the movie plot question, is my sweetheart cheating on me while I'm getting shot? Even one of the racial tolerance films brought in the bad wife. In *Home of the Brave*, five men embark on a dangerous mission: the officer (Douglas Dick), the bigot (Steve Brodie), Frank Lovejoy, Lloyd Bridges, and James Edwards, a black man. At the end of the film, Peter Moss (Edwards) and the now-disabled Mingo (Lovejoy) go off together to open a restaurant. Leaving the hospital, the one-armed Mingo struggles with his duffel bag. A few minutes before, he had refused a light from the bigot, but now he accepts Moss's help because Moss quotes from the poem Mingo had recited in the jungle to distract Moss from the cries of the captured Finch (Bridges), Moss's old high school buddy and one white friend. The last lines of the poem are:

Frightened, we are everyone.
Someone must take a stand—
Coward, take my coward's hand.

(The poem is credited to Eve Merriam, now a well-known feminist writer.) Watching Mingo as he wrestles with the bag—the bigot T. J. has called him "crippled"—Moss quotes gently, smiling, "Coward, take my coward's hand." Startled because Moss has remembered the poem, Mingo smiles back and accepts the hand of another vulnerable man. Back in the screaming jungle, Mingo had told Moss that the poem was written by his wife, who, he said, also writes an eloquent Dear John letter. It is not emphasized, but it is a fact: in the jungle in which the Japs are torturing their buddy, the girl Mingo left behind is also the enemy.

The Best Years of Our Lives raises the question, is she cheating? Up to complex levels, such as, if I married her because she was sexy as Virgino Mayo, didn't I ask for it? And, if she was as faithful as Cathy O'Donnell's Wilma only to snare me through gratitude—and guilt?—is marriage with her, after all, what I want? Handless Harold Russell's adjustments to dependency are explored sensitively and realistically, and thus his eventual happy ending with O'Donnell seems as sound as it is romantically satisfying. The Virginia Mayo-Dana Andrews dilemma is also developed realistically to a breakup—but then the movie rewards him with Teresa Wright. *Crossfire* made the question even more complex, evoking the abyss of lost identity through Paul Kelly's role as only "The Man," a veteran whose lack of a name symbolizes his complete loss of identity after he was labeled "D.D.": Dishonorably Discharged. The Man's complexity is reflected in his wife, the bargirl Ginny (Gloria Grahame), thorny and vulnerable, and like the waitress in *Boomerang*, unable in her hurt to help a veteran in trouble with postwar American Authority. But—however unwittingly—most postwar films treated the question of the soldier and his sweetheart dishonestly, by making her turn out good at the end. Typically, in *Till the End of Time*, veteran Guy Madison is hungry for a girl but holds himself back from the lovely war-wife (Dorothy McGuire), who has invited him home until she makes it O.K. by telling him that she is a war widow. It must be emphasized that all this was not clear then, at least not to us young women and men, because these strains ran through the complex, contradiction-ridden, frightening, and hence badly articulated psychological context called "readjustment." *Now* we recognize postwar plots and characters as reflections of the confusion, frustration, and alienation of the homecoming soldier. And his woman.[19]

For example, in this context the illegitimate baby romance that was so popular after the war looks like a reflection of guilt, a displacement of the "did she cheat?" theme to, "she cheated with *me*." Two of the biggest postwar hits were Olivia de Havilland's *To Each His Own* (1946) and Susan Hayward's *My Foolish Heart* (1949). Both films begin with the girl's Giving In and winding up with a dead warrior's baby. What is striking now, spotlighting these films as crazed reflections of the inchoate anxieties and angers of postwar men and women, is that both films are devoted mainly to the lifelong, soap operaish effects on the woman of that One Lovely, Lost Moment. The illegitimate child is her warrant on him. But (guilt, guilt for him) it is also his sentence on her. Part of the postwar problem was the returning veteran's sense of betrayal and loss of home when she cheated on him; but as the movies of the period confirm, another, more commonplace problem was the jaillike pressure of her All-American fidelity.

In any case, over and over again, she was not the girl he thought he'd left behind. Sometimes, like Virginia Mayo in *The Best Years of Our Lives*, she ran around. But often it was he who had changed, and she who appeared stagnant, and insufficient. In *Gentlemen's Agreement* (1947), Gregory Peck is a reporter who poses as a Jew and then writes about his experiences. His wartime buddy Dave Goldman (John Garfield) is Peck's unwavering Sancho Panza; but his WASP beloved,

Kathy (Dorothy McGuire again), breaks under the pressure, proving herself too weak to fight for the One Democratic World for which the men fought on the battlegrounds, and now in the civil arena. (Of course, she redeems herself for the happy ending, as almost always, by Learning From Her Man.) *Possessed* (1948) even managed to make a hero of that old villain, the man who refuses to marry the heroine, by making *her* so psychotically possessive that no one can help but sympathize with Van Heflin, whose only given reason for spurning Joan Crawford is, "I have to keep myself moving. I don't know why. Blame it on the Army. . . ."

Postwar movies also reflect women who, conversely, failed their men by demonstrating self-sufficiency all too well. Frederic March's overwrought homecoming in *The Best Years of Our Lives,* to a contented wife and daughter about to go to a dinner party, is typical, if more consciously expressed than was the norm. But Harold Russell's handless, and thus exaggerated, dependence on Cathy O'Donnell is even more interesting because it represents the man's deepest fears. Should he, helpless, give in?" "Why shouldn't two people need each other?" asks Ruth, the girl friend of blinded war hero Al Schmid, in *The Pride of the Marines* (John Garfield and Eleanor Parker). Harold Russell's struggle is also that of Marlon Brando's paraplegic in Brando's first film *The Men* (1950), with Teresa Wright, *The Best Year's* All-American Peggy, playing his helpmate; and it is Arthur Kennedy's battle in *Bright Victory* (1951), in which Kennedy is a blind veteran and Peggy Dow another Cathy O'Donnell, with long blonde-brown American bob and large, warm brown eyes. But for all these wounded veterans, the ending is happy, despite the question. The question is also Van Heflin's in *Possessed*: Why the charnel house of marriage? In *The Lady from Shanghai* (1948), Rita Hayworth answers. The man looks for adventure, and the women is beautiful, very sexy, and realistic. Michael O'Hara (Orson Welles) would run away with Elsa Bannister (Hayworth) to "one of the far places."

"Oh, Michael," she replies, in Acapulco, "We're in one of them now. It wouldn't work. I tried it. Everything's bad, everything."

A woman that is realistic can destroy a man lost in a romantic dream. Michael O'Hara is almost done in, in his words, by the "sharks who destroy themselves," and the sharpest teeth turn out to be those of the glamour girl. Unless he was maimed and gave in to dependency, the postwar man reflected in the movies was hard pressed to find a good marriage, much less romance. And even when playing typical Perfect Wives, the postwar movie heroines now seem subtly but unmistakably different from Mrs. Miniver, like Mom-and-apple-pie gone overripe. For example, in a stock situation comedy, *Mr. Blandings Builds His Dream House* (1948), the perfect wife Myrna Loy now looks appalling—not the perfect wife at all, but an at-home succubus who presses hubby Cary Grant over his head into a house in the country, and then diddles with their architect and best friend Melvyn Douglas while Grant sells his soul to—what else?—an ad agency.

Let me emphasize again: The postwar connection between fatal women and perfect wives was not articulated, not even by the scholars, not even in Martha Wolfenstein's and Nathan Leites's pioneer work *Movies: A Psychological Study,* 1950. The sexual enmity could not be articulated—much less negotiated—because it was officially denied by the combatants. Postwar America was pledged to the dream of Claudia and David: Dorothy McGuire and Robert Young in a Connecticut cottage with fluffy white curtains blowing in the sunny breeze, chintz davenports, and fires licking in pure white fireplaces. The era resolutely saw no difference between the smiling-through-tears American homes of the war years ("the American fortress," as David Selznick announced at the opening of *Since You Went Away*), and the postwar armed camps of brighteyed women and beleagured men. But it is clear now in the shadows of postwar films that to many American men the dream house looked more like an army camp without the camaraderie.

Postwar American women had less to say than men about what movies were made; but given the polls on wartime working women's favorable attitudes toward their jobs, whether they admitted it or not, Claudia's cottage must also have looked like a prison to at least a number of the 3 million women who by 1947 had left their wartime jobs, and to at least some of the wives of the men who had come home from the faraway places with the strange sounding names.[20] An ad for *Pitfall* (1948) spoke to the fears of both the good soldier and the good wife: "A man can be strong as steel . . . but somewhere there's a woman who'll break him!"*

Significantly, the ad was misleading. Far from being strong, Dick Powell was the postwar era's disssatisfied "Mr Average American," as he cynically termed himself, bored and sniping with his Perfect Wife (Jane Wyatt) and his dull insurance job, and ripe for Lizabeth Scott—who was not a *femme fatale*, but only a nice girl looking, as she put it, for a man to be "nice" to her, and unaware that Powell was married when she took up with him for all of one night. Protecting him afterwards becomes *her* pitfall when she shoots her blackmailing suitor, Raymond Burr. When Powell confesses his infidelity, the perfect wife's response is to forbid him to go to the police (for protection from Burr), because this would ruin the family name. Now we may see Wyatt as worse by far than Lizabeth Scott; but in 1948 *Pitfall* did not encourage that view, at least not on its surface. At the end of the movie, a whipped and whimpering Powell is revived to a smile by Wyatt's saying she will stay married to him, though

---

*The hype for Lizabeth Scott films indicates the closet sadomasochism of the era. The ads for *Too Late for Tears* (1949), for example, feature her face distorted under slaps from Dan Duryea. In this one, she did in a husband (Arthur Kennedy) with Duryea's help, then went to work on poisoning Duryea, before Getting Hers. In *Easy Living* (1949), she was so greedy she forced husband Victor Mature to go on playing pro football with a bad heart. The ads said she had to be slapped "back to her senses," and a fan magazine still shows an exhausted Mature cheek to cheek with a toothy Scott above the caption, "Lizabeth Scott gloats when she turns strong man Victor Mature weak."

(she reminds him grimly) it will be a long time before she can "forget ." In their modest American coupe, they move off into the Los Angeles traffic and The End, with her at the wheel.

In the postwar years, the climate was not conducive to proclaiming Lizabeth Scott or Virginia Mayo sisters to Jane Wyatt and Myrna Loy, or the disturbed veterans as brothers of "Mr. Average American." After HUAC, in October 1947, took up *Esquire* movie critic Jack Moffit's notion that portrayals of bitter veterans were Communist inspired, such portraits required courage as well as uncommon insight. A Leo McCarey, Gary Cooper comedy, *Good Sam* (1948), received a "definitely not recommended" rating from the Protestant Film Council because of the " 'slapstick and satirical manner in which "goodness" is treated' "; and the council gave the same palm to *Sorry, Wrong Number*, in which Barbara Stanwyck played an imperious rich man's daughter who, invalided in her bed, hears on the telephone that her poor-boy, henpecked husband (Burt Lancaster) is plotting to kill her. The council saw " 'no justification for a vicious and tortuous film of this sort.' "[21]

Hollywood knew that these controversial films were popular. Robert Mitchum's movies boomed after his marijuana bust in September 1948, and so did the films of declining stars Errol Flynn, Rita Hayworth, and Ingrid Bergman after their late forties "sexcapades." Or, as *Variety* reported on the next page after the story on the Protestant Film Council, the number one box-office hit of October 1948 was *Sorry, Wrong Number* in all its viciousness; *Good Sam* was ninth. But newly loosed from wartime Washington; highly institutionalized and hence vulnerable; in the middle of political and religious interests, the public, the buck, and sometimes even an ideal; how far could the studios go toward realism and away from pap? It is and it isn't their fault that we find the complex, ambiguous, tortuous realities of postwar feeling only now, and almost wholly in minor movies largely forgotten today, such as *Pitfall*, and in the dark corners of representations of the public dream, such as *The Best Years of Our Lives.*

As we children approached adolescence, we ran into the silent breakup of traditional verities, including an antiwoman mood that was probably the more virulent for its being largely unsanctioned. Just when our newly powerful sexuality collided with our unconscious, childish desire for our father, our mother, we also ran into a culture the mores of which reflected powerful, but repressed sexual antagonisms. We crossed from childhood to adolescence just as Richard Widmark's Tommy Udo, giggling, pushed a crippled old mother down the stairs in one of those revitalizing, documentary-style crime melodramas, *Kiss of Death* (1947) and just as in *The Street with No Name* (1948), Widmark slapped around his moll Barbara Lawrence, a vacuous blonde and late forties look-alike for Dolores Moran.

But any contrast between Dolores Moran and Barbara Lawrence is only skin-deep. Postwar antagonism to women did not contradict our romantic childhood dreams. They were fantasies of abasement, and the late forties mood only extended their hateful roots, intensifying them to dreams of abuse. After the war, *Gone with the Wind* was indeed revived.

The Stars: Old Heroes

Postwar attitudes toward women and sex are revealed now in both the stars and the popular movies of the periods. First, the stars.

After the war, the normal bent for novelty led to the eclipse of some of the established stars of the war years. At the end of 1948, *Variety* noted with surprise that the old stars were no longer carrying weak stories, and that strong stories lacking the stars of 1940-47 were top grossers at the box office. Unexpected failures included an Ingrid Bergman-Charles Boyer romance, *Arch of Triumph;* romances starring superstars Ginger Rogers and Bette Davis (*It Had To Be You; Winter*

Meeting); Rosalind Russell's Freudian melodramas, *The Velvet Touch* and *Mourning Becomes Electra* (1947); Ronald Colman's "Othello," *A Double Life;* and even the films of two of the most popular wartime "cheerleaders," Dorothy Lamour's *The Girl from Manhattan*, and Danny Kaye's *A Star Is Born.* Surprise 1948 hits, supposed "Bs," included *Red River,* released as just another oater; almost all-male crime films *Canon City, T-Men,* and *The Naked City*, starring newcomers of "B-men" Scott Brady, Dennis O'Keefe, Barry Fitzgerald, and Howard Duff (the postwar newcomer who came in fourth in a 1950 "sex appeal" poll); and *The Street with No Name*, starring Richard Widmark, the newcomer of 1947 whose whole name became Richard Widmark-playing-a-cold-blooded killer.[22]

Among the men, stars who had been absent for the duration functioned at least for a while as newcomers. Gallup Audience Research polls of the time indicated that contrary to the "rule"—three films a year to remain a star—no actor or actress who went to war to fight or entertain lost popularity.[23] Upon their return, Gable and Jimmy Stewart were thrown into one picture after another. Glenn Ford, William Holden, and Victor Mature, ingenues before the war, and Van Heflin, a prewar support, became postwar stars. We had men in abundance: in *Fort Apache* (1948), veteran Henry Fonda, John Wayne, and John Agar, a newcomer and, even more interesting to me, Shirley Temple's bridegroom. In *Command Decision* (1948), a now-it-can-be-told drama of the dilemmas and anguish of wartime officers, Gable, Walter Pidgeon, Brian Donlevy, Charles Bickford, and two male ingenues developed during the war years, John Hodiak and superingenue Van Johnson. Or in *That Forsyte Woman* (1949), with Pidgeon, Errol Flynn, and Robert Young (and Greer Garson). Other all-male movies were surprisingly popular, particularly Bogart's *The Treasure of the Sierra Madre* (1948)—a hateful movie; not only unromantic, but unshavenly ugly—and *Down to the Sea in Ships* (1949), the saga of a New England rite of passage via a whaling ship, starring patriarch Lionel Barrymore, child star Dean Stockwell, and in his first sympathetic role, Richard Widmark. In 1949, even the World War II movie came back; among the year's most popular films were the all- or almost all-male *Battleground, Sands of Iwo Jima,* and *Home of the Brave.* The popularity of these masculine movies, and the fact the actor-veterans Gable, Fonda, Ford, et al. were thrown into one picture after another, suggest that the postwar public was eager to see men.

In reality, of course, it was not that simple. Gable's homecoming film, *Adventure* (1945), co-starring the super superstar of the war years, Garson, drew audiences (some of us had never seen him), but it disappointed, as did his subsequent films. Even with Ava Gardner (*The Hucksters,* 1947) or Lana Turner (*Homecoming,* 1948), Rhett Butler could not score. The postwar strategy for selling Gable is caught in an ad for *Homecoming,* which seems now to reveal the time: A somberly dark, realistic photo of him embracing his movie wife, Anne Baxter, and below it the caption, "In her arms, the homecoming," is placed next to a romantic drawing, full of white highlights, of Gable holding Turner in a Scarlett-Rhett pose, and the caption, "In her arms, the awakening." So much for Claudia.

Yet *Homecoming* was not a Gable-Turner *Honky Tonk* hit. Metro Goldwyn Mayer plotted from the time-honored formula, yet the only time they varied from the formula it resulted in the all-male *Command Decision,* Gable's only late forties hit. Gable's other postwar movies were the old romances in which two contrasting women, the lady and the broad, vied for the King. In *Adventure,* it was Garson versus breezy blonde Joan Blondell and sultry brunette Lina Romay; in *The Hucksters,* it was Gardner and the new British lady, Deborah Kerr; in *Homecoming,* it was brown-haired Baxter and Gable's special blonde Lana Turner; in *Any Number Can Play* (1949), silver blonde Alexis Smith was the lady-wife and bright blonde Audrey Totter was the other woman; and in *Key to the City* (1950), Loretta Young and perennial blonde starlet Marilyn Maxwell vied for Gable. In all of these movies the lady got Gable, and none was a hit until *Mogambo*, the 1953 remake of Gable and Harlow's *Red Dusty* (1932), in which the broad, Ava, bested the lady—indeed, the lady of fifties ladies, Grace Kelly. It seems that whereas novelty could get people to the movie theaters ("Gable's Back and Garson's Got Him!"), and some teenage girls, like me, would love Gable in any turkey, generally the old stars alone did not suffice, and the old formulas did not speak to changed moods. A sign of the deep change was the success of new kinds of stories and new stars.

There were exceptions, of course, but only a few. Old stars Gary Cooper, Cary Grant, Alad Ladd, Errol Flynn, Robert Taylor, and lesser old stars Red Skelton, Fred MacMurray, Ray Milland, Dick Powell, George Raft, Robert Montgomery, and Robert Young were postwar stars, but with the exception of Cooper and Grant, their prime was past. After the war as before, Bing Crosby and Bob Hope were box office and popularity poll winners—Hope less than Crosby, who could sing, sentimentalize and romance as well as play comedy, and whose popularity in the midforties was touched by no other star. Among the new male stars of the war years, John Wayne, Gregory Peck, Gene Kelly, Robert Mitchum, and Sinatra survived and prospered, as for a while did Van Johnson, Dana Andrews, Robert Ryan, Peter Lawford, and Farley Granger. Of these, only Peck and Granger could be called conventionally handsome. Most of the wartime substitutes for Tyrone Power and Clark Gable faded away, from the aging Boyer, William Powell, Ronald Colman, Brian Aherne, George Brent, et al., through forties staples such as Joseph Cotten, Paul Henreid, Robert Cummings, and Dennis Morgan, to the younger crop: Sonny Tufts, Guy Madison, Turhan Bey, Cornel Wilde, Lon McCallister, John Hodiak, Lee Bowman, James Craig, John Carroll, Robert Hutton, and a horde of others. For *Apartment for Peggy* (1948), there was William Holden to play Jeanne Crain's man, a role taken in the war years by McCallister, Wilde,

Frank Latimore, or Glenn Langan. After the war, the latter two trekked to Italy for roles, along with such other wartime regulars as Alan Curtis, a Gable look-alike, and Lynn Merrick, one of my favorite blonde beauties.

New Men

Hollywood's postwar discovery that good features without stars could be sold led naturally to new, lower salaried "A" players. There is at least some evidence that the studios understood the national mood. In 1946, *Variety* reported a trend away from the studio stables and toward freelancers, not because the latter were cheaper but because the "stock companies" had become so familiar as to telegraph the stories they played in. (In this story *Variety* reported Universal's release of Alan Curtis, Lon Chaney, Jr., wartime leading men Noah Beery, Jr., Robert Paige, and David Bruce, and that guiding light and Rock of Gibraltar blonde of my childhood, Martha O'Driscoll.[24]) In 1947, the studios laid off 398 contract players, leaving only 336 on the rosters.[25] Partly this is accounted for by the postwar inflation-recession, but it was also the result of a newly restless public's desire for fresh faces and untelegraphed stories. Even I did not notice that Martha O'Driscoll and Lynn Merrick were gone.

Moreover, many of the most popular new stars were not conventionally handsome or glamorous. Some were, including among the men the novel foreign faces of Louis Jourdan, Ricardo Montalban, James Mason, Stewart Granger, and Richard Todd, and the American Howard Keel, John Lund, Gordon MacRae, Larry Parks, Scott Brady, Richard Basehart, John Derek, and Montgomery Clift, whom the fan magazines presented, and we teenage girls took, as a dream-boat and heartthrob. But there was little of the conventionally handsome face in Richard Widmark, Burt Lancaster, Kirk Douglas, Paul Douglas, Mario Lanza, Rex Harrison, David Niven, Howard Duff, Jeff Chandler, Dan Dailey, Zachary

Scott, Mel Ferrer, Jack Palance, Frank Lovejoy, Wendell Corey, and Marlon Brando; or in Robert Mitchum, John Garfield, Richard Conte, Dane Clark, and Van Heflin, who were not newcomers but were only stars after the war. The postwar male newcomers who never "made it big," despite all the magazine puffery I clipped and pasted, were invariably tall, dark, and handsome: Mark Stevens, Rory Calhoun, Rod Cameron, Richard Hart, John Bromfield, James Mitchell, Jim Davis, Keefe Brasselle, and others even more obscure. Moreover, with the exception of Clift and perhaps Jourdan, and on the programmer level, Stewart Granger, Howard Keel, and Gordon MacRae, none of the conventionally handsome newcomers listed endured like the "uglies," such as Mitchum, Lancaster, Widmark, Douglas, and Brando.

Leading Ladies

Despite the popularity of "men's movies," actresses did not disappear in the postwar years. In fact, evidence of our attraction to novelty then shows more in the new actresses than in actors, perhaps because the war veteran men served as well as the newcomers as new faces. Popular actresses of the postwar years included new British faces: Deborah Kerr, who was marketed as a Greer Garson; three Merle Oberon types: Jean Simmons, who made it, and Phyllis Calvert, Margaret Lockwood, and Patricia Roc, who did not; and Ann Todd, a new Bergman, classy but with suggestive embers. Other Bergmanesque newcomers were Viceca Lindfors and Marta Toren from Sweden and (Alida) Valli and Valentina Cortesa from Italy.

But what was wrong with the model, the old Bergman? She hit her peak of box-office popularity in 1945-46, mainly because of *The Bells of St. Mary's*, a Bing Crosby movie, and the number one box-office attraction of 1946. *Notorious* was also a hit. But then came *Arch of Triumph* (1948), a romance, co-starring Charles Boyer. It should have been a hit, but was a $2 millon flop—perhaps at least in part because Bergman's image would not allow her to pull off the switch within the movie from her initial lovely self to a woman too weak to be faithful when Boyer's devotion to fighting Fascism separates them. "I can't be hurt like that again," she says, when he returns—a typical late forties fatal *fidele*. He replies; "You know you'll leave me [again]...?" She (ecstatically, masochistically): "Yes, Yes, Yes. . ."

Her *Joan of Arc* (1949) also bombed, despite critical acclaim and the arty aura of her earlier stint on Broadway in Maxwell Anderson's play *Joan of Lorraine*. *Under Capricorn* (1949) was another dud, although directed by Hitchcock and boasting a novel Australian setting and a classic romantic plot, the triangle, with Joseph Cotten, a favorite romantic hero of the war years, as the husband, and a new Englishman, Michael Wilding, as "the visitor." Bergman's late forties decline can now be seen as typical.

In addition to welcoming newcomers, the late forties made new stars of wartime ingenues Esther Williams, Ava Gardner, Susan Hayward, Anne Baxter, Jeanne Crain, Elizabeth Taylor, and Ann Blyth; and of wartime "bits" Yvonne de Carlo, Dorothy Malone, Ruth Roman, Shelley Winters, and, in 1950, Marilyn Monroe. Some of the dependable leads or superstars of the war years revitalized their careers by switching. Loretta Young went from drama to comedies such as *The Farmer's Daughter* (1947), which won her an Oscar; and Olivia de Havilland and Jane Wyman became superstars by switching from their *Government Girl* (1943) type comedies to heavy drama, and Oscars again, to de Havilland for *To Each His Own* (1946) and to Wyman for *Johnny Belinda* (1948), in competition with de Havilland's acclaimed asylum film, *The Snake Pit*.

Katharine Hepburn had a postwar penchant for turgid melodramas: *Undercurrent* (1946), with Robert Taylor, and *Sea of Grass* (1947), with Tracy. But she was saved by Claudette Colbert's bowing out of *State of the Union* (1948). The success of this satiric Howard Lindsay-Russell Crouse Broadway *cum* Hollywood comedy, co-starring Tracy, led to the now-classic comedies written for Hepburn and Tracy: *Adam's Rib* (1949), *Pat and Mike* (1952), and *The Desk Set*

(1957). In the postwar years Joan Crawford and Bette Davis generally stuck to their women's dramas, but these were novel in their newly heavy—very heavy—psychologizing. Ann Sheridan, the good, breezy broad, switched to the heavies in *Nora Prentiss* and *The Unfaithful* (both 1947). Rosalind Russell, probably the number one comedienne of the late thirties and wartime forties, also tried to switch, going darkly dramatic in *Mourning Becomes Electra, The Guilt of Janet Ames* (1947), and *The Velvet Touch* (1948). None was a success for Russell, who never really came back until she could become a character in *Auntie Mame* (1958), but who returned to comedy in 1949, in something called *Tell it to the Judge.*

Sirens

But as this list of generally forgotten movies suggests, except for Loretta Young and durable Davis and Crawford, none of the wartime superstars could be spotlighted in the late forties. And like the superstars, the pinups and "suggestive ladies" of the war years were also eclipsed in the postwar era. One of the few who seems to have noticed was Kay Campbell in a 1949 *Variety* piece, "Hollywood and the Slicks."

The war, said Campbell, killed general interest in "glamour." Whatever the cause—and despite Winthrop Sargeant's panegyric to the glamour girls such as Rita Hayworth, as Campbell pointed out, postwar mass "slicks" such as *Life* and *Look* did not tend to feature not glamour girls but essays on camera work, directors (seeds of auteurism), and the other technical aspects of the film business-art. And the women's magazines, such as *Ladies Home Journal, Vogue,* and *The American home*, began to show the stars less as gods and goddesses and more as mortals at home with their homey families.[26] In a 1949 *Colliers,* for example, in an article entitled "What Hollywood Doesn't Know About Women," realistic looking and acting women, such as the *Best Years of Our Lives* and Jane Wyman in *Johnny Belinda,* opposed to the influence on the American girl of the impossible dream of looking like Lana Turner.[27]

In 1947-1948 came the long-skirted "New Look" in women's dresses, and with it, short hair. What chicken-and-egg kind of connection there may have been between that hairstyle and the antisexuality of postwar movies can only be speculated. But consider the difference between the glamorous longhaired Maureen O'Hara in *Sitting Pretty,* which introduced Clifton Webb's Mr. Belvidere. Or consider the difference in Jeanne Crain's image from the long brown waves framing her face in *State Fair* to a bunned Pinky. Perhaps most dramatic, was the less alluring Rita Hayworth with short blonde curls in *The Lady from Shanghai, was contrasted to her earlier Gilda.*

In postwar movies, women's parts were generally either asexual and familial or antisexual, with the wholesome allure of the early forties "siren" replaced by the fatal aura epitomized by Marlene Dietrich, whose career revived in the late forties, in A Foreign Affair (1948), in which she played a glamorous Nazi. For adolescents like me, who did not know The Blue Angel, who were kin to "Hitler's Children," and who came of sexual age in the late forties, Dietrich's Erika in Billy Wilder's "sophisticated comedy" was inexplicable, and is still remembered.

Unlike Dietrich, however, the glamour girls of the early forties either declined, or if they were smarter or luckier, recast their wartime images as patriotically hemogenized sex objects. Betty Grable went matronly in films such as *Mother Wore Tights* (1947) and *When My Baby Smiles at Me* (1948), in which she became a kind of musical Blondie. Largely it seems from the luck of finding a compatible partner, Dan Dailey, Grable remained popular, though never again at her wartime heights, as in 1943 when she was the number one star at the box office, male or female. Lauren Bacall, the new glamour girl after *To Have and Have Not,* also went homey, playing motherly girl friends to Bogart in *Dark Pasages*

(1947) and *Key Largo* (1948).

But, like Bergman, the sirens Turners, Hayworth, Lamarr, Veronica Lake, Paulette Goddard, Merle Oberon, Maria Montez, and Dorothy Lamour also all fell from favor in the postwar years, most of them permanently. Significantly, as they faded, they generally tried that popular postwar type, the wicked heroine. But just as the public did not buy Hayworth's Lady from Shanghai, neither did they respond to Hedy Lamarr's *Strange Woman* (1946), Merle Oberon's Belladonna *(Temptation,* 1946), or Joan Fontaine's python, *Ivy* (1947). Maria Montez, in the war years the very popular heroine of Arabian fantasies, could not arrest her decline either with a novel modern role in *Tangier* (1946), or as a wicked *Siren of Atlantis* (1948). "Dottie" Lamour left Hope and Crosby's Road, but the public would not buy "the sarong girl" as *Lulu Belle*)1948) or, in *The Lucky Stiff* (1949), as a chanteuse who is really the head of the shakedown racket. The career of this wartime favorite, second only to Grable in the war years, never revived.

The postwar course of Lana Turner's career, which did survive, is revealing. Turner had her Gilda—a classic sex role—in *The Postman Always Rings Twice* (1946); and like Hayworth's career after *Gilda* (also 1946), Turner's star declined after white-blonde, white-gowned Cora. She starred in *Green Dolphin Street* (1947), and even the novelty of her brown hair and of super special effects, such as an earthquake and tidal wave, did not make the movie a special smash hit. MGM was shaken by the failure of the romantic formula; it had also failed recently with *Desire Me,* with Greer Garson and Richard Hart—a conventionally handsome and also a new face (who, with Van Heflin, was also in *Green Dolphin Street*). Another old formula had also failed in 1947: *Song of the Thin Man,* with William Powell and Myrna Loy. When *Green Dolphin Street* opened to bad reviews in New York, MGM's president Nicholas Schenck called a meeting of MGM executives. Louis B. Mayer arrived late to the meeting; in mid-October, 1947, he was in Washington testifying at the opening of the new, intensified HUAC investigation into Communists in Hollywood.[28] The times were changing.

After *Green Dolphin Street,* Turner took second place behind male stars and played relatively unsexy parts in *Cass Timberlane* (Spencer Tracy, 1947), *Homecoming*, (despite that ad), and *The Three Musketeers* (1948); in the latter, she was not only a Bad Woman—in contrast to the love interest, June Allyson, she was Old. By 1952, however, Turner was able to score her first hit in a half dozen years, as a glamour girl in *The Bad and the Beautiful.* Somehow, in the early fifties—as the "Eisenhower era" dawned—Hollywood's almost unremarked anti-sexuality went away in a burst of Marilyn Monroe and Sophia Loren. But in the war's aftermath, bias against the sexual woman, however unacknowledged then, looks surprisingly pronounced now.

New Girls

Better than wholesome sirens turned *femme fatale,* the postwar public liked *new* bad girls: Lizabeth Scott, Gloria Grahame, Yvonne de Carlo, Angela Lansbury (who introduced the type of the forties amoral, deadly sexpot early, in her servant girl in *Gaslight,* 1944), and Jane Greer, who in *Out of the Past* (1947), wisely if untruthfully told Robert Mitchum, just before she shot him to death, that she had never pretended to be other than what she was, and that all the lovely, romantic things he thought she was, he had imagined.

Let Dolores Moran stand for how the bad girl changed. In wartime movies, such as *Old Acquaintance* and *The Horn Blows at Midnight*, Moran is an innocently trouble-making, ultimately winning, cute little vamp. But in a postwar movie, *Too Young to Know* (1945), she is not only the other woman, she is a greedy, vengeful slut, blown-up. Soldier Robert Hutton, meeting Moran in wartime Bombay after his and ingenue

Joan Leslie's marriage has ended (only until "The End" of course), hears from Moran that Leslie bore their son after the divorce (good news), and then that Leslie put the child up for adoption. "You always were bad news," he cries. After accusing her of "revenge," he stalks out and the scene fades on her glamorously lighting and then blowing out on a cigarette—a favorite forties image of glamour—and grinning with all her perfect white teeth between her luscious forties lips: Bad news personified.

Yet, how popular was Dolores Moran? Or even Lizabeth Scott, Yvonne de Carlo, Jane Greer, et al. who were postwar leads? In 1948, *Variety* reported that the only young actress Hollywood thought capable of carrying a picture was wholesome Esther Williams.[29] DeCarlo, Scott, and Greer all played good girls too and the sex queen of the postwar era* was Ava Gardner, who was unusual in the era of fatal sex because she usually turned out good and was pleasantly alluring, rather than threatening, along the way. The bent toward wholesomeness also showed in the newcomers. A front-page feature in the January 9,1946, *Variety* on new stars is instructive because the show biz bible seems to have based its predictions on past standards, and thus to have touted glamour girls and handsome men—who did not become stars. *Variety* highlighted Bacall, who did last, and Lizabeth Scott, Yvonne de Carlo, Rod Cameron, blue-eyed blonde Joan Caulfield, and smoldering brunettes Lucille Bremer, and Pat Kirkwood, none of whom lasted, at least for long. By September 11, 1946, *Variety* was announcing that MGM had dropped Pat Kirkwood and others from the January 9 list of promising players, "without explanation."

---

*In late 1950, a poll of 150 women movie extras voted Ava Gardner the "sex appeal" palm; Jane Russell, who with the exception of the little seen *The Outlaw,* was thoroughly wholesome in her movie roles,came in second. Hayworth was sixth, but Grable was down at number twenty-one. Tyrone Power was the male winner; second and third were newcomers Howard Duff and Montgomery Clift; fourth was the durable Gable, who was then, as the short U.P. Bulletin of January 31,1950, saw fit to add, "nearing fifty."

The girls who did thrive were typified by Debbie Reynolds, who debuted in 1949 in that late forties rarity, a Bette Davis comedy (*June Bride*). The ingenue of the postwar era usually had Debbie's brownish "American blonde" hair, she usually co-starred rather than starred, and she generally played a staunch sweetheart. Together, these ingenues form an impressive list of late forties "favorites": Janet Leigh, Ann Blyth, Jane Powell,Shirley Temple, Barbara Bel Geddes, Diana Lynn, Betsy Drake, Peggy Dow, Coleen Gray, Vanessa Brown, Cathy O'Donnell, Allene Roberts, Joan Evans, Sally Forrest, and others. But even if the newcomers were the conventional brunettes, blondes and titians of the war era, they too were almost always cast as All-American good girls by the studios, and always so by the movie magazines. Dark-haired Gail Russell, Jean Peters, Geraldine Brooks, Joanne Dru, Colleen Townsend, and Ruth Roman were rarely cast as sultry. Nor were the beautiful blondes: Patricia Neal, Virginia Mayo, Peggy Cummins, Barbara Lawrence, and Shelley Winters, or even the new flaming redheads, Arlene Dahl, Rhonda Fleming, and Julie London.

In the thirties and fifties, European imports could get away with sexier roles than the girl next door on Main Street. But in the postwar years, only Corinne Calvet was heavily hyped as a sex kitten. One of the rare French imports of the time, Calvet debuted in a Bergman-type role in the *Casablanca*-like *Rope of Sand* (1949), with Paul Henreid, Claude Rains, Peter Lorre, and newcomer Burt Lancaster as the hero. But despite this sure-fire vehicle, and despite a *Life* cover and sexy stills even in the movie magazines, Calvet went nowhere. The lady imports, Britain's Deborah Kerr and Jean Simmons, made it, but not the sex kitten, and not the sophisticated Continentals such as Valentina Cortesa, Viveca Lindfors, Denise Darcel, Micheline Prelle (Presle), Cornell Borchers, or Florence Marly of Czechoslovakia, who looked not unlike Dietrich and who got an Ilsa Lund role opposite Bogart in another moody *Casablanca, Tokyo Joe* (1949) ("These Foolish Things" was the "As Time Goes By" in this one.)

The career of Terry Moore is exemplary. A former child actress (she played Bergman as a child in *Gaslight*) in the late forties, with a new name, she was a brown-bobbed, sparkly-eyed ingenue, with a bust that even the postwar period could not entirely ignore. But despite the breasty stills—as on the cover of the New York *Daily News* magazine, primed to shoot an arrow from her bow—in Moore's ingenue debut in *The Return of October* (1948; Glenn Ford), she was wholesomely devoted to a horse (that's who October was); and in *The Mighty Joe Young* (1949), although it was a remake by the original producers and director of *King Kong,* she and the gorilla could not have been more wholesomely devoted. Moore's sexpot of the later fifties, Betty in *Peyton Place* (1957), was all there in the postwar era, but the times were not much interested.

The Genres: Swashbucklers, Musicals, and Comedies

Like the players, the popular genres of postwar film reveal woman's degraded place. The prime masculine genre of the war years, the war film, died in America until 1949.* But other male-dominated genres replaced the war movies. Most of the popular types were masculine: the crime thriller, the social problem drama, and the western. Even in the genres that were less altered from the wartime formulas, swashbucklers, musicals, and comedies, women were newly scorned. In costume epics such as *Kitty* (1946), *Forever Amber* (1947), and *Captain from Castile* (1947), the women—Paulette Goddard, Linda Darnell, and Jean Peters—were low-life "meat," South Seas women. As the ad copy for *Gilda* put it, in Gilda's words next to Hayworth

---

*The war film did not, however, die in Europe and Asia, which had been through the crucible, and which, in the postwar years, saw Hollywood's World War II movies for the first time and rated them their favorites. *Variety*, January 14, 1948, pp. 7, col. 3, and 24, col. 3.

recumbent in black satin sliding off her breasts: "Now they all know what I am!" (It should be noted that although they were all "big budget" films, none of these epics was a box office smash—not even *Amber*, based on the Kathleen Winsor novel we *all* read secretly, as later we did Dr. Kinsey's Report.)

In musicals, the wartime emphasis on anonymous pretty faces and figures was replaced in the postwar years not by meat but by male musical talent: Crosby, as popular as in the war years; Sinatra, Gene Kelly, and Danny Kaye, up from wartime ranks; Fred Astaire, come back from what he thought was retirement with *Blue Skies* (1946), with Crosby; and new stars, most notably Howard Keel, who with Kathryn Grayson, was MGM's new Jeannette MacDonald-Nelson Eddy, and the "new Caruso," the especially popular Mario Lanza. There were still plenty of conventional girlie musicals, a Technicolor opus a year from new postwar stars June Haver, Jane Powell, and Esther Williams. Better than most late forties films, I remember these movies, such as Powell's and Elizabeth Taylor's *A Date with Judy*; I see now that like my movie magazines, they were my security blankets. Except for Gable and Turner's *Homecoming*, of the postwar films, I remember best Doris Day's debut in *Romance on the High Seas* (1948); at one and the same time, she was new and familiar. I remember noticing that her pure white and "powder blue" evening gowns were out of date, with their padded shoulders and net sequin panels; but "It's Magic" "when we walk hand-in-hand, the world becomes a wonderland"—did not seem an out-of-date reprise of a romantic ballad.

Yet Betty Grable needed Dan Dailey. And Rita Hayworth's 1947 version of *Cover Girl, Down to Earth* (in which she played Terpsichore), was a box-office disappointment, despite the Gilda aura, despite having the new "Jolson"—Larry Parks—in the Gene Kelly position, and despite Terpsichore's aides, the conventional bevy of beautiful girls. In Judy Garland's case, real-life troubles played a part, but still, more and more, Judy too needed a boost: Gene Kelly in *The Pirate* (1948) and *Summer Stock* (1950), Fred Astaire in *Easter Parade* (1948), and Van Johnson in *In The Good Old Summertime* (1949). Garland and Al Jolson are now often compared as two of a rare kind. But in the late forties, she fell and his film biographies revived him. With Larry Parks mouthing his songs, *The Jolson Story* (1946) and *Jolson Sings Again* (1949) were among the most popular movies of the era.

The change in the Dennis Morgan-Jack Carson team is, like Terry Moore, emblematic. In *The Hard Way* (1942), starring Ida Lupino, Morgan, and Joan Leslie, Morgan and Carson played a song, dance, and patter vaudeville team. Although supporting player Carson stands out (and to critics of the time, stood out), playing Leslie's true love who kills himself when she puts her career ahead of their marriage, *The Hard Way* focused on the drama of star Lupino pushing her kid sister Leslie to success as a singer of romantic ballads and eventually, after ruining Leslie's life, jumping off the bridge herself. In 1946, the Morgan-Carson vaudeville team that supported Lupino and Leslie was reunited as the stars of *Two Guys from Milwaukee,* and because it was a hit, *Two Guys from Texas* (1948). In the postwar films the girls were token pretty faces, like Vera-Ellen, Ann Miller, and Betty Garrett in *On the Town.* In *Two Guys from Texas* they were Dorothy Malone, newly raised from the unbilled ranks of girl bits such as bookstore clerks, and a blonde newcomer to Hollywood named Penny Edwards. In *Two Guys from Milwaukee* they were Janis Paige and Joan Leslie, who in 1946 was a fading ingenue.

Except for the few—but popular—revivals of satire and screwball farce, movie comedies after the war also remained relatively unchanged. As in the early forties, the majority of Hollywood's comedies were more like early television situation comedies than like Chaplin, the Marx Brothers, or Lombard at their thirties best. The Blondie and Maisie series, staples of the war era, ended in the postwar years, *Maisie* in

1947 and *Blondie* in 1950, but they were replaced by the equally popular Ma and Pa Kettle series (Marjorie Main and Percy Kilbride), drawn from Claudette Colbert and Fred MacMurray's hit comedy *The Egg and I* (1947).

But when postwar Hollywood tried more sophisticated comedy, the best roles (I notice now) were given to males. Gene Tierney and Tyrone Power in *That Wonderful Urge* (1948) stand out in my memory; but Anne Baxter, in her memoirs, *Intermission,* tells us that in 1946, when they were making *The Razor's Edge,* Power and Tierney were "head over heels in infatuation." I presume that in 1948, at least the ghost of their romance remained, making them memorable as a team.[30] Ann Sothern, the very popular "Maisie," was in Joseph Mankiewicz's *Letter to Three Wives,* (1948) but the sharpest lines went to her movie husband, the popular newcomer Kirk Douglas. As a high school English teacher dedicated to the finer things, Douglas got to put down mass culture (a popular postwar intellectual activity), and particularly the radio soap operas his wife wrote. And the best role in *Letter to Three Wives*—a star-maker—went to newcomer Paul Douglas as a rough-hewn magnate unable to believe that he could be loved for himself. The wives in *Letter to Three Wives*—Sothern, Linda Darnell, and Jeanne Crain—were merely addressees.

So was Darnell in Preston Sturges's comedy *Unfaithfully Yours* (1948; with "Sexy Rexy" Harrison), and *Everybody Does It* (1949; Paul Douglas again). Also outshone by the male leads were Ann Sheridan in *I Was a Male War Bride* (1949; "I" was Cary Grant); Maureen O'Hara in Clifton Webb's *Sitting Pretty;* Virginia Mayo in Danny Kaye's pictures; Ella Raines in William Powell's *The Senator Was Indiscreet* (1947); and Ann Blyth in Powell's *Mr. Peabody and the Mermaid* (1948). Most of these titles accurately reflect postwar Hollywood's attitude toward chintzy love and South Seas sex.

Yet, in postwar films, Katharine Hepburn and Claudette Colbert were the comic equals of their partners, Tracy, John

Wayne (*Without Reservations,* 1946) and Fred MacMurray (*The Egg and I,* 1947), so that the reason why women seem merely window dressing in comedies of this time may simply have been that there were few Carole Lombards for whom to write. In addition, comedy is a complex genre, in which the hero is essentially some form of a fool. If Lucille Ball or Auntie Mame is the fool, it will be a *man's* voice of reason, calling the chinks in her armor, but also loving her. Whether it is a man or a woman who plays Sanity, that is at least relatively not a degraded image.

Westerns

Thus, musicals and comedies do not make a strong case for male domination of postwar movies—unless they are looked at in the context of the dramatic genres, where even the "women's picture" degraded women. The first genre we will discuss is the western, because its male orientation is traditional.

In 1947, westerns accounted for 91 of the 428 pictures released.[31] The oater, the short feature starring the cowboy on his horse that we children of the war years had grown up on, still accounted for most of the postwar westerns. But these years also saw the revival of the western epic, and we began to be influenced by the values of this genre on the Big Picture level.

The postwar western epic was particularly the creation of two directors, John Ford and Howard Hawks, and a company of actors, mainly John Wayne, Ward Bond, Victor McLaglen, Ben Johnson, and sometimes Henry Fonda. An ingenue love story might be tossed in—Shirley Temple and John Agar in Ford's *Fort Apache,* (1948) or a decorative female—Joanne Dru in Hawk's *Red River* (1948) and Ford's *She Wore a Yellow Ribbon* (1949), or Linda Darnell's dancehall girl named Chihuahua, and brownette Cathy Downs's sweet Clementine in Ford's *My Darling Clementine* (1946).

But the fundamental irrelevance of women in the western world was virtually trumpeted in these Ford-Hawks films.* In John Wayne's raspy voice, particularly, a young girl heard herself diminished to almost nothing; and coming from Wayne, the diminishing was exciting. Looking at these, his early patriarch films—like it or not—it still is exciting. We carry our baggage with us. I did not think it at the time (who called John Wayne a romantic hero in the forties?**), but I think now that, then, he must unconsciously have seemed like another Rhett Butler, and an even more frustrating one, because he was cast not to walk out on Scarletts, but to be beyond them. When in *Red River*, Joanne Dru comes to him to try to soften him to getting along with her young man, Montgomery Clift, Wayne talks of his dead, young wife and it is clear that he is seeing her in Dru. Their scene of forbidden sexual feeling is as erotic as the simple love of Dru and Clift is not and cannot be.

But in addition to its epic form, the postwar western feature began also to breed with the amoral, antisexual crime: even this most traditional genre, the western, was roiled. Of Dick Powell's *Station West* (1948), *Variety* noted that the plot could be that of any one of Powell's Raymond Chandler detective melodramas,[32] and the same might be said of many other postwar westerns, in which the characters and stories were psychological, violent, bitter, and cynical. Richard Widmark's coldhearted, but neurotic killer moved from the city to a realistically infernal desert in *Yellow Sky* (1948). In this

---

*Hawks had degraded women in the thirties, as with Jean Arthur and Rita Hayworth as flyers' "groupies" in *Only Angels Have Wings* (see Joan Mellen's *Big Bad Wolves,* pp. 89-92); and it is only accidental—and ironic—that we now see his *To Have and Have Not,* with Bacall and Bogart, as uniquely "liberated."

**Perhaps the first time Wayne's "animal magnetism" was noted critically was in the 1944 western *Tall in the Saddle;* it was noted by Wanda Hale (New York *Daily News,* December 15, 1944), who also noted his "sizzling romance" with leading lady Ella Raines. John T. McManus of *PM* was (as always) more prescient (December 17, 1944). He devoted his entire review of this western to the Wayne-Raines romance, and added that "By most past accounts, these are two listless players, handsome but inert": *New York Motion Picture Critics Reviews,* Vol. I (New York: Critics Theatre Reviews, 1944), 148.

film, Widmark becomes an outlaw, he tells his buddies, after losing his gambling casino and his woman to a lover who beats her. Chief outlaw Gregory Peck is redeemed by a good woman—Anne Baxter—but his love redeems *her* from being, as one of the outlaws calls her, a "he-woman." Baxter, the more aggressive partner to her miner grandfather (James Barton), stimulates Widmark to villainy by reminding him of his perfidious wife. And Peck, incidentally, is also redeemed by grandpa Barton's judgment that, like a lot of boys, he has been led out of order by "the war." In this movie he meant the Civil War. In *The Man from Colorado* (1948), a sheriff (Glenn Ford) is also characterized as twisted by his Civil War service into a trigger-mad martinet. Of that movie, *Variety* said dubiously, "It's been generally presumed that high-action [western] films were immune to psychiatric encroachment. . . ."[33]

In these strange new oaters, the women were either good and minor, like Ellen Drew in *The Man from Colorado;* absent, as in *The Treasure of Sierra Madre;* good-bad girls, who were sometimes maniacally greedy, like Ida Lupino in *Lust for Gold* (1949; Glenn Ford); a girl with a golden heart under repressive rattles, like Anne Baxter in *Yellow Sky;* sympathetic though doomed, like Yvonne de Carlo in *Calamity Jane and Sam Bass* (1949; Howard Duff), and half-breed Virginia Mayo in *Colorado Territory* (1949; Joel McCrea). With her untamed hair, makeup-darkened skin, *Outlaw* blouses, and loving-though-illiterate role, Virginia Mayo in *Colorado Territory* was what postwar America—and hence Hollywood—was after: the South Seas slut in an All-American setting.

"Women's Films"

In the "women's films," or "weepies" of the late forties, few heroines were honorable, much less likeable. If they were likable, like Calamity Jane, they were almost always trapped in straits that led to unhappy endings. This was not novel in the woman's picture; what was new in this genre in the postwar era was the exaggeration of it all.

Possessed (1948), for example, starred Joan Crawford as a psychotic, paranoid schizophrenic who at one point falls into what the wise, and needless to say, male psychiatrist calls a "catatonic coma" and a "nearly mutistic state." She also murders her beloved (Van Heflin), and, worst of all, she tries to act up to this psychological orgy. In *Humoresque* (1947) Crawford is rich, married more than once, and a drinker—that is, a decadent who quite decently ultimately decides not to compete with John Garfield's violin. She then marches into the Pacific dressed in black sequins, with Garfield—really Isaac Stern—playing the *Liebestod* from *Tristan and Isolde* on the sound track while bubbles sputter artistically on the top of the California Pacific.

Olivia de Havilland had to play twins in *The Dark Mirror* (1946) for us to see one good, sound de Havilland, as did Bette Davis in *A Stolen Life* (also 1946). Davis had her *Possessed* in *Beyond the Forest* (1949), in which her Rosa Moline was perilously close to, if not beyond exaggeration and parody. At that time more than now, when she is almost idealized, Davis in her black Anna Lucasta wig, garish mouth, and cinch-waisted "peasant" outfits appeared grotesque to those of us who were used to the slender black gowns, the fox jackets, and the sweeps across elegant lobbies.

But it seems now that it is Barbara Stanwyck's *Sorry, Wrong Number* (1948) that epitomizes women's problems in the forties. Based on a popular radio play, this box-office hit had Stanwyck as a bedridden invalid trying to phone out and instead hearing a conversation about her husband's plot to kill her. The ties to *Gaslight* are clear; Stanwyck's physical imprisonment in her bed is only a representation of the social prison of marriage, which in *Gaslight* prevents both Bergman and almost everyone else from believing that her own husband is plotting to do her in. But there is an important difference: Bergman in *Gaslight* is totally sane and lovable. In the postwar film, the victim Stanwyck is also rich man Ed Begley's destructively insecure, demanding, castrating daughter, a wife most any man would want to murder. (I don't know whether they knew it, but in *Earthquake*, 1975, Ava Gardner, Charlton Heston, and Lorne Greene replayed the Stanwyck, Burt Lancaster, and Ed Begley configuration in *Sorry, Wrong Number*.)

Marjorie Rosen has pointed out an "antifemale" theme of women's physical or mental illness running through women's films of the forties.[34] Only a rivulet in the war years (sprung from Bette Davis's *Dark Victory*, 1939), the theme flooded postwar movies. Deaf Loretta Young (*And Now Tomorrow*, 1944) and mute Dorothy McGuire (*The Spiral Staircase*, 1945) grew to Maureen O'Hara dying from unnamed disease in *Sentimental Journey* (1946), Margaret Sullavan dying from cancer and replacing herself with Viveca Lindfors in *No Sad Songs for Me* (1950), and Jane Wyman in *Johnny Belinda* (1948), a deaf mute who is raped and sees her father (Charles Bickford) murdered and the child of the rape almost kidnapped by his father (Stephen McNally), before she is allowed to become infuriated and kill the rapist.

Women's mental problems also grew from Bette Davis—from her repressed maiden in *Now, Voyager* (1942). Joan Fontaine had paranoid delusions that her husband Cary Grant was trying to poison her in *Suspicion* (1941), and Bergman had more obviously valid suspicions about her husband in *Gaslight*. There was neurotically homely Dorothy McGuire and disfigured war veteran Robert Young, transformed by love in *The Enchanted Cottage* (1945). There were also pitiable women who nonetheless had to be punished: Laraine Day's schizophrenic in *The Locket* (1946); Rosalind Russell's Electra and guilty Janet Ames; Stanwyck's compulsive in the 1949 *The Lady Gambles* (like Mildred Pierce, given a last-minute reprieve by a long-suffering husband, Robert Preston); Crawford's psychotics; de Havilland's Electra driven to *The Snake Pit*. Then there were the alcoholics: Anne Baxter's Sophie in *The Razor's Edge*

(1946), followed by Susan Hayward's first in *Smash-Up* (1947) and her second in *My Foolish Heart* (1949), in which her drinking was caused by her war-lost love and its "il-legitimate" child.

Davis's Charlotte in *Now, Voyager* also bred victims: Davis herself, driven to murder her madly jealous ex-lover Claude Raines in *Deception* (1946); Stanwyck sent to her bed again, this time by husband Humphrey Bogart's poison in *The Two Mrs. Carrolls* (1947; made in 1943-44); Bergman in *Notorious,* also poisoned by a husband, here joined by his mother. In *Dragonwyck* (1946), based on a popular novel, the victim of a drug addict husband gothically named Nicholas Van Rhys and played by Vincent Price, is Miranda (Gene Tierney), who must be rescued by the handsome young doctor (Glenn Langan). In *Sleep, My Love* (1948), Don Ameche, the early forties hero for Alice Faye and Betty Grable, is also slowly poisoning his wife Claudette Colbert, until Robert Cummings comes to the rescue. In *Secret Beyond the Door* (1947), Joan Bennett is almost murdered by her husband, Michael Redgrave, whose motive is simply out-and-out woman hatred. In *A Double Life,* released the same week as *Secret Beyond the Door*, Signe Hasso is murdered by Ronald Colman in his Oscar-winning role as an actor playing Othello—the arch possessor—opposite his ex-wife Hasso, and living his role of a man obsessed with the vileness of women.

These were the movies we saw as late forties adolescents. In the "women's films," the victims got rescued by a Good Man, such as Lew Ayres (*Johnny Belinda*) or Cary Grant (*Notorious*), or Got What They Deserved, even if it was sad, as, of course, it was when Joan Crawford walked into the Pacific. I'd laugh now, if it weren't for the number of these women psychotics and victims, and for how well I, and other men and women of my generation, remember them. Could we *not* have been influenced by them—both I and my dates?

"Message Movies"

If they were demeaned in the women's films, most leading ladies in the social problem pictures of the postwar era actually impeded progress. The postwar flourishing of socially significant films began in 1947, but thanks to the Communist witch-hunts was short-lived and limited to *Gentleman's Agreement, Crossfire,* and *The Boy with Green Hair,* the latter almost not released because it was not finished until after HUAC blew the deep freeze of fear into Hollywood. But then in November 1948 came Harry Truman's surprising reelection, and, according to Variety, *Hollywood* decided that liberal days were here again.[35] The short enlightenment that followed (an interesting footnote to Truman history) produced *Pinky, Lost Boundaries,* the film version of William Faulkner's southern *Intruder in the Dust,* the most prescient of them all, and *Home of the Brave.* And *Pinky* was Fox's top grosser of 1949.[36]

But then Hollywood went too far, ironically with the film that *Variety* in its story on the liberalizing effect of Truman's reelection, said would never have been filmed without his victory. *No Way Out* (1950) introduced Sidney Poitier; starred Richard Widmark, this time as a psychopathic racist; used the strong words, such as *boogies, jigs,* and *coons* more than the earlier intolerance films had; featured a race riot that was reminiscent of the newsreels of the Detroit race riot in 1943; and as Andrew Dowdy says in his book on fifties movies, helped "kill off the cycle of tough black films until much later in the decade."[37] So sensitive was Hollywood at the end of the decade of the war that saved the world for democracy that Paramount's 1949 version of *The Great Gatsby* changed the name of the gangster Meyer Wolfscheim to Myron Lupus.

Another Daisy Buchanan, Gene Tierney's Isabel Bradley in *The Razor's Edge* (1946) set every snare—even Her Body—to trap spiritual Tyrone Power in the world of the capitalist. Until she saw the light for the happy ending of *Gentleman's Agreement*, Dorothy McGuire lacked the courage to share Gregory Peck's assumed life as a Jew. Nor could the story's Jewess, "Miss Green" (June Havoc), resist passing. Her male counterpart, Dave Goldman (John Garfield), on the other hand, was a firebrand. In *Lost Boundaries,* a doctor and his wife (Mel Ferrer and Beatrice Pearson) passed for white, but their movie was about *his* agonizing choices, and after they were exposed, the plot focused on him and their son, and ignored her and their daughter.

Pinky was different. A woman, a Negress (Jeanne Crain), had the courage to give up passing, as she had been doing up north, and use her nursing skills to help her people in the south. If at the unusual "unhappy" ending, Pinky did not marry her blond doctor (William Lundigan), it seems now that the Breen office may unwittingly have favored the liberal cause. Whether or not Darryl Zanuck intended it,* it may have been sounder rhetoric not to hit us young idealists hard, but rather to let it steep that a favorite ingenue, the image of Miss America, could not have her usual happy ending just because she was a Negro.[38]

In movies of the forties, we got the message of idealism from both men and women (of course, more from men). Why didn't we also see that we were all in our sexual mess together? All-male war movies such as *Wake Island, Bataan,* and *Sahara* taught us children the democracy-in-a-foxhole philosophy. In *The Pride of the Marines,* the company's most patriotic soldier, Lee Diamond (Dane Clark), reminds blind-

---

*In Cid Ricketts Sumner's novel *Quality* (New York: Bantam Books, 1947 [1945]), on which *Pinky* is based, the white boyfriend is an idealistic young black doctor. Because the censors would not countenance a black boyfriend for Jeanne Crain, Fox, to provide love interest, ironically created an avant-garde interracial *Romeo and Juliet.* Like Hollywood, Sumner (according to Bantam) was atoning for her "slave-owning grandparents." (facing p. 278)

ed, bitter Al Schmid (John Garfield) that some employers will
not hire him either, because "my name is Diamond and I
celebrate Passover instead of Christmas." But we also learned from the women's war pictures, as when in *Tender Comrade* (1943), Ruth Hussey asks war bride Kim Hunter why she
traded the name White for Dumbrowski, and Ginger Rogers
responds indignantly, "What's wrong with Dumbrowski?"

It seems now that we were the products of an age that was
unintentionally caught by Eleanor Parker in *The Very
Thought of You* (1944), when she tells her airman husband
Dennis Morgan that one reason she loves him is that she likes
listening to all the important things he says about saving the
world for Democracy, even though she cannot understand it
all. In the forties I could see movies such as the *Pride of the
Marines* and *Crossfire*, and not see my involvement. I could
watch *Sahara* (1943), in which the heroic-looking black actor
Rex Ingram had a heroic bit, and watch many musicals with
"rhythm spots," and not see the contradiction. At that time I
regularly rode the "Yankee Clipper" train between Boston
and New York, and I looked at "125th Street" only as a
given, a fact of life. Years later, reading *The Autobiography
of Malcolm X*, I realized that at the same time I was riding
the Clipper he was one of its wagon men. But as a white
middle-class child of the forties, I saw no contradictions,
made no connections, accepted all as given. *Pinky* made me
righteously indignant, but not 125th Street. After reading
Laura Z. Hobson's *Gentleman's Agreement*, I heaped scorn
on my Irish father's epithets; but I also remember that none
of the Jews were among the "popular" kids in my class. On
the Bicentennial Fourth of July, after I had written these
words, I read the following from a woman about my age,
Martha Weinman Lear:

> At assemblies we sang "America the Beautiful," rendering
> it, as we had been taught, up-tempo and with a great
> operatic rolling of the R's: " . . . And cr-r-rown thy good
> with br-r-rother-r-rhood/ Fr-r-rom sea to shining sea!"

And then, after school, we would go out into the streets of Roxbury [Massachusetts], where the black kids were forever beating up on the Jewish kids and the Irish kids on the black kids and the police on them all. We heard no dissonance. We sensed no irony.[39]

As girl children, Martha Weinman Lear and I also never doubted that marriage was, as she put it, our " 'calling,' " and that men knew more than we did. Now, as I talk with and read men of my generation, it is clear that they too swallowed Eleanor Parker's romantic line, and that for both of us, it is a heavy, messy burden.

The dichotomy went deeper even than race, for nothing goes deeper than sex. Who could lash out at Al Schmid's faithful Ruth? But it could be cathartic for the good soldier and "Mr. Average American" if, like Lizabeth Scott in *Dead Reckoning,* the screen soldier's girl friend was a false-faced tramp who was responsible for his death. His shamefully hidden, dark feelings may help explain the popularity of the postwar crime thriller, with its characteristics of violent action, trampy women, and good guys getting doublecrossed. If women were demeaned in the other postwar genres, they were degraded in this, the most novel, and in a number of polls, the most popular genre in that era.

Crime and Romance

After Pearl Harbor the crime movie went patriotic. In late 1941, Bogart began another gangster movie, *All Through the Night,* and when it was released on January 28, 1942, it ended with New York's rival gangsters joining forces to round up the city's Nazi spies. Thereafter, until the end of the war, the characteristics of the genre—violent action and trickery by warring tough guys—were put to the service of war propaganda. After the war the crime feature came home; for as the FBI (Lloyd Nolan) put it in *The Street with No Name* (1948), since the war, "gangsterism" and "juvenile delinquency'' were on the rise. But many of the postwar gangsters were more complex, and thus their stories were more tangled, than Cagney's and Bogart's prewar public enemies. Gangster heroes perfectly represented the bitter but defiant existential mood that crossed the Atlantic after the war, along with millions of American soldiers and Deborah Kerr and Corinne Calvet. The increased bloodletting in postwar films was another kind of war baby; combat movies had conditioned American audiences to more violence.[40] Perhaps, too, the sadism and cheapening of human life in the anti-Nazi and anti-"Jap" movies led along some subconscious stream to Richard Widmark's Tommy Udo in *Kiss of Death.*

Widmark's Udo is remembered for the scene, shocking at the time, in which, giggling effeminately, he pushes an old lady in a wheelchair down a flight of stairs. It was the apparently gratuitous violence of the act that stood out, but reviewing the film now reveals something unremarked at the time: that as much as amoral violence, Udo's act also represents women-hatred, and particularly that most hidden theme of wartime forties films, mother hate-love. The old woman (Mildred Dunnock) is the mother of a hoodlum on whom Udo has a contract. He decides to kill her when he discovers that she has lied to him to cover for her son's skipping town. "You're worse than he is," Udo cries, enraged, and he means she is worse because she is a mother-betrayer.

Later, when Udo runs into his old buddy Nick Bianco (Victor Mature), he becomes increasingly irritated by the presence of his moll, and finally sends her off with the line, "We don't want no old ladies around." The epithet "old lady," linking a man's mother and his woman, suddenly now seems a significantly popular Americanism. When Widmark catches up with the stoolie Mature, he threatens not only the man but also his wife (Coleen Gray) and his two daughters. The daughters are Mature's by a first wife (Patricia Morison, cut from the film) who could not take it when he was in prison and killed herself. Coleen Gray is the woman who was faithful and strong and won the man. She is another Teresa

Wright in *The Best Years of Our Lives,* as Mature's dead wife is analogous to Dorothy McGuire in *Gentleman's Agreement,* Bergman in *Arch of Triumph*, and the soft, self-centered wives Virginia Mayo played in both *The Best Years of Our Lives* and *White Heat* (1949). In the latter, Cagney's faithful, resilient woman is his Ma. It seems clear: the women are the problem. They are refuge, but they can betray; and if they do cling tightly, as Harold Russell's Wilma does, they can become hostages to fortune, or they can choke you. In a mine field like this, a man may give up feeling.

"You can never understand the dogface until you have grasped the extent of his cynicism," says William Manchester in *The Glory and the Dream*, of how he and other GIs felt about bosses, their own as well as Hitler.[41] Or, as Eric Sevareid put it when he came back from the Far East in 1943, the dogface's cynicism grew from the discovery that all the publicity about America's invincibility was hogwash and all the hype for fliers and other heroes was hypocrisy. The GIs, said Sevareid, were " 'just kids, who for the most part were brought up on such super sales talks and probably always believed in them. Suddenly they're thrown into reality. . . .' " And the reality, as Sevareid put it, was that the war was going to be won, if it was won, not by shooting down a few "Japs," but by ground strafing and disrupted shipping. And that while a G.I. was reading about America's prowess, he might hear that a buddy had been lost because of a defect in his airplane.[42]

The Best Years of Our Lives explored readjustments realistically, but among men of goodwill in a peaceful world. *Crossfire* is one of the first, and perhaps the best, of the postwar pictures that melded social idealism and war-sprung violence. Written by John Paxton and directed by Adrian Scott and Edward Dmytryk shortly before the latter were fired to feed the HUAC maw, *Crossfire* was made in twenty-three days to beat the other anti-anti-Semitism movies in the works, *Gentleman's Agreement* and Samuel Goldwyn's *Earth and High Heaven*, which gave up. The cost of

Crossfire, $650,000, was that of the average B-movie, and as John Houseman noted, its B-qualities were its strengths:

> There is a unity to the production—limitation to a narrow world of darkness and policed streets, of closing bars and lonely apartments—a concentration upon the essential reality of character and conflict, an over-all directness and lack of contrivance very rarely found in Hollywood pictures.[43]

The characters in *Crossfire* are postwar soldiers, the bored and bitter backwash of The Greatest Army Ever Assembled. Stationed ironically in Washington, D.C., with nothing to do but drink, one of them, Montgomery (Robert Ryan), kills a "Jew boy" (Sam Levene) and tries to pin it on a buddy, Mitch (George Cooper). *Crossfire*'s plot—"B"-lean—is the clearing of Mitch and the catching of Montgomery. The action is led by soldier Keeley (Robert Mitchum) and a D.C. Irish cop, Joe Finley (Robert Young).

Usually noted in the film histories for its tolerance message, and remembered that way by teenage idealists of the forties like me, *Crossfire* now seems more remarkable for its complex, psychologically war-wounded characters. The characters in *Crossfire* are deftly implied, as in a good B-movie: Montgomery, an ex-cop, not a Jew-hater, but simply a hater, who now that it is peacetime, is adrift without sanctioned victims. Keeley, a newspaperman, now the army's printer, who has not seen his wife in two years and can only wonder, abstractly, if they will ever get together again. (All this takes only a sentence and a lifted Mitchum eyebrow or two.) Young Mitch, before the war an artist, now the army's sign painter, battling deep but inchoate anxiety about being an artist in postwar America, and avoiding his All-American blonde wife (Jacqueline White), afraid he will sully her. Ginny (Gloria Grahame), the bar girl Mitch picks up, whom no one is afraid of sullying, who resists feeling and bitterly refuses to help clear Mitch after his wife tells her that Mitch talked about his time with *her*, the time in which he touched her feelings. Wounded people, unconnectable, walk through *Crossfire*. "The Man" (Paul Kelly), who helps Mitch because, a "D.D.," he is desperate to give himself value. They weave together, these wounded in postwar America, until The End: Mitch and Mrs. Mitch together again, but The Man fading out calling offers to help down the stairs after the sure-as-shootin', pipe-puffing, cool cop Robert Young, Ginny, slamming the door, cursing cops and good blonde wives; and in the last frame, the hero, Keeley-Mitchum, walking away in the city's late night, alone as he was at the beginning, still unready even to hope.

Fearfully released as a straight "thriller," *Crossfire* by July 1948, had earned RKO a profit of more than $3 million. (*Gentleman's Agreement* also became Fox's biggest moneymaker in 1948, as *Pinky* was in 1949.) *Crossfire* earned humanitarian awards and Oscar nominations for itself, Dmytryk, Paxton, and "supporting" performers Ryan and Grahame. Thus, it embarrassed the industry which, under HUAC pressure, had fired its producer and director, two of the "Hollywood Ten." But if it did not teach the movie industry moral courage, the movie did get across the message that the documentary model—short films with no stars—was a way out of the bind of rising production costs and audience demand for novelty.[44] Yet for all its immediate value, *Crossfire*, like a lot of civilization's B-productions, is more meaningful now, when in hindsight and the context of similar movies, it can be seen as the splintered mirror of an era in which official certitude was one thing and reality another, complex shadow.

For example, there is *Deadline at Dawn* (1946), like *Crossfire* produced and directed by Scott and Dmytryk and written by Clifford Odets. In it, a good tough girl, Susan Hayward—counterpart to Mitchum's Keeley—helps an innocent young sailor, curly-blond-haired Bill Williams, to clear himself of murder. They are also helped by a kindly, philosophical cabbie, Paul Lukas, who, thirty years before Martin Scorsese's *Taxi Driver*, turns out to be the murderer, apparently because he hated scum. Lukas' victim blackmailed lovers, cheated an innocent sailor, drank to a stupor, and was a woman. Furthermore, years before, Lukas' wife left him for another man; and finally, he says, he murdered because of the overwhelming summer night's heat in New York City.* "Nothing is what it seems" is an ancient tag for mysteries, but in conventional Hollywood thrillers, it began to refer to psyches, plots, and "messages" only in the post-World War II years. We noticed that at the time, even we teenagers. Movies were more complex—our word for it was "confusing." But not taking seriously the foreground for our weekly dates—who did take movies seriously?—we tend to recall only the highly publicized patterns. The only "recurrent theme" I remembered from the postwar years was tolerance.

But now the unsanctioned reality riding through postwar film is also visible in mass-market movies—surprisingly so to someone who saw them in the forties as a teenager caught up equally by romance and idealism, and conscious not at all of dark and shifting metaphysical shadows. *The Razor's Edge*, for example, was one of the most popular movies of 1946—and it explicitly criticized American capitalism and focused on a love story in which the lovers did not clinch at the end. And to boot, it featured studio Hollywood's first sensitive portrayal of a woman alcoholic, Anne Baxter's Sophie.

In *The Razor's Edge*, Somerset Maugham's hero Larry Darrow (Tyrone Power) emerges from World War I awed by

---

*In a 1945 B-movie *Two O'Clock Courage*, RKO used its late-night-street set, and essentially its *Deadline at Dawn* characters: Tom Conway played a bewildered amnesiac, taken in hand and helped to clear himself of murder by an energetic, wittily resourceful cabbie: Ann Rutherford. But *Two O'Clock Courage* has none of the city-at-night atmosphere, nor a philosophical murderer. It is all formulaic comic cops and reporters, and the fast paced, barely motivated reversals of "who done it" that kept us awake during the sixty-minute Bs.

The *Falcon in Hollywood* (1944), with Tom Conway as the Falcon, also featured a woman cabbie—after all, so did wartime America. This one was Veda Ann Borg, now something of a Breezy Blonde icon.

death and vaguely but deeply desirous of doing something better with his life than getting in on the ground floor of the elevator which, in Chicago, he is told will rocket America to the position of "the greatest and richest country in the world by 1930." Darrow not only rejects the morally violent world of Capitalism, he even rejects a Daisy Buchanan named Isabel Bradley (Gene Tierney) in order to expatriate to France, and later India, to look for "peace of mind." His is not Rhett Butler's dessicated escapism at the end of *GWTW*, but rather a positive search for answers, eschewing, as he explains to Isabel, "most people [who] take things as they are." So Darrow lives, to triumph unusually for a forties hero. At the end of the movie, still a menial laborer, still spurning the intoxicating Isabel, still looking for meaning rather than money, Darrow, according to Maugham (played by Herbert Marshall), is a man whose goodness inspires those near him and who is thus a hero. Only eleven when I first saw it, I remember *The Razor's Edge* as boringly talky and depressing because of its "unhappy" romantic ending. But looking at it now, and in the context of *Crossfire, Kiss of Death, Gilda,* and other existential postwar movies, it seems clear why *The Razor's Edge* with its doubts about the American way of life and love, was a $5 million box-office hit in the year after the war.

Larry Darrow, searching the world over for answers, now seems a representative postwar figure. In *Dark Passage* (1947), Humphrey Bogart is the opposite of Darrow; Bogart's Vincent Parry resists giving and taking love and comradeship. But that too now seems representative, and *Dark Passage* is also like *The Razor's Edge* in its unconventional ending: Vincent Parry is a wrongly convicted escaped convict who gets away. Oh, he was wrongly convicted, but still, he does not vindicate himself before he enacts the universal dream of escaping The Law to one of the faraway places (Peru) with a beautiful—and a good-tough—woman. At the end of the movie, Parry overcomes his general distrust and invites Irene Jansen (Bacall), who has befriended him, to join him in Peru. He does this because, waiting in the bus station to start his solitary journey, he overhears a lonely man and woman getting together. "What's the world coming to?" the man muses. "No one cares for anyone but himself."

Bogart, listening, looks up (characteristically saying nothing about the sea change waxing inside him), and walks to the phone to call Bacall. But first he stops at the juke box and plays their song "Too Marvelous for Words," a nice choice for this study of a man locked in distrust, and for a good part of the movie literally silenced by the plastic surgery that gives him his new life. At the juke box, Bogart is caught again by the man's words to his new friend, "In the past, people used to help each other. . . ." As he turns his face toward the man, the camera closes on him, and behind Bogart's face we see a grimy poster picturing a Red Cross worker pushing a veteran in a wheelchair.

But in 1947 I did not note that background poster; and although I recall Tommy Udo pushing the mother down the stairs as clearly as I remember Jeanne Crain among the roses, the crime movies of the late forties and early fifties were not favorites among teenage girls. What my generation was used to in movies had little or no part in postwar crime movies. Love interest, particularly between ingenues, was pared from their lean forms, and those equally stirring moral speeches that were characteristic of the wartime features also rarely had a role in the style of the crime film. Even those films that had love stories with happy endings, such as Bogart's and Bacall's movies, were unsatisfactory at the time because (I see now) the love stories seemed inarticulate, undramatic, and peripheral. Romance—"true love"—when it appeared, fared best as it fared in *Dark Passage*. Usually it fared much worse.

Gilda (1946) appears now to be the symbolic forties romance. Produced by Virginia Van Upp, with a screenplay by another woman, Marion Parsonnet, *Gilda* was made directly after the war ended, its lovers postwar Americans in one of the faraway places, Buenos Aires. Early on in the movie, the hero and narrator, Glenn Ford, announces in a voice-over that, "By the way, about that time, the war ended." That was one of our postwar Messages about Meaning.

The three leading characters in *Gilda* are Ford, Rita Hayworth as his own true love, and George Macready as her husband and his boss and best friend. All three of them, says Ballin Munson (Macready), have no pasts. But like everything that matters in this movie, Ballin's remark is not what it seems. It is true that Johnny Forbes (Ford) says that his life began when he went to work for Ballin in Buenos Aires, and also true that, according to Ballin, Gilda said that her life began that night she met him (they married the next day). But it turns out that Johnny and Gilda have been lovers, and Ballin is not only the casino owner he appears to be but also a power maniac who plans to take over the world through a cartel in tungsten. It takes a while—the length of the movie—but eventually their three pasts become their destinies. Ballis gets his, and Gilda and Johnny get together and go back to America, good people, if come lately. It is the conventional ending of a wartime romance. But in between we have watched a love story in which the hero, against all evidence, trusts his male friend rather than the woman, and in which every love scene is phrased in hate.

Gilda says that she married Munson in revenge for Johnny's ditching her. Johnny never disputes her interpretation, but in response to her revenge, he seethes, scowls, spits venomous words, and slaps her around in hate unending until the final frame. On the other hand, he is so loyal to Munson, who he only met in the first scene of the movie, that even though he has come to know about his boss's shadiness, he honors him after his death (which also is only apparent) by marrying the loving Gilda—and then, maliciously laughing, isolating her in an apartment with Munson's portrait.

From the beginning to almost the end of the movie, Gilda says she hates Johnny so much she would "destroy" herself to "take him down" with her. Johnny says he hates her "so much I [can't] get her out of my mind"; and the asexual Ballin comments that hate can be "an exciting emotion"; that "hate is the only thing that has ever warmed me." That hate is love in this movie is signaled when, sinuously trying to get Johnny to kiss her, Gilda whispers over and over, "I hate you so much I think I'm going to die from it." These lines of hers alternate with Johnny narrating that he's going to "throw her out" of Ballin's life because her "infidelity" has ruined his friend's plans. Ironically, she gets her kiss at last in this scene—Ballin sees, and disappears, pretending to kill himself but letting us know that he lives and will return for revenge on the man who is taking revenge on Gilda—by marrying her.

Eventually these inchoate shadows and realities are clarified for the dumb hero (Gilda knows and names Ballin an "insane" egomaniac early on). But first, Gilda must use her body for revenge more spectacularly than ever before, in her "Put the Blame on Mame" song and strip. It is worth noting—I did not until I reviewed *Gilda*—that probably the best remembered erotica in postwar film is motivated by hate, and is the desperate act of a supremely sexual image who is really a simple, loving woman. "Now they all know what I am," Gilda cries after Johnny drags "Mame" away from the grasping hands. He slaps her (again). But by then we know beyond a shadow of a doubt that she is not the whore.

Finally, the Law—Argentinian police detective Joseph Calleia—helpfully tells Johnny that "you two kids" love each other, and even more helpfully, he names the game: "It's the most curious love-hate pattern I've ever had the privilege of witnessing." Impressed, Johnny gives Calleia the evidence on the cartel, humbly asks Gilda (suddenly chastely gray-suited) if he may go home with her to America, and with even more startling lack of ceremony dispatches the villain who has haunted the picture (Macready, on the other hand, is suitably swathed in a dramatic black cape for this scene). Without even the kiss that releases us, the lovers exit for

America. Coming after all that passionate hatred, it is a climax notable for its impotency; notable, that is, except in confused postwar America.

If love figured in the postwar movie melodrama, it usually looked more like lust or a contract in the name of greed. The wartime prototype love objects were Bogart's Mary Astor in *The Maltese Falcon* (1941), Judith Anderson in *All Through the Night* (1942), and Angela Lansbury in *Gaslight* (1944). In the late war years came Veronica Lake as a Nazi agent whom hubby Franchot Tone has to kill at the end of *The Hour Before the Dawn* (1944) and Signe Hasso as the ringleader of the Nazis hunting the formula for the bomb in *The House on 92nd Street* (1945). The "psychotics" included Geraldine Fitzgerald in *Uncle Harry* (1945; George Sanders was Harry) and in *Three Strangers* (1946), Gene Tierney in *Leave Her to Heaven* (1945), Anne Baxter as a primeval Eve in *Guest in the House* (1945), and Phyllis Thaxter in *Bewitched* (1945), a remembered Arch Oboler MGM B about a split good Joan/murderous Karen that foreshadowed de Havilland's *Dark Mirror* and Davis' *Stolen Life*. There was also that forerunner, Maria Montez's split in *Cobra Woman* (1944).

And there were the *"film noir"* Liliths: Dick Powell's Claire Trevor in the Phillip Marlowe story *Murder, My Sweet* (1945) and George Raft's Claire in *Johnny Angel* (also 1945); Barbara Stanwyck, with Fred MacMurray in *Double Indemnity* (1944); Linda Darnell, with Laird Cregar, in *Hanover Square* (1945), and in the Chekovian *Summer Storm* (1944); Susan Hayward in *The Hairy Ape* (1944); Joan Bennett, with Dan Duryea as man and Edward G. Robinson as patsy, in Fritz Lang's *Woman in the Window* (1944) and *Scarlet Street* (1946); and Mary Beth Hughes in *The Great Flamarion* (1945), with Erich von Stroheim in the E. G. Robinson role and Duryea again (Anthony Mann directed this praised Republic B).

Bennett in *Scarlet Street* was censor bait; but in the late forties there were fatally seductive women galore. These included oldtimers seeking to revive careers, such as Oberon, Lamour, Montez, Veronica Lake, and Joan Fontaine, who in *Ivy* (1947) murders her husband (Richard Ney), pins the murder on her lover (Patric Knowles), and ends up falling down an elevator shaft. Other seductive women were new stars such as Lizabeth Scott; Ava Gardner in *The Killers* (1946); Doris Dowling as the cheating wife of soldier Alan Ladd in *The Blue Dahlia* (1946); and Valli, a murderess well masked in *The Paradine Case* (1947). *Variety* called *Framed* (1947; Glenn Ford and blonde Janis Carter) "another in the unscrupulous woman cycle"[45] signaling the man-killer gone formulaic. There were many "borderline B" films like *Race Street* (1948; George Raft and Marilyn Maxwell), and out-and-out Bs, such as *Blonde Ice* (1948), with Leslie Brooks, one of the barely distinguishable blonde beauties of wartime movies such as *Nine Girls,* as a calculating murderess of husbands and lovers, and the conclusively named *Deadly is the Female* (1949), again with an ethereal blonde femme fatale, Peggy Cummins, and her victim, John Dall.

These films ranged widely in popularity, but as the *Variety* quotation on *Framed* indicates, they were successful enough to create a new postwar genre: the crime thriller with the woman as villain. The public voted for Scarletts without a trace of a woman's heart, and for Rhetts, or Johnny Forbes, unable to best or even cope with these woman, who thus at the end of the film were usually either dead or foolish. Orson Welles' Michael O'Hara, almost done in by the Lady from Shanghai, takes himself repeatedly for the "fool," and Michael O'Hara was the type. In *Out of the Past* (1947), after Jane Greer murders two men, one of them a crime boss lover (Kirk Douglas), Robert Mitchum finally faces up to the truth that she is no good. His moment of truth does not impress her. The fatal beauty with the ironic ingenue name, Kathy, tells Mitchum with scornful acuity, "I never told you I was

anything but what I am. You just wanted to imagine. . . ."
At the end of the movie, when she realizes that he has called
the cops on them, Greer shoots Mitchum as he drives, in
murderous and self-destructive close-up. In *Station West,* a
year later, the man-killer Greer played the crime boss herself,
a woman named Charlie.

The key to this formula—and perhaps to its snaky appeal—was the beautiful woman's motiveless malignity and
the "hero's" hapless victimization. She was not Lana
Turner's Cora in *The Postman Always Rings Twice* (1946),
not *Anna Karenina* (Vivien Leigh; 1948), and not *Madame
Bovary* (Jennifer Jones; 1949). Their sexuality was destructive, but their immoralities had clear roots outside
themselves, and hence seemed, if not perhaps excusable, at
least uncontrollable. Villains, they were also victims. The
deadly females came from the world of *The Lady from
Shanghai,* an amoral, heartless, contemporary as a sea of
sharks devouring each other and maddened by the blood of
perpetuate murder. It was not a world that sustained romantic dreams. Our postwar love stories as often ended not like.
A Date with Judy but rather like *Out of the Past,* with its true
lovers as corpses, or like the bleak *Letter to an Unknown
Woman* (Joan Fontaine and Louis Jourdan; 1948) and *The
Heiress* (Henry James' "Washington Square"), with Olivia
de Havilland pining after an unattainable Montgomery Clift.
Where was the final, fade-out, forever clinch? Where were
the great screen lovers such as Gable and Turner?

Normalcy

To be precise, Gable and Turner were staging a postwar
reunion in which he played a doctor, time-honored romantic
figure, and she played his World War II battlefield nurse.
Because he was married and she was Good, they resisted love
until, with the shells falling and in a blizzard, they framed

themselves in a tent door and Gave In. They kissed; it was enough. But in *Homecoming* (1948) unlike *Honky Tonk* (1941) or *Somewhere I'll Find You* (1942), there is no fade-out Gable-Turner clinch. In *Homecoming,* Turner ("Snapshot") is killed by the shells and Gable (Dr. Ulysses Johnson, in this film originally titled *The Homecoming of Ulysses)* returns after the war to his brownhaired wife in black with a pearl choker, his Penelope (Penny), Anne Baxter. In the war years, forbidden, impossible love had looked like an exciting challenge, the glamorous and ultimately winning combat of Jeanne Crain against Gene Tierney in *Leave Her to Heaven.* By the time of *Homecoming,* it seems now that we must have seen how hopeless it all was. But I know that I did not see. Given the bleakness of most postwar love affairs in the movies, our earlier brave assumption that if we were lovely enough we could overcome, must, like Tara, have come to ruin. Yet who at the age of fifteen—and uninstructed by MGM about the original Ulysses—did not believe that she was the one who could win Clark Gable forever?

Emphasizing the darkness in postwar America is misleading if it is not seen as only hindsight. At the time, optimism and normalcy were official, especially for the Anne Hiltons, the Claudias, and us teenage girls. Most women my age remember few movies of the late forties, perhaps because of the change I discern in myself at the age of eleven or twelve from unconscious, metonymic memory to conscious, intellectual recollection. But perhaps it is also because we did not *like* so many of the movies we saw in those years. Until we are pressed ("do you remember Tommy Udo in *Kiss of Death?"),* the movies from that period we recall tend to be the musicals of Esther Williams, June Haver, Doris Day and the like romances, and sometimes, the "message movies," such as *Gentleman's Agreement* and *Pinky.* Yet it is not true, as a prevalent view of the forties has it, that in the late forties, we had all we wanted of movies extolling traditional American values, such as family and happy-ending romance.

If it were true, it seems unlikely that moviegoing would have declined as it did after the war, especially among women, who, according to *Variety,* complained that there was "not enough handkerchief stuff."[46]

In a 1950 *Journal of Popular Culture* article, Norman L. Friedman summarized postwar films as an entity that "reinforced, extolled, illustrated, reflected and transmitted dominant cultural orientations." These orientations, said Friedman, were "especially the values of activity, achievement and success, material comfort, and progress, science, individualism, nationalism and equality."[47] It is hard to argue with this shopping list, and in *The Fountainhead* (1949), Ayn Rand could even get them all into one movie, except equality. Friedman's error is not seeing that these "orientations" in postwar movies were not always presented as givens or as positives. To dismiss the films of this period as conventionally All-American is to ignore deep psychological and social changes that also were reflected, and not always in their shadows. These changes—still largely unrecognized—are especially pertinent to the question of how these movies affected us young people, because although a married woman might choose to stay home, a dating teenager went regularly to the movies, absorbing *Kiss of Death* and *White Heat,* even if she would have preferred another version of last week's *Romance on the High Seas* or *Every Girl Should Be Married.* Like or not, girls—and boys—of my generation were force-fed alienation, cynicism, violently individualistic rebellion, and other seeds of change, including woman hatred. And, in addition, these postwar strains permeated the conventional movies.

As an example, in the very popular *Apartment for Peggy* (1948), Peggy—*our* Jeanne Crain—ingeniously creates a make-shift home, and otherwise lovingly supports her war veteran hubby, William Holden, as he goes to college on the G.I. Bill. As a bonus, she revives the will to live in an old man planning suicide (Edmund Gwenn). No demeaning of women here! In *Old Acquaintance,* John Loder said that his marriage to Miriam Hopkins began to fail when she began to write, and no one in that movie ever enlightened him, or us. In *Peggy* a veteran's wife finds lipstick on his handkerchief and confides to Peggy over the Bendix washing machine that as her husband studies Plato and "Spinoz" he grows away from her. "Naturally," she says, "he's going to find some-one he can talk to. I just wish it could be me." That in itself is a great leap forward from *Old Acquaintance* and from Eleanor Parker's reverence for Dennis Morgan when he talks to her about Democracy in *The Very Thought of You*. But *Apartment for Peggy* goes further. Peggy the organizer organizes seminars for the wives; Dorothy wins back her philosopher husband; and professor Gene Lockhart, in atten-dance and listening to the women arguing against Socrates's antidemocratic ideas, decides that "maybe the wrong people are going to school. Perhaps the husband should stay home with the children and the wives should go to class."

In the late forties, of course, this was not as condescending as it may sound now; and in general, *Apartment for Peggy* was a positive, optimistic social situation comedy. But it was not fluff. The shadows of the era are in it, in the strains in the students' marriages, in the notion of philosophy professor Henry Barnes (Gwenn) that suicide is the rational answer to his feeling out of place in a no longer dignified world, in the doubts of Jason (Holden) about studying chemistry in college when he could be making lots of money selling used cars in Chicago, and, most strikingly, Peggy's losing the baby she carried throughout the picture, its brightest symbol of hope. Hardly ever during our wartime childhoods did our Jeanne Crains lose their baby boys. Even though *Apartment for Peggy* ends happily with Peggy making plans for another baby, my memory tells me that the film's ending was sha-dowed by looming, vague fear of forces that even the best and brightest human beings could not control. It was not that the forces were new to us war children; it was that they were not supposed to be in the postwar Jeanne Crain romances.

Certainly there were unhappy endings in war movies. Occasionally, as in *The Constant Nymph,* there was even an unhappy ending that could not be attributed to the Nazis or the Japanese. But the latter were rare and the war was exceptional, understandable chaos. And certainly, in postwar movies, there were conventional happy endings, plenty of them. They were in the majority, especially if B-movies are included. *Deadly Is the Female* is the less common postwar B; the norm was *Campus Honeymoon* (1948), a B-level *Apartment for Peggy* starring the blond Wilde twins, Lee and Lynn, and featuring a song called "Who's got a Tent to Rent?"(The Bs died slowly in the TV fifties). In the features, which starred people like Betsy Drake and Cary Grant, in *Every Girl Should Be Married,* almost every girl and boy got married. Maureen O'Hara got *Sinbad the Sailor* (Douglas Fairbanks, Jr.), Betty Grable always got Dan Dailey, and Bing Crosby always got hooked—unless he was a priest. Our favorites among the ingenues also always got their men: Esther Williams, Jane Powell, June Allyson, Kathryn Grayson, June Haver, Jeanne Crain (until *Pinky*), Doris Day, and Elizabeth Taylor, until she married a "Commie" in *Conspirator* (1949). The 1949 *The Great Gatsby* even got a kind of happy ending: Nick Carraway (Macdonald Carey) and Jordan Baker (Ruth Hussey), together at Jay Gatsby's (Alan Ladd's) grave.

The postwar era still produced comfortingly formulaic romances such as *Every Girl Should be Married* (1948). Seen recently, this movie that Cary Grant made with his real-life young bride Betsy Drake, still stirs the thrill of a successfully charted man-chase. (But again, there's no spark when she finally gets him: The Kiss is hidden behind a raised Grant shoulder.) There were also ingenue romances. I searched my memory for the one that had a special place for me, and then I saw again *Our Very Own* (1950).

This film could have been made in 1944. There is the white American home, with the white fireplaces and the family gathered around the polished mahogany table for breakfast, with mother—Jane Wyatt again—serving from a silver coffee service. There are the beautiful young lovers, Ann Blyth and Farley Granger, both dark-haired and unbelievably white-toothed. There is the rival, Joan Evans, not really a bad girl, especially since she plays Ann Blyth's kid sister. There are the organdy-gowned parties and a romantic swim at the beach (pre-*From Here to Eternity*) for the sweethearts Gail and Chuck; there are the family's big moments (the opening scene is the arrival of its first television set); there is the pert, lovable brat of a little sister—Natalie Wood in pigtails; and there is the wise "colored" maid, Vi, and the shaggy family dog, Bedelia.

There is also conflict. On her eighteenth birthday, Gail hears from her jealous sister Joan that she is adopted. I can't resist the cynicism about the silver coffee service for breakfast in the white house, but Gail's crisis holds up as a rite of passage metaphor, just as losing her fiance in the war served for Jennifer Jones in *Since You Went Away,* and still does. After Gail goes through the ritual of finding her real mother (Ann Dvorak)—a good soul but, according to formula, serving beer, not coffee—she realizes who her real real mother is; and *Our Very Own* concludes with Gail's high school graduation with lengthy, rich choruses of Pomp and Circumstance, and then Gail's speech as graduating class vice-president (I note now that it is vice-president, not president, and that this is high school, not college, of which there is no mention for Gail). Her speech extols the primary value of "citizenship," and " next," the value of the family. It reconciles Gail with her Macauley parents, Wyatt and Donald Cook (note: no star plays Father), and it reconciles her with Chuck, so that the movie can end with Gail and Chuck striding, matching smiles, to stand under a southern California tree and embrace, petite Ann Blyth and broad-shouldered dark and handsome Farley Granger.

We also had our *Cover Girl—Lovely to Look At* (1952) in which the pairs and parallels were even neater than in the Hayworth, Kelly, Silvers movie. Three pals: Jerry (Gower Champion), Al (Red Skelton), and Tony (Howard Keel);

four pairs: comic supports Kurt Kasznar and Zsa Zsa Gabor, Marge and Gower Champion, Red Skelton and Ann Miller, and Howard Keel and Kathryn Grayson—switching en route from Skelton and Grayson, and Keel and Miller. We have a scene of Gower courting Marge with dance ("I Won't Dance"), followed by one of Keel courting Grayson with song("You're Devastating"). There is the pals' no-go show in the opening scene, and their closing smash hit. . . .

In *Lovely to Look At,* the romantic conventions also never look smoother, the obstacles like bright signals: Grayson's prudishness, Keel's show biz ego, and his other woman from what Leslie Fiedler would call his "genital past." As soon as Stephanie (Grayson) is charmed, the other woman, Bubbles (Miller), appears. This sends Stephanie from her ruffled dove-gray dresses to a strapless gown and too much champagne, so that, charmingly giddy, she can depart the cafe for a hansom ride with Tony, alone at last. But the star lovers' first kiss is held back for the Champions having theirs (in an infinite starry midnight sky, "Smoke Gets in Your Eyes," she in periwinkle chiffon and sparkling sequins), and—one more time—for a comedy bit, the chagrined Bubbles escorting tipsy Skelton home. (You can imagine Skelton's bit.) Then, at last: Grayson and Keel in the hansom in the park, and his broad-shouldered, encompassing embrace. No wonder I believe in romance—and in stars.

Lovely to Look At, which, like *Our Very Own,* I searched out because I remembered it especially, ends with the song-dance-and fashion show produced by the three pals and their true loves. Staged by Vincente Minnelli (who did not do the rest of the movie), this scene features the Champion's showy, sexy ballet and a parade of models, as in *Cover Girl*—except that in the 1952 film, the focus is not on the faces but on the costumes by Adrian. The conclusion has all four pairs whirling in acres of chiffon and tons of broad, black, tuxedoed shoulders. It could not have been more comforting. In postwar movies, we could not escape loves that failed, women who killed, men who preferred their buddies, and even stillborn babies. Perhaps, in our "prepuberty" and adolescence, these films made us hang on harder to our childhood dreams of looking like Ann Blyth and graduating to the kiss of a man who looked as much like Farley Granger as we could imagine.

Idealism: "The Gift of Long-Gone Hacks"

In the idealism that was romanticism less charged, somewhat intellectualized, I suspect now that we were also more influenced by the conventional than by what was for us the *avant-garde,* films such as *Lost Boundaries* and *Pinky.* In this somewhat more thoughtful aspect of our romanticism, we were served with better dreams than broad shoulders—except perhaps in one movie, which, interestingly, is deeply remembered and hence likely influential. In it, the two aspects, "love" and moralism, merged at their extremes: rape and rampant egocentricity. That was *The Fountainhead.* But first, the conventional: *Showboat.*

Lost Boundaries, Intruder in the Dust, and *Home of the Brave* (all 1949) were powerful representations of the effects of racism. I remembered them and knew that they had shaped me. But while *Pinky, Crossfire,* and *Gentleman's Agreement* were box-office hits, none of the other postwar tolerance movies was, and overall their number was few. Unidealistic grown-ups could, and did, avoid "tolerance" movies. But MGM's 1951 *Showboat* was one of Hollywood's biggest hits ever. *Variety* (August 1, 1951) reported that the first week's gross for this film at Radio City Music Hall—$167,000—was the highest opening week in a nonholiday season in the theater's history. I stood in a line around the block to see the Music Hall premiere, and when William Warfield ended his Joe's "Ole Man River," I heard a movie audience applaud for the first time in my life.

From this *Showboat,* few seem to remember the stars,

Kathryn Grayson and Howard Keel, but rather remember
Warfield as Joe and Ava Gardner as Julie. My mother, who
goes back to Bara, Bow, and Garbo, says that the most
beautiful face on film is Ava Gardner's Julie, and I feel so
too. We were too young, or generally too insular, to know
Paul Robeson; Warfield's singing was a door opening. We
may have heard Caleb Peterson's Joe, and Lena Horne's
Julie singing "Can't Help Lovin' Dat Man" in MGM's 1946
biography of Jerome Kern, *Till the Clouds Roll By*. And I
would guess that most of us then did not even know that the
Breen office would not countenance a black Julie in the 1951
Showboat because Julie has a white husband (Robert
Sterling). But we made no connections. Ava Gardner was our
Julie. Like my mother, almost everyone with whom I have
talked who remembers the forties and fifties gets to Ava
Gardner's beauty; and as with Jeanne Crain's Miss American
Pinky, perhaps in the long run it was better to have a Julie
who was the postwar American Venus, a Julie with the trans-
lucent skin, the cheekbones and chin cleft, the green eyes,
sinuous body, and above all, the soft, sad sensuality of Ava
Gardner.

We may deplore "the long run," but at least by now we
cannot deny it. After *Lost Boundaries, Home of the Brave,
Intruder in the Dust,* and *Pinky* passed in white America, *No
Way Out*, with its "boogies" and Sidney Poitier's debut, was
too strong, a year before *Showboat*. It is a long run, but at
least in the forties in Hollywood Jews and blacks stepped
forward. Women, it seems now, did not.

Despite the brave war wives, Resistance fighters, battlefield
nurses, spy catchers, and spunky Peggies of the postwar
years, the forties in overview seem characterized by boss
ladies who end up in mosquito-ridden cottages in New Jersey;
Cover Girls who retire to succor their men; Scarletts
searching stupidly for romance; and at the end, after the war,
Dragon Ladies using romance to murder men. Or so it seems.
And yet, somehow, the cause of women as equal and
important has prospered in a time in which the children of the

forties are in the prime of their power. After all this looking back, I am no more sure how this happened than I am sure how we came to the cause of tolerance for the differences among human beings from a womb so smotheringly xenophobic, class-bound, and bigoted.

My memory and my conversations tell me that *The Fountainhead* (1949) influenced us deeply. A few years ago, after I had talked on the "seeds of seventies paranoia" in forties films and mentioned *The Fountainhead* fleetingly and among many others, a much younger person, living in the "counterculture," came up to say that he had seen the film on television the night before he went away to college and felt his whole life influenced by it. But how and why and to what ends it influenced him and us I am not certain. Thanks to its author Ayn Rand's notion of woman's place, the love story between Howard Roark (Gary Cooper) and Dominique Françon (Patricia Neal) is another rape fantasy like unto, more so, that of Scarlett and Rhett; and thus, as Lois Gould's survey of seventies women reveals, the film is nearly as popular as "pornography for women." But in the movie *The Fountainhead*, as in the novel, there are also ideas about the world and man's place in it, and these are of a piece with the ideas about love, and it seems, at least as influential.

The remark made by the young man at my talk on paranoia suggests that we teenagers of its original time were not special. But at least we were ripe for Rand's philosophy of individualism; and, particularly in the movie, it could hardly have been put more simply. Her paean to "a man's right to exist for his own sake" is a dynamite blast at the "collective" society in which, like teenagers in all times, we believed we lived. These quotations are from architect Howard Roark's speech at his trial for dynamiting the Wrightian housing project he designed and which was diluted with gimcrackery by those who pander to "the mob." Roark, his own man, an artist and an extremist, became a model to many of us who believed passionately in the equality of all the colored soldiers, and when Jeff Chandler's portrayal in *Broken*

Arrow (1950) opened our eyes, all the Cochises. But since no model instructed us otherwise, we also yearned to be—or if we were boys, to take—a Dominique. How can I not be uncertain about *The Fountainhead*?

Exactly how we came—how at least some of us came—to commit ourselves to equality for anyone baffles me ultimately. I do not remember getting the message from family, teachers, ministers, or anywhere but in the popular media, and most vividly, through the "photoplay." FDR, MacArthur, and Eisenhower—those heroes, and our parents who pored over their ration stamps—must have been better than a medium whose psychology was Maria Montez's in *Cobra Woman* and whose politics was Jeanne Crain in *Pinky*. But I *remember* the movies in the dark. I first read, and then memorized, Polonius' speech because *This Above All* (1942) was a favorite movie, one of my first, a romance set in London under the Blitz, starring blonde and beautiful Joan Fontaine and dark and handsome Tyrone Power. Lee Diamond (Dane Clark) in *Pride of the Marines*, the tolerance movies, and Howard Roark's self-defense have something to do with it. Perhaps even Sam does, whom Bogart called "Boy" in *Casablanca*; perhaps even the outcast Rick himself; the obstinately good girls whom men called bad: Ilsa, Alicia, "Slim," Gilda . . . ; Hattie McDaniel, the wise one in *Gone with the Wind*; and other forties characters who, because of what Vincente Minnelli, in that era, termed the "surrealistic" accident of creativity, cracked stereotypes and formulas.[46]

Richard Schickel's conclusion to his television documentary " 'You Must Remember This': Hollywood in the Forties" is seductive. There is a connection between the mushroom cloud and the apocalyptic shadows in postwar films. For his text *Hollywood in the Fifties*, Gordon Gow picked a 1950 movie, *Fourteen Hours*, to represent fifties strains that I have indicated through films such as *Kiss of Death* and *Crossfire*. *Fourteen Hours* is about a man on a ledge (Richard Basehart), who is undecided whether he should jump. Says Gow, this film "prefigured a theme that persisted significantly throughout the decade: the plight of the individual who cannot adjust."[49] As Gow says, this individual can be completely straight: the man wrongly accused, such as Henry Fonda in *The Wrong Man* (1957). (Earlier examples are Arthur Kennedy in *Boomerang* and Bogart in *Dark Passage*.) But he can also be a pitiable drug addict (Don Murray in *A Hatful of Rain*, 1957), a driven poor boy (John Derek in *Knock On Any Door*, 1949; Montgomery Clift in *A Place in the Sun*, 1951), a *Rebel Without a Cause* (James Dean 1955), or some other kind of misfit, often played by Marlon Brando in a strange way that burned into one's unprepared soul. The point is not that these men (note, men) were heroes who were "different," but that in the later fifties—and often enough in the postwar era—these Bogarts in their dark passage and Mitchums who could not get out of their pasts became the heroes of popular American movies.

The Forties: Dreams Come True

It is also tempting to see the events of 1949 as symbolic. In that year, "Uncle Don," who read the comics to New York area kids over WOR radio on Sunday mornings for twenty-three years, was dumped, because the station thought that children had become too "sophisticated" for Uncle Don. (He was dumped for "Heidi.")[50] "One Man's Family," along with "Walter Winchell" and "Louella Parsons from Hollywood," were Sunday evening radio events that were as stable for me as the earlier Sunday dinner and double solitaire game at Grandma's. In 1949, "One Man's Family" was moved to Monday nights. (Portents.) Elizabeth Taylor played her first married role in a movie (*Conspirator*) that contained the subterranean message that the Communist menace was so powerful it could seduce even the most beautiful girl in the world. At the end of 1949, and only a few weeks after the death of Bill "Bojangles" Robinson, Shirley Temple got a divorce. Margaret Mitchell died in 1949, ending for good all our hopes for another *Gone with the Wind* from her. And Maria Ouspenskaya, who had opened the decade with that rare portrait in *Dance, Girls, Dance* of a woman creator, set fire to her bed with a cigarette, and later died on December 3, 1949.

In 1949, Ingrid Bergman lost her lady image to Roberto Rossellini (the name says it all), and Rita Hayworth got her image slapped for traveling with Ali Khan before marrying him. A Boston City Councilman wanted to ban Hayworth's movies, but the motion was shunted to the Committee on Public Safety. But Hayworth's was a Gilda image anyway; and in addition, she married before the Khan baby came; and the wedding was a grandiose Riviera blast, according to my movie magazines, to which everyone, but especially Louella, came. And just as the paternity suits and brawls only enhanced Errol Flynn's image, and just as Bob Mitchum's marijuana bust only raked in more money for his scolding studio, so did the falls of Bergman and Hayworth bring the public flocking to reissues—at least in the wicked city. *Variety,* June 8, 1949, reported Bergman's *Intermezzo* (1939; Leslie Howard) doing well in New York, and also a double bill of *Cover Girl* and *You Were Never Lovelier*, billed as the "Dance Battle of the Century": Kelly versus Astaire for the flaming woman.[50] (In the midseventies, the same double bill did beautifully in Chicago, at John Dillinger's old Biograph.)

It is easy now to see significance in 1949. But, in reality, the year, like all years, seems as mixed as the reactions to the stars' peccadilloes. It probably meant just what a list of the dozen top box-office grossers of November 1949 suggests: Number One: *Jolson Sings Again* (featuring "The Anniversary Waltz"); Number Two: *She Wore a Yellow Ribbon*; Number Three, *That Forsyte Woman*, which the critics called dull, but which offered Garson and Pidgeon, plus Errol Flynn, Robert Young, and one of the popular new "All-American" ingenues, Janet Leigh. Fourth was the Forsyte saga's opposite, one of the new-style crime docu-dramas,

Chicago Deadline, starring a strong forties favorite, Alan Ladd. Fifth was *Pinky*. Numbers six, seven, ten, and eleven at the box office were a show biz musical (June Haver's *Oh, You Beautiful Doll*), Milton Berle's *Always Leave Them Laughing*, and two relatively sophisticated comedies, Hepburn and Tracy's *Adam's Rib* and Paul Douglas's *Everybody Does It*. Eighth and ninth on the popular movie list were as tried and true as Milton Berle was to become in the history of television: Bogart in *Tokyo Joe*, a variant of *Casablanca*, and Bette Davis seething in *Beyond the Forest*. The last of the top dozen of November 1949 was a Technicolor biography of a popular horse of the decade, *The Story of Seabiscuit*, with the epitomal forties cast, Barry Fitzgerald, Shirley Temple, and Lon McCallister.

In this montage of Hollywood at the end of the forties—this list of formulaic musicals and melodramas and one reasonably brave perspective of American society —seems to lie the only meaning of "the forties." This could as well be said of any other decade. It is only the mix of tried and true with always insufficient innovation that defines the American motion-picture industry. It is only the difference—and the likeness—among *Jolson Sings Again* and *Pinky; Home of the Brave* and *Gilda; The Best Years of Our Lives* and *Dark Passage*, that tells us anything about America in the postwar years.

I remember the audience in my movie house, "my" Rivoli, standing to sing "The Star-Spangled Banner" when President Roosevelt asked us to at the end of some of the war movies. And Richard Schickel writes of watching movies as a forties child:

. . . one had the most delicious sensation of being permitted to eavesdrop on grown-up conversations, of being let in on a big secret. Which secret was that even a serious problem like world war was soluble. Soluble because Americans were a fundamentally decent, good-natured, aspiring, perfectible people—occasionally deluded, but only briefly so, and easily summoned back to their basic idealism. Funny thing: I still think that. In the schlocky recesses of my soul, that belief, that gift of long-gone hacks and moguls, abides, triumphs over education, over experience, over the not-illogical apocalyptic vision that has replaced it in fashion. One should know better; one really does. But. Still. . . .[52]

One should know better. In truth, what was imprinted on my *tabula rasa* in the forties is probably more constricting and dark than the values of "One Man's Family," our country, and one world. Now it seems that our childhood is better represented by Jimmy Cagney's Cody Jarrett at the end of the decade, than by his George M. Cohan at the beginning. Now the "logic" of the forties seems better symbolized by the apocalyptic fireball with which Schickel summarizes the decade in his documentary than by the Schickel who wrote "Growing Up in the Forties," and wonders, "But. Still. . . ."

Reading Gabriel Gladstone in *Dissent* (1955) now, or Joan Mellen in *Big Bad Wolves: Masculinity in the American Film* (1977), who says essentially the same thing Gladstone did, I can see now that popular American movies did not teach that striving gets you ahead, but rather that they taught the opposite. Clearly, just as Gladstone and other Marxists such as Mellen say, the movies inculcated passivity by representing the notion that you only get what you want by not wanting it, whatever it is. (Gladstone uses fifties movies: *How to Marry a Millionaire*, 1953, in which Lauren Bacall gets hers by giving up and marrying a poor boy, who, of course, is a millionaire in hiding; and *Woman's World*, 1950, in which Van Heflin gets the promotion only after the tycoon, Clifton Webb, has made it perfectly clear that no one can scramble for the top.) Yes, it is clear: that ineffable something special that in the sixties we learned to call charisma, cannot be worked for. So keep in line at the public beaches and bargain counters. If you belong higher up, you'll be picked.[53]

Gladstone could as easily have used *Cover Girl*, or the

"doomed to be what you are" movies of the late forties and
early fifties: Mitchum in *Out of the Past* trying to break away
from his Kathy (Jane Greer) and brought back by only a kiss;
Joel McCrea, Wes McQueen in *Colorado Territory*, who
would shuck his outlawry for farming with sweet Judy Ann
(Dorothy Malone), and whose fate is predicted by the very
image of the drifter dancing girl and half-Pueblo outcast
(note, "half"), Colorado Carson (Virginia Mayo), who says
to McCrea (with "native wisdom"), "You can't bust out of
what you are." Or John Garfield, at the end of *Humoresque*,
after Joan Crawford has released him to be a great violinist
by walking into the Pacific, saying as he stares at the empty
ocean, "One way or another, you pay for what you are." Or
Joan Fontaine in *Born to be Bad* (1950), Coleridge's
Christabel (her name is Christabel Kane), fated to destroy her
lovers because as one of them (Robert Ryan) says, her doom
is to really love only herself. (It should be noted that this
absolutely unredeemed woman is the creation of a woman
novelist—Anne Parrish, author of *All Kneeling*—and a
woman screenwriter, Edith Sommer.)

Now it seems easy to call the forties the "Age of Alfred
Adler," after the psychologist who defined our "inferiority
complexes" and counseled adjusting and fitting it, rather
than asserting and taking control of our individual worlds, as
the iconoclast Ayn Rand promoted. According to historian
Warren Susman, Americans in the late thirties and the forties
took to Adler's ideas about how to win friends and influence
people because of the "shame and fear" bred in them by the
Depression.[54] Like Gladstone, Susman makes sense now.
But. Still. . . .

Now even that quintessentially schlocky movie *Cover Girl*
looks propagandistic. "Rusty" learns the hard way that she
must renounce fame and professional fulfillment to get love.
Just as Ida Lupino and Joan Leslie learned in *The Hard Way*,
and Miriam Hopkins in *Old Acquaintance*, and Ginger
Rogers in *Lady in the Dark*, and Rosalind Russell, and even
Katharine Hepburn, until she got to *The African Queen* in

1951. Is there a conspiracy behind all this? At the end of our epitomal forties propaganda picture, *Mission to Moscow* (1943), Russian and American peasants march up a backdrop mountain to a choral crescendo of "I am my brother's keeper. I am. I am. . . ." Was this a communist plot, as HUAC told us it was after the war was over? Or was it rather that we believed in a kinship of the common people until the age of affluence told us that it was shameful to be one of those people whom God must have loved since he made so many of them? Exactly when it happened, I am not sure, but at some point in the last twenty years, we stopped honoring the gentle, humorous myth, which in our pride and resiliency as a people we had shared. The myth that gorgeous Rita Hayworth and talented Gene Kelly really belonged with the common people in Joe's "erster" bar in Brooklyn. How often my talks with forties men and women ended with their hoping that the "dream" of our childhood had been a conscious thing—as one of them asked, Wasn't it really all a "joke in which we never really believed"? But the truth, I think, is that we try now to believe that we did not believe then, that we try to avoid recognizing that at least a lot of our problems are rooted in the fact that those movie-made dreams of long ago and far away came true.

At the end of *Cover Girl*, the pearl that Hayworth, Kelly, and Silvers look for in the oysters every Friday night turns up and brings Rusty and Danny together again. But what did the stars do with their treasure? That was the question that, in my childhood, never got answered before The End. As David Thompson recently wrote of these movies:

> . . . Endless wooing was the state of love, and closed-mouth kisses constituted rapture. Sexual splendor was a never-reached nirvana beyond the happy ending, while marriage was a restful, comic condition of the middle-aged. . . . The natural and fruitful adoration that men and women inherited from Romanticism as an expectation is so much more lasting in cinema if lovers never meet. And the movies do touch us without making real connections.[55]

And as Johann (Erland Josephson) reminds Marianne (Liv Ullmann) when they are divorcing in Ingmar Bergman's *Scene from a Marriage,* "The masquerade begins in the cradle."

Redeeming

. . .the craziness of this war in which you sleep with the enemy—Pauline Kael, reviewing Paul Mazursky's *An Unmarried Woman,* 1978.[56]

In the violence of *Crossfire* and the violent idealism of *The Fountainhead,* I can now see the seeds of our largely unknowing, hence uncontrolled, and hence all-too-impotent revolt in the sixties against the answers that do not answer, the conventions that do not fulfill. It seems light years now from Guy Madison to Robert Redford, but in reality it may be only a dissolve. And in the middle, between Madison and Redford, is Jack Kennedy, because we look for Apollos, we children of the forties. We look, too, for sunny, chintz-flowered cottages and the verities of children and wise men. We cannot help looking for order and, paradoxically, for romance. Like Alice, we can try to grow up. We can wipe the fuchsia off our lips, uncurl our hair, unbra, and ungirdle. It is still a struggle with our childhood images.

Men or women, we are kin to Dana Andrews in the scene near the end of *The Best Years of Our Lives* in which the air force captain without a job in postwar America, and about to leave his hometown for anywhere, walks through a junkyard of discarded bombers. The camera lifts then, as in the *Gone with the Wind* scene at the railroad station in Atlanta with the war wounded and Scarlett walking among them. Inside ourselves we walk among romantic talismans, and now that we are forty and looking at *The Best Years of Our Lives* as a historical document rather than as the weekend movie, we may try not to see that only the young lovers in that film overcome, that at the end, and despite the perfect wife, Myrna Loy, Frederic March is still drinking too much, and that, even in a popular Hollywood movie in 1946, his loneliness in the postwar world is left unresolved. In 1946, I do not remember noticing. At one point in *The Best Years of Our Lives*, Teresa Wright tells her parents that they cannot understand her agony, loving a married man. "You loved each other," she cries, "And you got married in a big church and had a honeymoon in the south of France and you never had any trouble. . . ." March and Loy—Al and Millie—look at each other, and he walks across the room to stand beside his wife as she answers their daughter by looking at him and asking rhetorically, "We never had any trouble? How many times have you said we were through? That it was over? How many times have we had to fall in love all over again?"

For Al and Millie's daughter Peggy, and for all us Peggies in the forties audience, love was romance. For her mother, it was commitment to meld the dream and the reality, something much harder to get than any romantic hero. Then, as a child, I could not stand with Loy and March. Now I can. But, here, I bear with me Peggy and Scarlett, never to be wholly free of longing for the dark and winding staircase.

In one of the recent and typical liberation novels of women in their forties, *Lovers and Tyrants*, Francine du Plessix Gray defines liberation as a passage through exorcisms of the tyrant lovers in our lives: fathers, mothers, husbands, friends, hero lovers, the opposite sexual self in each of us. . . . It is an odyssey, a hard coming through archetypes and rocks and storms often fulsome, back to that foggy place of oblique and unconscious registrations. Men and women both, we have to find what the Sailor Has Hidden. Yet, if we are wise and lucky enough to get something, I think it is not exorcism we get. Perhaps that is why Gray's Stephanie, and so many of the self-searching women in our new novels and films, seem at the end still deluded, and hence pathetic, and if we are identifying with them, so achingly short of the step. For we carry our baggage with us. In Nora Ephron's phrase,

"After liberation, we will still have to reckon with the Sleeping Beauty and Cinderella."[57] We cannot free ourselves—for who can want to lose any part of her, or his, own, unique, precious, fragile life?

Henry Fairlie, a man and an Englishman, perhaps saw us better than we see ourselves when he wrote recently of "romantic love" as a "key": "one way of trying to identify the secrets of our own human natures without destroying the mystery." And, he said, it was a key which "feminists—because they find it awkward to talk of sexual relations in terms of love, and especially of romantic love—refuse to turn."[58] There are some signs that this is changing, as in Ephron, and in *Ms.* magazine's "Special Issue on Sexuality" (November 1976), in Molly Haskell's defense of "rape fantasies" as healthy romantic playlets, not "blueprints for reality." As Haskell says, "the 2,000-year-old misunderstanding" about "rape fantasies" is simply not seeing them as fantasies in which a man chosen by the fantasizer goes " 'mad with desire' " in a manner she chooses. After marshaling her evidence that it is "the most assertive, creative, independent" women who fantasize being dominated by a strong man, Haskell concludes,

. . . we are always returning to, reclaiming, redeeming our history. Those of us in our thirties or older are compelled to return, in fantasy form, to the male-worshipping world of our former selves. . . . We cannot so easily discard the past; we cannot turn a man's world into a man-woman world, and make up new rules for love and marriage, without an emotional upheaval. Fantasy provides the perfect vehicle for this return. . .[59]

Perfect if we know them, these Rhett Butler dreams, for what they are, and for what they were to us as children. Gable said of his public:

"They see me broke, in trouble, scared of things that go bump in the night but coming out fighting. . . . They see life with a high price tag on it, but they get an idea that no price is too high if it's *life* . . . I am not going to make any motion pictures that don't keep right on telling them that about a man. Let's get that understood. The things a man has to have are hope and confidence in himself against odds, and sometimes he needs somebody, his pal or his mother or his wife or God, to give him that confidence. He's got to have some inner standards worth fighting for or there won't be any way to bring him into conflict. And he must be ready to choose death before dishonor without making too much song and dance about it."[60]

And Fay Weldon, in her 1976 "woman's" novel *Remember Me*, wisely wrote,

Does the doctor's wife envy the architect's wife, as the doctor claims? Yes, she does. He's right. And why not? Well, none of our lives are so perfect that we wouldn't want to change them—or at any rate, some part of them—with some other person of our choice. Only when we are in love, and loved in return, does the pleasant singularity of being oneself fill the heart with joy—when we are the recipient of that insane love that on occasion comes from another, by-passing all defects, ignoring all faults of appearance, age, history, conduct, character and humor. Such love would alter, if it improvement found, so at such times we can be reconciled for once to our imperfect selves.[61]

But still, the issue is barely even joined. In the words of a psychologist:

We are a society which bolsters the withdrawal of men and women from each other and provides social defenses against sexual war. The women's movement has offered a way of handling problems by objectifying them. Women band together not merely to achieve greater control of social, personal, and political life but for mutual support against male hostility. Men become brothers to each other in mistrust of women. What unites men to men and women to women are shared problems, the anger and fear they find incommunicable across the gulf of sex.[62]

The gulf of sex. If it is unbridgeable, where will all this "anger and fear" take us? We have, still, so little tolerance—that old forties word—so little humor, so much confusion. For the "happy ending" of the 1977 romance *Saturday Night Fever*, John Travolta, who thought all girls were either "nice girls" or "cunts," clasps hands with a girl "friend." Joan Mellen sees a sympathetic portrayal of Al Pacino's homosexuality in *Dog Day Afternoon* (1975) as the most hopeful note in contemporary "Masculinity in the American Film." Perhaps the way we are right now is best caught in two parts of a *New York Times* interview with director-writer Paul Mazursky, upon the opening of *An Unmarried Woman* (March 1978). Asked about the vulnerability of his men, his Blumes in Love, Mazursky responded:

> I see the baby in the man. I was brought up on Clark Gable: "Frankly, Scarlett [sic], I don't give a damn." . . . In those days, they didn't show the baby side of guys like Gable, Cagney, Bogart, Garfield—only the heroic side. But God knows they all had a baby side. I deliberately show the baby side, the vulnerable side. I show imperfect people. I have a hunch that this interferes with the fantasy life of even the sophisticates in the audience who really want larger-than-life silver-screen heroes and heroines. I show imperfect people in romance. . . .

But it seems no accident that the *Times* interviewer, a woman, Leticia Kent, ended the interview with an account of meeting Mazursky's wife. Twenty-four years married, the receptacle and responder with her husband for the sad stories of their innumerable breaking-up friends, half of what, in another interview, her husband called a " 'miracle' " marriage.[63] Betsy Mazursky said to Leticia Kent of *An Unmarried Woman*, "firmly," " 'It's totally about *me*.' " There follows a passage of dialogue between Betsy and Paul Mazursky about her twenty years at home with the children, her need now, at the age of fifty-one, to do something outside the home, her fear that without a master's degree, " 'It may be difficult for me to find a job. . . .' " He feels she " 'made a choice,' " and she responds that " 'It wasn't a conscious choice. . . . A lot of women of my generation didn't realize we had the choice.' " " 'Some women of your generation did,' " Mr. Mazursky counters. But he names no one. (And that also says a lot about what's off in his woman's sensibility movie.)

And then Kent concludes her story on Paul Mazursky with his reply to her question, "What happens" if Mrs. Mazursky follows the path of his Erica (Jill Clayburgh), gets a job, and refuses to go "to Vermont (read Hollywood) with him for the summer." Mazursky's last words are very moving, very important; like Ellen Burstyn's at the beginning of this book, very scary; and just maybe, very, very liberating:

> I have a strange feeling—a nightmare—that for the first time in my life I've written a prophetic movie. Not one out of my experience. I don't know what's going to happen."[64]

We can only hope for control of the demons, which perhaps we can have if we can learn them, if we can turn the keys. It will be more catharsis than exorcism, this liberating passage; more the discovery of a dialectic than a series of sheddings. We must find the buried springs, such as the formulas of our childhood romances, and then we must set them aside, in the sense in which that old romantic Hegel used the word *aufheben* for the *moment*, or aspect in the spiral in which thesis and antithesis form a synthesis and are then *put aside*, in both the sense of detaching from the new aspect and the sense of putting away as cherished, incorporated parts of a life passage. Parts of our imperfect selves, then and now.

We are not "ONE," said Denis de Rougemont. "We are two in contentment." That is a potent dream.

Notes

1. Helene Deutsch, *The Psychology of Women*, I: "Girlhood" (New York: Bantam Books, 1973 [1944]), Chapter I, "Prepuberty," 1-23. Deutsch on careers is from p. 113.

2. David Thompson, *America in the Dark: Hollywood and the Gift of Unreality* (New York: William Morrow, 1977), p. 19.

3. Deutsch, *The Psychology of Women*, I, 101.

4. Thompson, *America in the Dark*, p. 195.

5. Sir Francis Galton's findings on the differences among people in imaging memories are old but still sound. In the 1880s, Galton sent a questionnaire to 100 distinguished men (including 19 Fellows of the Royal Society), asking them to explore their memory of their breakfast tables that morning. Galton's study, corroborated in a study by G. H. Betts in the United States in 1909, found that the ability to image varies widely; when it exists, it resists classification; and it is dimmest in people habituated to abstract thought—and stronger in women (who were not in Galton's study, but were in Betts'). For a summary of the Galton and Betts' experiments, see Ian M. L. Hunter, *Memory* (Baltimore: Penguin Books, 1972 [1957]), pp. 189-193. See also Herbert Read, *Education Through Art* (New York: Pantheon Books, 1958), pp. 45-46; and Galton, *Inquiries into Human Faculty and Development* (New York: E. P. Dutton and Co., 1911 [1883]).

6. See, for example, Frederick Bartlett, *Remembering: A Study in Experimental and Social Psychology* (Cambridge: Cambridge University Press, 1964), pp. 195-96.

7. See Joseph Goulden, *The Best Years: 1945-1960* (New York: Atheneum, 1976) and Douglas T. Miller and Marion Nowak, *The Fifties: The Way We Really Were* (Garden City: Doubleday, 1977). After an insightful and informed analysis of *The Best Years of Our Lives* as cultural reflector in the opening pages of his book, Goulden limits his coverage of movies to a few pages on *film noir*, drawn from Robert Thom, in which he attributes the dark film of the postwar era too simply to American "confus[ion]" over the loser winning; i.e., over our helping Germany and Japan after the war (pp. 203-4). Miller and Nowak do give the movies a chapter—"Hollywood in Transition"—but it is sketchy and not deeply informed.

8. Meyer A. Zeligs, M.D., *Friendship and Fratricide: An Analysis of Whittaker Chambers and Alger Hiss* (New York: The Viking Press, 1967).

9. Leslie Fiedler, *Love and Death in the American Novel* (New York: Criterion Books, 1960), p. xxxiv.

10. Pointed out by *Variety*, February 5, 1947, p. 12, col. 1.

11. See, for example, the lead story in *Variety*, September 5, 1945.

12. *Variety*, December 22, 1948, p. 3, cols. 1-2.

13. *Variety*, p. 7, col. 5; *Variety*, June 11, 1947, p. 18, cols. 1-2.

14. Paul M. A. Linebarger's *Psychological Warfare* (Washington: Infantry Journal Press, 1949), pp. 138-39, reproduces Nazi leaflets dropped on American soldiers in Europe, titled "The Girl You Left Behind," and featuring "Joan Hopkins," who is enjoying herself making money (before the war, $12 a week at the five-and-ten-cent store; now, $60 a week as a private secretary), and cavorting with

her boss, "Sam Levy," while her fiancé, "Bob Harrison" is fighting overseas. The leaflets picture horn-rimmed, cigar-chomping, curly-dark-haired, lascivious Sam, and Joan, deshabille about the upper legs, and finally, Sam and Joan running into Bob, returned home to America, a one-legged amputee.

15. For the extent, and something of the fear and hate in this bitter cry, see Marjorie Rosen, *Popcorn Venus: Women, Movies and the American Dream* (New York: Avon Books, 1974 [1973]), pp. 215-20, particularly the excerpt from a 1946 *New York Times Magazine* article by an American war correspondent threatening to return to France for his women.

16. See Charles Higham and Joel Greenberg, *Hollywood in the Forties* (New York: Paperback Library, 1970 [1968]), pp. 87, 90-91, on de Rochemont's contribution and influence.

17. Thompson, *America in the Dark*, p. 205.

18. *Variety*, January 30, 1946, p. 1.

19. In *America in the Movies, or "Santa Maria, It Had Slipped My Mind,"* Michael Wood also links evil, powerful women to the fears of returning soldiers, but the Britisher begs off the implications of this "monstrous family romance" (New York: Basic Books, 1975), pp. 51-74; pp. 70-71 for the begging off. See also Frederick Fearing, "Warriors Return: Normal or Neurotic?" *Hollywood Quarterly* 1 (1945), 97-109, on the psychology of the soldier returning from years of submission to authority, perhaps "permanently impairing [his] capacity ever to return to independent living" (p. 103), and on how radio and movies offer "the best, perhaps the only solution" to "adjusting" veterans and home frontiers (p. 97).

20. See Rosen's Chapter 12, "The Rise and Fall of Rosie the Riveter," and Richard Lingeman, *Don't You Know There's a War On? The American Home Front 1941-1945* (New York: G. P. Putnam's Sons, 1970), pp. 156-159.

21. *Variety*, November 3, 1948, p. 3, col. 2.

22. *Variety*, December 22, 1948, pp. 1, col. 5; 16, col. 5.

23. *Variety*, January 16, 1946, pp. 1, 62.

24. *Variety*, April 24, 1946, pp. 4, 24.

25. *Variety*, March 3, 1948, p. 9, col. 5.

26. *Variety*, January 5, 1949, p. 14, cols. 4-5.

27. Howard Whitman, *Colliers*, 123, March 5, 1949, pp. 18-19; 46.

28. For the story of the movie *Green Dolphin Street*, see *Variety*, October 22, 1947, pp. 3, col. 3; 4, cols. 1-2; 27, col. 4.

29. *Variety*, January 7, 1948, p. 62, col. 4.

30. Anne Baxter, *Intermission: A True Story* (New York: Ballantine Books, 1976), p. 332.

31. *Variety*, December 31, 1947, p. 6, col. 2.

32. *Variety*, December 11, 1948, p. 6, col. 3.

33. *Variety*, November 24, 1948, p. 6, col. 3.

34. Rosen, *Popcorn Venus*, pp. 233-38.

35. *Variety*, January 19, 1948, pp. 1, col. 5; 52, col. 2.

36. Miller and Nowak, *The Fifties*, p. 325, say that none of these four antiracism films of 1949-50 "did very well financially," and that this was the reason "racial prejudice" got shelved until the late fifties. As the text indicates, the truth is more complex.

37. Andrew Dowdy, *"Movies Are Better Than Ever": Wide-Screen Memories of*

the Fifties (New York: William Morrow, 1973), pp. 69-70.

38. Donald Bogle and Michael Wood disagree with this rhetorical notion: Bogle, *Toms, Coons, Mulattoes, Mammies and Bucks: An Interpretive History of Blacks in American Films* (New York: The Viking Press, 1973), p. 152; and Wood, *America in the Movies*, pp. 133-34.

39. Martha Weinman Lear, "Of Thee I Sang," *The New York Times Magazine*, July 4, 1976, p. 50.

40. See Lawrence Alloway, *Violent America: The Movies 1946-1964* (New York: The Museum of Modern Art, 1971), pp. 25-26; 79; and Arthur Knight, *The Liveliest Art: A Panoramic History of the Movies* (New York: New American Library, Mentor, 1959), pp. 245-64.

41. William Manchester, *The Glory and the Dream: A Narrative History of America, 1932-1972* (Boston: Little, Brown & Co., 1973), Vol. I: 342-51; the quotation is from p. 344.

42. Reported in *Variety*, December 15, 1943, p. 3, col. 1.

43. John Houseman, "Violence 1947: Three Specimens," *Hollywood Quarterly* III (Fall 1947), 65.

44. For example, in early 1948, foundering MGM, unsure in a world in which Andy Hardy was no longer boffo, hired the pioneer documentarist Louis de Rochemont to produce his kind of films at minor half-million budgets. Before the first one, though, Metro had hired *Crossfire's* social-minded executive producer, Dore Schary, and de Rochemont canceled. *Variety*, January 19, 1949, p. 6, col. 2.

45. *Variety*, March 5, 1947, p. 8, col. 5.

46. Rosen, *Popcorn Venus*, p. 276, quoting from a 1951 *Variety* poll, in which 3,000 exhibitors reported a decline in the female audience from 67 percent in 1944 to 52 percent in 1951. The reasons given were not television as often as they were dislike of the new male-oriented westerns and crime films.

47. Norman L. Friedman, "American Movies and American Culture, 1946-1970," *Journal of Popular Culture* 3 (Spring 1970): 816-17.

48. " 'The accidental juxtaposition of people and things makes for surrealism. The surrealists are the court painters of the period. They sum up an age which is at best utter confusion.' " Minnelli, quoted in *Agee on Film: Reviews and Comments by James Agee* (Boston: Beacon Press, 1964), p. 358.

49. The International Film Guide Series (New York: A. S. Barnes & Co., 1971), pp. 104-16; the quotation is from p. 104.

50. *Variety*, January 26, 1949, pp. 1, col. 1; 15, col. 4.

51. *Variety*, p. 20, col. 2.

52. Richard Schickel, "Growing Up in the Forties," *The New York Times Magazine*, February 20, 1972, p. 23.

53. Gabriel Gladstone, "Hollywood, Killer of the Dream," *Dissent* 2 (1955), 166-70.

54. "Introduction," *Culture and Commitment, 1929-1945. The American Culture*, Neil Harris, Ed. (New York: George Braziller, 1973), pp. 10-12; 15-16.

55. Thompson *America in the Dark*. pp. 222-23.

56. Pauline Kael, *The New Yorker*, March 6, 1978, p. 102.

57. Nora Ephron, "Fantasies," *Crazy Salad: Some Things About Women* (New York: Bantam Books 1976 [1975]), p. 16.

58. "The American Woman and How She Got That Way," Chicago *Sun-Times*,

April 18, 1976, "Views," p. 3. Reprinted from the Washington *Post.* In *The Spoiled Child of the Western World: The Miscarriage of the American Idea in Our Time* (Garden City: Doubleday & Co., 1976), Fairlie characterizes contemporary " 'liberated' " sex as the act of a "spoiled child, dodging from experience to experience, seeking to contrive an authenticity that has no art, no convention; with no narrative, no plot, to his life, but merely a conspiracy for each occasion" (pp. 269-70).

59. Molly Haskell, "The 2,000-Year-Old Misunderstanding—'Rape Fantasy,' " *Ms.* V (November 1976), 84-86, ff.; the quotation is from p. 98.

60. Spoken to Adela Rogers St. Johns in 1945. Quoted in Lyn Tornabene, *Long Live the King: A Biography of Clark Gable* (New York: G. P. Putnam's Sons, 1976), p. 324.

61. Fay Weldon, *Remember Me* (New York: Ballantine Books, 1977 [1976]), p. 176.

62. Herbert Hendin, "The Revolt Against Love," *Harpers* (Aug. 1975), p. 26.

63. Roger Ebert, "A Hunch Pays Off," Chicago *Sun-Times*, March 5, 1978, "Show," p. 2.

64. Leticia Kent, "Mazursky: 'It's O.K. Not to Be Married,' " *New York Times*, March 5, 1978, Sec. 2, pp. 1, 13.

Appendix:
Subjective Typology

Those lists not alphabetized are ordered subjectively according to my sense of relative popularity. Names in parenthesis indicate that the performer is also listed in a previous category.

Actresses

I. Superstars of the Forties—According to the Seventies
Bette Davis, Joan Crawford, Katharine Hepburn, Barbara Stanwyck, Ingrid Bergman, Rosalind Russell, Rita Hayworth, Lana Turner, Judy Garland, Lauren Bacall, Ann Sheridan, Ida Lupino.

II. Superstars of the Forties—According to the Forties
Greer Garson (Davis, Crawford, Hepburn, Stanwyck, Bergman,[1] Rosalind Russell), Irene Dunne, Claudette Colbert, Loretta Young, Myrna Loy, Alice Faye,[2] Ginger Rogers,[3] Margaret O'Brien,[4] Joan Fontaine, Olivia de Havilland,[5] Jane Wyman.[5]

[1] Only after *The Bells of St. Mary's* (1945).
[2] First half of decade. Retired to marriage (Phil Harris) and motherhood.
[3] For drama. Except for *The Barkleys of Broadway* (1949), in which she replaced Judy Garland after one of Garland's late forties breakdowns, Rogers abandoned Astaire and the musicals of the thirties for drama and, less often, comedy. She was rewarded with an Oscar for *Kitty Foyle* in 1940.
[4] See Leo Handel, *Hollywood Looks at Its Audience*, pp. 141-44,

for "The Margaret O'Brien Study," which MGM gave Handel permission to use. This was an audience survey done by the studio in 1943 to determine if O'Brien, who had been introduced in *Journey for Margaret* in 1942, could carry a picture by herself. The survey suggested she could; and she did. What is interesting about the O'Brien study is the information it provides into how we got our stars in the days of The Studios.

⁵In the second half of the decade, as dramatic actresses. In the first half, both appeared in comedies, sometimes together (*Government Girl*, 1943; de Havilland top-billed). Wyman's breakthrough seems to have been *The Doughgirls* (1944), in which she was fourth-billed after Ann Sheridan, Alexis Smith, and Jack Carson, but got top reviews for her dumbell role, a forerunner of My Friend Irma and Billy Dawn.

III. Dependable Leads of the Forties
　A. Superstar Pinups¹
　　Lana Turner, Rita Hayworth, Betty Grable, Hedy Lamarr.²
　　1. Wholesome pinups
　　　Dorothy Lamour (Ann Sheridan), Esther Williams,³ Jane Russell,⁴ Virginia Mayo.³
　　2. Sultry "Face" Pinups²
　　　(Lauren Bacall), Linda Darnell, Yvonne de Carlo,³ Marlene Dietrich, Ava Gardner,³ Susan Hayward,³ Veronia Lake, Maria Montez, Lizabeth Scott.

¹Superstars, perhaps, because of the "pinup girl" publicity: but generally looked upon as objects, "meat"—superstarlets, not "actresses," i.e., "lady" stars. According to Irving Klaw, who mailed over a half-million stills to soldiers, 75 percent of the requests were for pinups in bathing suits, and the favorites (in mid-1943) were Grable, Lamour, Turner, Janet Blair, Jinx Falkenburg, Hedy Lamarr, and Dona Drake. *Variety* July 7, 1943, pp. 1, col. 3; 55, cols. 4-5.

²Except for Dietrich and Gardner, these were faces; that is, there was little or no emphasis on the body (in those bathing suits that now look like armor) or on legs. This list is alphabetized.

It is interesting to speculate in what category one's memories would place Lamarr had she not turned down *Laura* (1944; Gene Tierney) and Bergman's *Gaslight* (1944) and *Saratoga Trunk* (1946). And what if MGM had loaned her to Warner Brothers for *Casablanca*? James Robert Parish and Ronald L. Bowers, *The MGM Stock Company: The Golden Era* (New Rochelle, N.Y.: Arlington House, 1973), p. 409.

[3]In second half of decade: graduates from ingenue and starlet bits. For example, Williams and Van Johnson in Irene Dunne and Spencer Tracy's *A Guy Named Joe* (1943); Hayward in *Reap the Wild Wind* (1942); and Gardner as "Girl Bit" in *Calling Dr. Gillespie* (1942), leading lady in an East Side Kids epic, *Ghosts on the Loose* (1943), and third female behind Ann Sothern and Marta Linden in *Maisie Goes to Reno* (1944). Mayo played a "looker" in Bs such as *Seven Days Ashore* (1944), starring the popular comedy team of Wally Brown and Alan Carney and girl comic Marcy McGuire. Her first "A" lead was in Bob Hope's *The Princess and the Pirate* (1944), quickly followed by Danny Kaye's *Wonder Man* (1945). Williams was starred in *Bathing Beauty* (1944), and from then on it was (watery) roses. Gardner's breakthrough role was in *Whistle Stop* (1946), with George Raft; Hayward's was her first alcoholic, in *Smash-Up* (1947).

[4]Wholesome despite the once-infamous *Outlaw* poses. *The Outlaw* was withheld from general distribution until after the general public was introduced to a virtuous and tear-jerking Russell in *Young Widow* (1945), and to an "athletic" Russell in the movie magazines, which could never be too unwholesome in the forties.

B. "Ladies"
(Bergman [until *Bells*], de Havilland, Fontaine), Merle Oberon, Margaret Sullavan, Sonja Henie,[1] Eleanor Powell,[1] Deborah Kerr.[2]
1. "Ladies—But"; or "Good Broads"; or "Look Bad, but Generally Turn Out Good"[3]
(Lauren Bacall, Ida Lupino), Carole Lombard, Vivien Leigh, Paulette Goddard, Joan Bennett, Gene Tierney, Maureen O'Hara, Lilli Palmer.[2]
2. Young Ladies (Ingenue Leads)[4]
(Judy Garland), Deanna Durbin, Betty Hutton,[1] Kathryn Grayson,[1] Jennifer Jones, Joan Leslie, Anne Baxter, Laraine Day, Dorothy McGuire, Susan Peters, Eleanor Parker,[6] June Allyson,[1] Joyce Reynolds, Jeanne Crain, June Haver,[1] Gail Russell, Diana Lynn, Joan Caulfield, Shirley Temple,[5] Jane Powell,[1] Elizabeth Taylor,[5] Ann Blyth,[1] Doris Day,[1] Jean Simmons.
3. Lady Stars of the Thirties with Increasingly Diminishing Roles in the Forties
Mary Astor, Constance Bennett, Elisabeth Bergner, Madeleine Carroll,[7] Dolores Del Rio, Kay Francis,

Greta Garbo, Ann Harding, Miriam Hopkins, Jeanette
MacDonald,[1] Luise Rainer, Norma Shearer, Sylvia
Sydney, Mae West.[8]

[1]Dependable leads, plus song and/or dance performers. Henie was
a dancer on skates.

[2]Postwar.

[3]Akin to Sultry "face" pinups.

[4]Ingenues are naturally short-lived. This list progresses from the
ingenue leads of the early forties to those of the later forties and
early fifties, with all of the early forties ingenue leads becoming
"dependable leads" in the late forties except Durbin and Reynolds,
who retired to matrimony; Peters, who was crippled in a 1945
accident; and perhaps Leslie, whose career petered out in a lengthy
battle to get free of her Warner Brothers' contract in order to play
more dramatic roles. When at last she did, few noticed.

[5]Temple, of course, was a child star of the thirties, and Taylor of
the first half of the forties.

[6]A typical case history: After several years of Warner Brothers
starlethood, Eleanor Parker got her big break playing Paul
Henreid's wife in *Between Two Worlds* (1944). She got good
reviews; and so was picked when illness forced Ida Lupino out of
The Very Thought of You (1944). After that came the female lead
in a wartime blockbuster, *The Pride of the Marines* (1945).

[7]During the war, Carroll devoted herself to work with refugee
children. She made a comeback in *An Innocent Affair (Don't Trust
Your Husband)*, 1948, with Fred MacMurray and Mary Pickford's
husband, Charles "Buddy" Rogers, also making a comeback. She
had greater success as the star of one of the successful plays of the
1948-9 season, *Goodbye, My Fancy*. But Joan Crawford got the
screen part.

[8]*My Little Chickadee* (1940); *The Heat's On* (1943).

IV.   "Almosts"[1]

Annabella, Lucille Ball, Tallulah Bankhead, Vivian Blaine,
Phyllis Calvert,[3/4] Peggy Cummins,[4] Frances Dee, Betty Field,
Joan Greenwood,[3/4] Signe Hasso, Wendy Hiller,[3] Valerie
Hobson,[3] Celia Johnson,[3/4] Evelyn Keyes, Carole Landis,
Priscilla Lane, Anna Lee,[3] Viveca Lindfors,[3/4] Margaret
Lockwood,[3] Anna Magnani,[3/4] Mary Martin,[2] Michelle
Morgan,[3] Anna Neagle,[3] Maureen O'Sullivan, Lea
Padovani,[3/4] Micheline Prelle,[3/4] Patricia Roc,[3 4] Shirley
Ross,[3] Kathleen Ryan,[3/4] Martha Scott, Moira Shearer,[2/4]

Anne Shirley, Simone Simone,[3] Anna Sten,[3] Ann Todd,[3]/[4] Tamara Toumanova,[2]/[3] (Alida) Valli,[3]/[4] Teresa Wright, (Vera)Zorina,[2]/[5] Vera-Ellen.[2]

[1]Technically, leading ladies in A movies, at least sometimes. But they never really caught on, although some did as A second leads or B leads (e.g., Lucille Ball).
[2]Song/dance performers.
[3]European or English imports.
[4]Postwar.
[5]Originally cast by Paramount executive Buddy De Sylva as Maria in *For Whom the Bell Tolls*, Zorina was replaced by director Sam Wood with Bergman. Zorina was also cast for *Hostages* (1943), in the part that brought Luise Rainer back to the screen, at least once more.

V. "The Bs": Ingenues: B-Leads; A-Supports; Starlets; "Other Women," etc.
A. Ingenues
(Susan Hayward, Esther Williams), Mary Anderson, Heather Angel, Jane Ball, Vanessa Brown,[1] Lois Butler,[1] Mimi Chandler,[2] Peggy Dow,[1] Cathy Downs,[1] Penny Edwards,[1] Sue England,[1] Joan Evans,[1] Sally Forrest,[1] Anne Francis,[1] Mona Freeman, Susanna Foster,[2] Peggy Ann Garner,[3] Nancy Gates, Ann Gillis, Bonita Granville, Mary Hatcher,[1] Jean Heather, Gloria Jean,[2] June Lockhart, Betty Lynn,[1] Pat Marshall,[2] Trudy Marshall, Jane Nigh, Cathy O'Donnell,[1] Debra Paget,[1] Jean Porter, Frances Rafferty, Debbie Reynolds,[1] Donna Reed, Ann Rutherford, Gale Storm, Phyllis Thaxter, Colleen Townsend,[1] Beverly Tyler.

[1]Postwar
[2]Song and dance
[3]Former forties child star

B-Leads; Best Friends or Other Women in As; Starlets
(Jane Wyman, Lucille Ball, Ava Gardner, Virginia Mayo, June Haver, Jeanne Crain, Yvonne de Carlo, Evelyn Keyes, Jennifer Jones [Phylis Isley], Joyce Reynolds, Gail Russell, Diana Lynn), Acquanetta, Kay Aldridge, Ruth and Juanita Alvarez,[1] Ramsay Ames, Dusty Anderson, Lois Andrews, Eve Arden,[1] Lenore Aubert, Ann Ayars,[2] Stephanie Bachelor, Lynne Baggett, Lynn Bari, Binnie Barnes, Mona Barrie,

Wendy Barrie, Diana Barrymore, Jeanne Bates, Belita,[2] Tala
Birell, Julie Bishop, Betsy Blair, Janet Blair, Joan Blondell,[1]
Karen Booth,[2] Olympe Bradna, Lucille Bremer,[2] Mary Brian,
Virginia Brissac, Hazel Brooks, Jean Brooks, Reno Browne,
Virginia Bruce, Jeanne Cagney, Cleatus Caldwell, Maureen
Cannon, Claire Carleton,[3] Mary Carlisle,[3] Lynn(e) Carver,[3]
Joan Chandler, Marguerite Chapman,[8] Linda Christian, Jan
Clayton,[2] Nancy Coleman, Lois Collier, Dorothy Comingore,[3]
Rita Corday, Valentina Cortessa,[4] Dolores Costello, Catherine
Craig, Constance Cummings, Virginia Dale,[3] Pat Dane,[3]
Denise Darcel,[4] Nancy Davis,[4] Olive Dearing,[3] Rosemary de
Camp, Gloria DeHaven,[2] Myrna Dell,[4] Jo-Carroll Dennison,[3]
Gloria Dickson, Diana Dill (Douglas),[5] Faith Domergue,[4] Jeff
Donnell, Ann Doran, Constance Dowling, Doris Dowling,
Dona Drake, Natalie Draper,[3] Ellen Drew, Steffi Duna, June
Duprez, Ann Dvorak, Marta Eggerth,[2/3] Laura Elliot, Faye
Emerson,[3] Dale Evans, Jinx Falkenburg, Virginia Field,
Geraldine Fitzgerald, Rhonda Fleming, Nina Foch, Jane
Frazee, Eva Gabor, Beverly Garland,[4] Frances Gifford,[6]
Virginia Gilmore,[3] Angela Greene, Nan Grey, Sigrid Gurie,[3]
Anne Gwynne, Jean Hagen,[4] Barbara Hale, Aileen Haley,[3] Kay
Harris,[3] Dorothy Hart, June Havoc, Margaret Hayes,[3] Gloria
Henry,[4] Irene Hervey, Harriet Hilliard,[3] Gloria Holden, Joyce
Holden, Judy Holiday,[4] Celeste Holm,[2] Jennifer Holt, Louisa
Horton,[4] Marjorie Hoshelle, Virginia Houston,[4] Rochelle
Hudson,[3] Kathleen Hughes,[4] Marsha Hunt, Kim Hunter, Ruth
Hussey, Martha Hyer,[4] Isabelita (Lita Baron), Rita Johnson,
Brenda Joyce, Arline Judge,[3] Nancy Kelly, Pat Kirkwood,[2][4]
Lola Lane, Rosemary Lane, June Lang, Louise La Planche,[3]
Madeleine LeBeau,[3] Diana Lewis, Marta Linden, Margaret
Lindsay, Julie London,[4] Marjorie Lord, Joan Lorring,[3] Grace
MacDonald, Catharine MacLeod,[4] Marjorie Manners, Margo,
Faye Marlowe, Florence Marly,[4] Brenda Marshall, Janet
Martin, Osa Massen, Ilona Massey,[2] Marjorie Massow,[3] Carole
Mathews, Lois Maxwell,[4] Mercedes McCambridge,[4] Marie
McDonald, Wanda McKay, Fay McKenzie, Joyce McKenzie,
Mary Meade, Jayne Meadows, Patricia Medina, Madge
Meredith, Doris Merrick Betty Miles,[3] Kristine Miller,[4]
Constance Moore, Peggy Moran,[3] Karen Morley,[3] Patricia
Morison,[7] Dorothy Morris, Ona Munson, Frances Neal,[3] Noel
Neill,[4] Marianne O'Brien, Peggy O'Neill, Joanne Page, Joy
Page, Janis Paige, Maria Palmer, Cecilia Parker, Jean Parker,
Helen Parrish, Gail Patrick, Lee Patrick, Sally Payne,[3] Susan

Perry,[4] Mala Powers,[4] Rita Quigley, Ella Raines, Vera Hruba Ralston, Rebel Randell,[3] Jane Randolph, Paula Raymond,[4] Betty Rhodes,[2]/[3] Ann Richards, Gale Robbins, Lynne Roberts, Estralita Rodriguez, Jean Rogers, Ruth Roman, Lina Romay, Sheila Ryan, Olga San Juan, [2]/[4] Ann Savage, Natalie Schaefer, Kay Scott, Annabel Shaw, Elaine Shepard,[4] Gale Sherwood, Penny Singleton,[8] Alexis Smith, Gale Sondergaard, Ann Sothern,[1]/[2] Jan Sterling,[4] K. T. Stevens, Linda Stirling,[8] June Storey, Glorida Stuart, Jean Sullivan, Helen Talbot, Nita Talbot, Jessica Tandy, Ruth Terry, Joan Tetzel, Carol Thurston, Claire Trevor, Betty Underwood,[4] Marcia Van Dyke, Elena Verdugo, Kaaren Verne, Martha Vickers (Mac Vicar), June Vincent, Helen Vinson, Joan Vohs,[4] Helen Walker,[6] Cheryl Walker (Sharon Lee), Amelita Ward, Ruth Warrick, Bunny Waters, Marjorie Weaver, Jacqueline White,[4] Arleen Whelan, Cara Williams, Marie Wilson,[1] Jane Withers,[1] Joan Woodbury, Maris Wrixon, Jane Wyatt, Nan Wynn.

[1]Also Special Talent: Comic
[2]Also Special Talent: Song/Dance. Belita was a skater. Like Patricia Morison (*Kiss Me, Kate*) and William Eythe (*Lend an Ear*), Jan Clayton was a success on Broadway, garnering good reviews as the original Julie in *Carousel*, and never a star in Hollywood.
[3]Mainly prewar-war years.
[4]Postwar.
[5]Married to Kirk Douglas in 1943, she acted first as Diana Dill, later as Diana Douglas (e.g., in *The Sign of the Ram*, 1948).
[6]In 1947, after Arch Oboler's *The Arnelo Affair*, Gifford may have been ready at last for the lift up from B-leads and other woman supports. Of her acting as a woman married twelve years (to George Murphy) and then compulsively attracted to gangster murderer John Hodiak, *Variety* wrote that she was marked for a "top dramatic slot in Metro's future." (February 12, 1947, p. 14, col. 3) Unfortunately, the film never took off. And tragically, brain damage from a 1948 automobile accident ended her career. Hospitalized in 1958, Parish and Bowers in *The MGM Stock Company* say, "this has been the last her public has heard of her." (P. 278.)
The also promising career of Helen Walker never recovered from an auto accident at 80 mph + speed, which resulted in the death of one of her passengers, a soldier hitchhiker; a manslaughter charge; and a lawsuit from a surviving soldier. *(Variety,* January 8, 1947.)

[7]Statuesque, smoldering, chignoned brunettes such as Morison or Gale Sondergaard exemplify Louis B. Mayer's principle on villainous women. According to Norman Zierold in *The Moguls* (New York: Avon Books, 1969), Mayer cast "elegant women" in the villainess roles because "it was bad enough to be a bitch without looking like one." (PP. 197-98.) Morison smoldered through countless Bs and the shadows of As, and then smashed as Kate in *Kiss Me, Kate* on Broadway (1948). Still, her career(s) went nowhere. Doug McClelland, in *The Unkindest Cuts: The Scissors and the Cinema* (New York: A. S. Barnes, 1972), reports that before she was totally cut from the film, Morison, playing the role of Victor Mature's first wife in *Kiss of Death* (1947), was judged by viewers to be "Supporting Actress Oscar Material." (P. 123.)
[8]Also Series

   1. The Barely Distinguishable Blonde Starlets[1]
     Iris Adrian, Louise Allbritton, Evelyn Ankers, Veda Ann Borg, Barbara Britton, Hillary Brooks, Leslie Brooks, Phyllis Brooks, Georgia Carroll,[2] Janis Carter, Judy Clark, Anita Colby, Paula Corday (Paule Croset),[3] Suzi Crandell, Mary Beth Hughes, Anne Jeffreys, Adele Jergens, Andrea King, Patricia Knight,[3]/[4] Elyse Knox, Peggy Knudsen,[4] Barbara Lawrence,[3] Audrey Long, Anita Louise, Irene Manning,[5] Adele Mara, Marion Martin, Marilyn Maxwell, Lynn Merrick, Marilyn Monroe, Dolores Moran, Martha O'Driscoll, Dorothy Patrick,[3] June Preisser, Marjorie Reynolds, Lynn Thomas,[3] Jean Wallace,[3] Eve Whitney, Lee and Lynn Wilde, Kay Williams, Marjorie Woodworth, Shelley Winters.

[1]Some girls from Bs may be blondes who you consider barely distinguishable from these. Either I distinguish them (e.g., Bunny Walters by her [publicized] height), consider them variable (in hair color and/or character type), or have forgotten them.
[2]Wartime.
[3]Postwar.
[4]Knight and Knudsen (Pat and Peggy) looked enough alike that when they co-starred in a 1947 B, *Roses are Red, Variety* called it a "casting oversight" in a film already burdened by a Gable look-alike hero, Don Castle, playing twins. (November 5, 1947, p. 8, col. 5.)
[5]In 1944, Manning left her Warner Brothers' contract for concert

and "opera work." (*Variety*, September 20, 1944, p. 2, col. 5.) After the war, she played for eighteen months on the London stage in a musical called *Serenade*. But as it had in the movies, stage stardom eluded her.

2. Looking Toward the Fifties: Touted Newcomers of the Late Forties
(Phyllis Calvert, Peggy Cummins, Viveca Lindfors,[1] Micheline Prelle, Valli, Vanessa Brown, Lois Butler, Peggy Dow, Joan Evans, Sally Forrest,[1] Anne Francis, Mona Freeman, Ruth Roman,[1] Barbara Lawrence, Martha Vickers, Shelley Winters[1]), Lola Albright, Barbara Bates, Barbara Bel Geddes,[1] Adrian Booth, Geraldine Brooks,[1] Corinne Calvet, Helena Carter, Arlene Dahl,[1] Betsy Drake,[1] Joanne Dru, Gloria Grahame,[1] Jane Greer,[1] Coleen Gray, Nancy Guild, Wanda Hendrix,[1] Phyllis Kirk,[2] Janet Leigh,[1] Dorothy Malone(y),[1] Terry Moore,[1] Patricia Neal,[1] Beatrice Pearson, Jean Peters,[1] Meg Randall, Allene Roberts, Constance Smith, Marta Toren,[1] Audrey Totter,[1] Helen Westcott, Marie Windsor.

[1]Became stars in postwar era, at least for one or two pictures.
[2]In 1949, Kirk was picked from the Broadway stage by Samuel Goldwyn to replace Teresa Wright, who had split his stable for independence after disputing how much Goldwyn could ask of her in the way of flackery. After her Goldwyn picture, *Our Very Own* (1950), Kirk got herself a contract with the Big One, MGM. She never went far.

3. Special Talent Supports or B-Leads: Song/Dance
(Vivian Blaine, Karin Booth, Lucille Bremer, Jan Clayton, Gloria Jean,[1] Lina Romay, Olga San Juan, Vera-Ellen, Nan Wynn), The Andrews Sisters, Pearl Bailey, Pamela Britton, Carol Bruce,[2] Cyd Charisse, Helen Forrest (Harry James Orchestra), Betty Garrett, Connie Haines, Lena Horne, Ina Ray Hutton, Marion Hutton, Marina Kisnetz (Jeanne), Frances Langford, Mitzi Mayfair, Joan McCracken, Allyn McLerie, Ann Miller, Sono Osato, Lorraine and Roy Rognan,[3] Hazel Scott, Dinah Shore, Ginny Simms, Rise Stevens, Martha Stewart, Martha Tilton, Sophie Tucker, Beryl Wallace,[2] Ethel Waters.

[1]Gloria Jean was involved in a strange postwar incident when she appeared on the British vaudeville circuit in June 1947. Her opening performance resulted in a panning and her collapse on stage the next day, after which she cancelled her tour. Her offending song was "The Lord's Prayer." The British termed it pure propaganda because of the line, "Forgive us our debts as we forgive our debtors." The country heavily in debt to the U.S. from the war effort was insulted. *Variety*, June 1, 1947, p. 2, col. 4.
[2]War era.
[3]Comedy dance team. He was killed in the 1943 Lisbon Clipper crash in which a number of entertainers were lost and Jane Froman and Gypsy Markoff severely injured.
[4]*Sensations of 1945* (1944)

4. Special Talent Supports or B-Leads: Comic (Often Song/Dance too)
   (Eve Arden, Joan Blondell, Judy Holliday,[1] Marie Wilson[2]), Gracie Allen, Judy Canova, Cass Daley, Joan Davis, Gracie Fields, Betty Kean, Patsy Kelly, Marcy McGuire, Carmen Miranda, Virginia O'Brien, Martha Raye, Peggy Ryan, Vera Vague, Virginia Weidler.

[1]Postwar (i.e., the others, with the exception of Miranda, were popular during the war years).
[2]Postwar as comedienne *(My Friend Irma,* 1949).

5. Series (Major)
   Comic: *Mexican Spitfire:* Lupe Velez (1939-43; Leon Errol).
   Maisie: Ann Sothern (1939-47).
   Blondie: Penny Singleton (1938-50; Arthur Lake, Larry Simms, Marjorie Ann Mutchie/ Marjorie Kent).
   Ma and Pa Kettle (1947-57; Marjorie Main; Percy Kilbride).
   Other: *Brenda Starr, Girl Reporter*: Joan Woodbury; *Jungle Gold:* Linda Stirling (1944-46; Allan Lane, Duncan Rinaldo); *Spy Smasher*: Marguerite Chapman (1942-46; Kane Richmond).

VI. Character Actresses (Major)[1]
    Jean Adair, Katherine Alexander, Sara Allgood, Judith Anderson, Pearl Bailey,[2] Fay Bainter, Ethel Barrymore, Florence Bates, Louise Beavers, Edna Best, Beulah Bondi,

Nan Bryant, Billie Burke, Spring Byington, Ilka Chase, Mady Christians, Virginia Christine, Ina Claire, Constance Collier, Patricia Collinge, Gladys Cooper, Jane Darwell, Margaret Dumont, Florence Eldridge, Isobel Elson, Hope Emerson, Glenda Farrell, Mary Forbes, Gladys George, Grace George, Connie Gilchrist, Dorothy Gish, Lucille Gleason, Mina Gombell, Ruth Gordon, Charlotte Greenwood, Margaret Hamilton, Sara Haden, Rose Hobart, Josephine Hull, Martita Hunt, Frieda Inescort, Rosalind Ivan, Isabel Jewell, Alma Krueger, Elsa Lancaster, Elissa Landi, Aline MacMahon, Marjorie Main, Hattie McDaniel, Butterfly McQueen, Una Merkel, Agnes Moorehead, Mildred Natwick, (Alla) Nazimova, Pola Negri,[3] Jarmila Novotna, Una O'Connor, Maria Ouspenskaya, Elizabeth Patterson, Katina Paxinou, Zasu Pitts, Marjorie Rambeau, Anne Revere, Thelma Ritter, Flora Robson, Selena Royle, Margaret Rutherford, Irene Ryan, Natalie Schaefer, Cornelia Otis Skinner,[4] Dorothy Stickney, Mary Treen, Evelyn Varden, Norma Varden, Lucile Watson, Ethel Waters,[2] Dame May Whitty, Mary Wickes, Peggy Wood, Margaret Wycherly, Blanche Yurka.

[1]Unlike the male characters, no actresses were strong enough to carry a picture as lead—not even Barrymore.
[2]Besides singing, Bailey and Waters also played character roles—Miss Waters on a more distinguished level than the "maid" Bailey (e.g., *Isn't It Romantic?* 1948)
[3]*Hi Diddle Diddle* (1943); Adolphe Menjou, Billie Burke, June Havoc, Dennis O'Keefe, Martha Scott.
[4]*The Uninvited* (1944).

VII. Child Actresses
(Elizabeth Taylor, Margaret O'Brien, Peggy Ann Garner, Marjorie Ann Mutchie,[1] Marjorie Kent[1]), Joan Carroll, Mary Eleanor Donohue, Clare Foley,[2] Connie Marshall, Jo Ann Marlowe, Lori Lee Michell, Sharyn Moffett, Luana Patten, Gigi Perreau, Shari Robinson, Mary Jane Saunders, Ann Todd (Ann E. Todd[3]), Natalie Wood.

[1]Mutchie was Blondie's Cookie, 1943-45; Kent played the role in 1945-50.
[2]*Janie* Joyce Reynold's kid sister, 1944.
[3]Changed her name after the postwar importation of British leading lady Ann Todd.

Actors

I. Superstars of the Forties—According to the Seventies
   Humphrey Bogart,[1] James Cagney, Spencer Tracy, John
   Wayne,[1] Clark Gable, Fred Astaire,[1] Gene Kelly,[1] Frank
   Sinatra,[1] Gary Cooper, James Stewart, John Garfield,[1] William
   Holden,[1] Robert Mitchum, Alan Ladd,[1] Henry Fonda,[1] Orson
   Welles.[2]

[1]By 1948 Bogart had become Hollywood's highest paid movie star,
but neither he nor his pictures ever came close to topping box-office
or popularity polls. Except with blacks: In 1942, in one of the
largest chains patronized by Negroes, Bogart was number one box-
office grosser (Bette Davis was number two). *Variety*, March 31,
1943, pp. 1, col. 2; 44, col. 4. *Casablanca* was another Bogart
exception; it won the 1944 Oscar, and won him a best actor
nomination (he lost to Paul Lukas for *Watch on the Rhine*). Wayne
became a superstar with *Red River* (1948). Before, he had shuttled
among Republic B-westerns, a few war movies, and RKO comedies
such as *Without Reservations* (1946), with Claudette Colbert, and
an occasional pretty Big Picture, such as *The Spoilers* and
Pittsburgh (both 1942; with Randolph Scott and Marlene Dietrich).
   Astaire, too, is more a phenomenon of our times than of his
prime time. In the early forties, he continued as in the thirties,
dancing regularly: in *Holiday Inn* (1942), but second billed to
Crosby; with Rita Hayworth in *You'll Never Get Rich* (1941) and
You Were Never Lovelier (1942); and with second-rate Joan Leslie
in *The Sky's the Limit* (1943). But by *Blue Skies* (1946), he *and*
Hollywood considered Fred Astaire to be emerging from retirement
to play the guy who loses the girl (Joan Caulfield) to Bing Crosby.
He was again lured from retirement for *The Barkleys of Broadway*
(1949), after Gene Kelly broke his leg in rehearsal. Like Sinatra,
Kelly was a newcomer who spent the forties growing up to stardom.
In person in the war years, with the bobby-soxers, the WACs, and
the WAVES, Sinatra was a superstar. But in movies he was just the
ingenue singing lead until the late forties, and particularly his and
Kelly's *Take Me Out to the Ballgame* and *On the Town* (both
1949). Do you remember him in *Higher and Higher* (1943: Michelle
Morgan) and *Step Lively* (1944: Gloria DeHaven)? Or in his first
film, a Columbia B called *Reveille For Beverly*, starring Ann
Miller, in which *Variety* referred to his "lugubrious, clumsily
directed and photographed vocal of 'Night and Day' "? (April 28,
1943, p. 8, col 4) Henry Fonda was a dependable lead before and

after war service, but no superstar then in his relative youth. Similarly, Holden, like Glenn Ford, was a budding ingenue before war duty, who clicked as a romantic male lead after the war. Garfield, Mitchum, and Ladd developed during the forties to be dependable picture toters.

[2]At best, the erratic Welles was thought of as a reasonably dependable lead in the forties.

II. Superstars of the Forties—According to the Forties
(Cagney, Cooper, Gable, Grant, Stewart, Tracy), Walter Pidgeon,[1] Bing Crosby,[2] Abbott and Costello,[3] Mickey Rooney, Bob Hope,[3] Ronald Colman,[1] Charles Boyer,[1] Tyrone Power, Robert Taylor, William Powell,[1] Pat O'Brien[1]

[1]Older: got second lease on romantic leads because Gable, Stewart, Power, et al., went to war.
[2]For dramatic as well as singing roles, or combinations, as in priest pictures, *Going My Way* (1944) and *The Bells of St. Mary's* (1945).
[3]Special Talent: Comic. Abbott and Costello's unbroken string of forties hits was snapped, permanently as it turned out, by Costello's bout with rheumatic fever in the late forties and early fifties.

III. Dependable Leads
(Astaire, Bogart, Fonda, Garfield, Holden, Kelly, Ladd, Sinatra, Wayne), Brian Aherne, Don Ameche, Dana Andrews, Lew Ayres, Eddie Bracken,[1] George Brent, Joseph Cotten, Robert Cummings, Brian Donlevy, Melvyn Douglas, Douglas Fairbanks, Jr., Errol Flynn, Glenn Ford, Van Heflin, Paul Henreid, Danny Kaye,[1] Joel McCrea, Fred MacMurray, Frederic March, Victor Mature, Ray Milland, Robert Montgomery, Dennis Morgan,[2] George Murphy,[3] David Niven, John Payne, Dick Powell,[4] George Raft, Ronald Reagan, Randolph Scott, Red Skelton,[1] Sonny Tufts, Cornel Wilde, Robert Young.

[1]Special Talent: Comic.
[2]For both musicals (e.g., *The Desert Song*, 1943; *Two Guys from Milwaukee*, 1946) and drama (*The Hard Way*, 1942; *God Is My Co-Pilot*, 1945).
[3]On its twentieth anniversary, June 21, 1944, MGM officially created new stars from its contract players Murphy, Gene Kelly, Van Johnson, Robert Walker, Esther Williams, Margaret O'Brien,

Kathryn Grayson, Susan Peters, Laraine Day, and Ginny Simms. It then had thirty-three stars on contract, in addition to nineteen in the service. *Variety*, June 21, 1944, p. 3, col. 5.
[4]After the midforties, not for musicals but for dramas, usually as cool, Chandler detectives. Today we might say, Bogart detectives.

A. Postwar Male Leads
Rossano Brazzi,[1] Montgomery Clift, Dan Dailey,[2] Kirk Douglas, Paul Douglas,[3] Howard Duff, Stewart Granger,[1] Alec Guinness,[1]/[3] Rex Harrison,[1]/[3] Van Johnson,[4] Louis Jourdan,[1] Burt Lancaster, Mario Lanza,[2] Peter Lawford,[4] John Lund, Gordon MacRae,[2] James Mason,[1] Robert Mitchum,[4] Ricardo Montalban,[1] Audie Murphy, Larry Parks,[4] Gregory Peck, Robert Ryan,[4] Mark Stevens,[4] Richard Todd,[1] Richard Widmark.

[1]Foreign imports.
[2]Special Talent: Song/Dance.
[3]For dramatic and comic roles.
[4]Up from the ingenue or male "starlet" ranks.

IV. "Almosts" as A-Leads[1]
(Orson Welles), Robert Alda, Jean-Pierre Aumont,[2] Richard Basehart,[4] Turhan Bey, David Brian,[4] Arturo de Cordova,[2] Jim Davis,[4] Robert Donat,[2] Jose Ferrer,[4] Mel Ferrer,[4] Jean Gabin,[2]/[3] Richard Hart,[4] Hurd Hatfield, Dick Haymes,[5] Trevor Howard,[2]/[4] Alexander Knox, Francis Lederer,[3] Greg McClure, Burgess Meredith, John Mills,[2] Laurence Olivier,[2] Vincent Price, Michael Redgrave,[2]/[4] George Sanders, Zachary Scott,[4] Franchot Tone, Michael Wilding.[2]/[4]

[1]Although some—especially Sanders and Price—scored as character actors.
[2]Foreign imports.
[3]Primarily wartime.
[4]Primarily postwar.
[5]Also song/dance.

V. Thirties Stars with Diminishing Roles in the Forties
Nils Asther, John Barrymore (died, 1942), Freddie Bartholomew, John Boles, Nelson Eddy,[1] Neil Hamilton, Edmund Lowe; Herbert Marshall,[2] Paul Muni.[3]

[1]Special Talent: Song.

[2]Character actor (e.g., *The Razor's Edge*, 1946).
[3]Return to stardom in *The Last Angry Man* (1959).

VI. The Bs
  A. Ingenues
      John Agar,[1] Robert Arthur,[1] Scotty Beckett,[2] Keefe
      Brasselle,[1] Tom Breen,[1] James Brown, Carleton
      Carpenter,[1] Jerome Courtland, Richard Crane, (Anthony)
      Tony Curtis,[1] Mark Daniels, John Derek,[1] Douglas Dick,
      Warren Douglas,[1] Charles Drake, Tom Drake, William
      Edwards, William Eythe, Farley Granger, John Harney,[3]
      Darryl Hickman,[2] Rock Hudson,[1] Ross Hunter, Tab
      Hunter,[1] Robert Hutton, Conrad Janis, Glenn Langan,
      Frank Latimore, Richard Long, Willian Lundigan, Guy
      Madison, Lon McCallister, Roddy McDowell,[2] Dickie
      Moore,[2] William Prince, Richard Quine, Edward Ryan,
      Johnny Sands,[1] Robert Stack, Don Taylor, Marshall
      Thompson, Loren Tindall, Robert Walker, Bill Williams.

[1]Primarily postwar.
[2]Child players of the forties *cum* postwar ingenues.
[3]Primarily wartime.

  B. B-leads: A-supports; "starlets"
      Eddie Albert,[1] Kirk Alyn, Warner Anderson, Keith
      Andes,[2] Richard Arlen, Russell Arms, Edward Ashley,
      John Baragrey, Alan Baxter, Warner Baxter, Noah Beery,
      Jr.,[3] Ralph Bellamy, Bruce Bennett, Lyle Bettger, Jack
      Beutel, Lee Bonnell, Scott Brady, Neville Brand, Lloyd
      Bridges, Steve Brodie, John Bromfield,[2] David Bruce,[4]
      Donald Buka,[5] Raymond Burr, Yul Brynner,[2] Rory
      Calhoun, Rod Cameron, Macdonald Carey, Richard
      Carlson, Jack Carson,[6] Jeff Chandler,[2] Dane Clark, Lee J.
      Cobb, Steve Cochran, Richard Conte, Donald Cook, Peter
      Cookson, Jackie Cooper,[5] Wendell Corey,[2] Broderick
      Crawford, Stephen Crane, John Craven, Laird Cregard
      (died, 1944), Hume Cronyn, Donald Curtis, John Dall,
      Tom D'Andrea, Helmut Dantine, Don DeFore (Deforest),
      Richard Denning, Richard Derr, Billy DeWolfe,[6] George
      Dolenz, Philip Dorn, Michael Duane, Michael Dunne,
      Stephen Dunne,[2] Dan Duryea, James Edwards (*Home of
      the Brave*),[2] Richard Egan,[2] James Ellison, Dick Erdmann,
      Leif Erickson, Dick Foran, John Forsythe, Arthur Franz,
      Reginald Gardiner,[6] William Gargan, William Gaxton,

Leo Genn,[2] Kirby Grant, Richard Greene, Russ Hadley,
Billy Halop, Dean Harens, Sterling Hayden, Bob Haymes
(Robert Stanton),[7] Louis Hayward, Bill Henry,[4] John
Hodiak, John Ireland, Dean Jagger, Ben Johnson,
Johnnie Johnston,[7] Allan Jones,[7] Howard Keel,[2]/[7] Barry
Kelley, De Forrest Kelly, Paul Kelly, Alf Kjellen (Christian
Kelleen; Christopher Kent),[2] Arthur Kennedy, Michael
Kirby,[7] Joe Kirkwood,Jr.,[8] Charles Korvin, Kurt Krueger,
Allan "Rocky" Lane,[3] John Litel, Robert Livingston,
John Loder, Frank Lovejoy,[2] Robert Lowrey, Jeffrey
Lynn, Don McGuire, Karl Malden, Rory Mallinson, Hugh
Marlowe, William Marshall, Charles McGraw,[2] Scott
McKay, Stephen (Horace) McNally, Gary Merrill,[2] James
Millican, Cameron Mitchel,[2] James Mitchell,[2]/[7] Ray
Montgomery, Garry Moore, Henry Morgan, Wayne
Morris, Barry Nelson, Richard Ney, Edward Norris
Michael North, Ted North, Edmond O'Brien, Donald
O'Connor,[6] George Offerman, Dennis O'Keefe, Gordon
Oliver, Michael O'Shea, Lynne Overman, Robert Paige,
Willard Parker, Marc Platt,[7] Don Porter, Dick Purcell,
Anthony Quinn, Gene Raymond, Philip Reed, George
Reeves,[8] Kane Richmond, John Ridgeley, Dale
Robertson,[2] Gilbert Roland, Cesar Romero, Charles
Russell, Robert Shayne, Joshua Shelley,[2] Sabu, John
Shelton,[4] John Shepperd (Sheppard Strudwick), Kent
Smith, Michael Steele, Robert Sterling, Craig Stevens,
David Street, Barry Sullivan, Brad Taylor,[3] Kent Taylor,
Don Terry, Philip Terry, Lawrence Tierney, Richard
Travis, Forrest Tucker, Paul Valentine, Rudy Vallee,[6] Rick
Vallin, Murvyn Vye, Sam Wanamaker,[2] David Wayne,[2]/[6]
Richard Webb,[2] James Whitmore,[2] Richard Whorf,
Warren William, Donald Woods, William Wright,[4]
Keenan Wynn,[6] Efrem Zimbalist, Jr.,[2] (Van Johnson,
Peter Lawford, Robert Mitchum, Larry Parks, Robert
Ryan, Mark Stevens)

[1]Like Patricia Morison and William Eythe, Albert became the star
of a hit Broadway musical, Irving Berlin's *Miss Liberty* (1949),
with no discernible effect on his movie career.
[2]Postwar.
[3]Special Talent: Western.
[4]Wartime.
[5]Former forties child player (Buka, e.g., in *Watch on the Rhine*).
[6]Special Talent: Comic.

[7]Special Talent: Music (Kirby: iceskating).
[8]Primarily known for Series.

C. "Seconds" on the Gable Model[1]
John Archer, Lee Bowman, Bruce Cabot, John Carroll, Don Castle, James Craig, Alan Curtis, Preston Foster, John Howard, John Hubbard, Patric Knowles, Alan Marshal,[2] George Montgomery, Tom Neal, Robert Preston, Ron Randell, John Russell, John Sutton, Gig Young.

[1]As with the Barely Distinguishable Blondes and the general Bs, so here you may think that some of the Bs are Gable types. Except for Castle and Randell (on the B-level), none of these Gable look-alikes thrived, at least not in Gable roles, after he returned from the war. [2]In *The Unkindest Cut* (1972), Doug McClelland cited Alan Marshall, "tall dark and suavely handsome, slightly British-sounding with a thin mustache," as an example of the Hollywood actor who should have been a leading man, but never was because as the male lead in women's pictures (e.g., as Irene Dunne's husband in *The White Cliffs of Dover),* most of his scenes were cut. (P. 133.)

VII. Special Talent, Leads, and Supports
A. Musical and Musical-Comedy
1. Leads (As)
(Astaire, Crosby, Dan Dailey,[1] Nelson Eddy, Dick Haymes, Danny Kaye,[2] Howard Keel,[1] Gene Kelly, Mario Lanza,[1] Gordon MacRae,[1] Dennis Morgan, Frank Sinatra), Perry Como, Jimmy Durante,[2] Jose Iturbi, Jerry Lewis,[1]/[2] Dean Martin,[1] Tony Martin, Gene Nelson,[1] Ezio Pinza.[1]
2. Supports or B-Leads
(Bob Haymes, Johnnie Johnston, Allan Jones, James Mitchell, Donald O'Connor, Marc Platt, David Street) Louis Armstrong,[3] Desi Arnaz, Gene Autry,[4] Kenny Baker, Ray Bolger, Victor Borge,[2] Charlie Barnet,[3] Cab Calloway,[3] Hoagy Carmichael, Carmen Cavallero,[3] Gower (and Marge) Champion,[1] Nat King Cole (early in the forties: The King Cole Trio), Bob Crosby,[3] Xavier Cugat,[3] Jimmie Davis, Jimmy Dorsey,[3] Tommy Dorsey,[3] Ray Eberle,[3] Cliff Edwards, Jan Garber,[3] Benny Goodman,[3] Glen Gray,[3] Phil

Harris, Woody Herman,[3] The Four Ink Spots, Harry
James,[3] Spike Jones,[3] Kay Kyser,[3] Oscar Levant,[2]
Lauritz Melchior, Vaughan Monroe, Jules Munshin,[2]
The Pied Pipers, Teddy Powell,[3] Alvino Rey,[3] Roy
Rogers and the Sons of the Pioneers,[4] Andy Russell,
Phil Spitalny,[3] The Four Step Brothers, Paul
Whiteman,[3] Dooley Wilson.[2]

[1]Postwar.
[2]Also Special Talent: Comic.
[3]And Orchestra or Band.
[4]Also Special Talent: Western.

   B. Comedy
      1. Dependable Leads
         (Abbott and Costello, Paul Douglas, Jimmy Durante,
         Alec Guinness, Bob Hope, Danny Kaye, Jerry Lewis,
         Red Skelton), William Bendix, The Marx Brothers,
         Clifton Webb, Monty Woolley.
      2 . Infrequent Forties Comics
         Jack Benny, Milton Berle, Eddie Cantor, W. C. Fields,
         Ted Lewis, Harold Lloyd, (Ole) Olsen and (Chic)
         Johnson.
      3 . Comedy Supports or B-Leads[1]
         (Jack Carson, Billy DeWolfe, Oscar Levant, Henry
         Morgan, Rudy Vallee, David Wayne,[2] Keenan Wynn),
         Eddie "Rochester" Anderson, Mischa Auer, Phil
         Baker, Robert Benchley, Edgar Bergen (and Charlie
         McCarthy), Eric Blore, Ben Blue, Monte Blue, Joe E.
         Brown, Wally Brown and Alan Carney, Sid Caesar,
         Jerry Colonna, Hans Conreid, William Demarest,
         Buddy Ebsen, Leon Errol,[1] Tom Ewell,[2] James
         Gleason, Bill Goodwin, Jack Haley, Hugh Herbert,
         Edward Everett Horton, Bert Lahr,[3] Gil Lamb, (Stan)
         Laurel and (Oliver) Hardy, Jack Oakie, Franklin
         Pangborn, Lew Parker, B. S. Pully, Rags Ragland,[3]
         "Slapsie" Maxie Rosenbloom, S. Z. ("Cuddles")
         Sakall, Phil Silvers, Danny Thomas.[2]

[1]See also Series: Comic.
[2]Postwar.
[3]Wartime.

C. Western
(Gene Autry, Roy Rogers, Ben Johnson, Allan "Rocky" Lane, Cesar Romero[1]), Rex Allen, Don "Red" Barry, Ward Bond, William Boyd,[1] Johnny Mack Brown, Smiley Burnette, Harry Carey (Sr. & Jr.), Leo Carillo, Buster Crabbe, Andy Clyde,[1] Andy Devine, Richard Dix, William (Bill) Elliot, Hoot Gibson, George "Gabby" Hayes, Jack Holt, Tim Holt, Chris-Pin Màrtin,[1] Ken Maynard, Ray Middleton,[2] Charles Starrett, Glenn Strange,[3] Guinn "Big Boy" Williams, Chill Wills.

[1]See also Series: Western.
[2]Early in the decade.
[3]See also Special Talent: Horror.

D. Horror
Lon Chaney, Jr., Boris Karloff, Bela Lugosi (Glenn Strange).

VIII. Series: Major only
A. Comic
Andy Hardy (1937-46; 1958): Mickey Rooney, Lewis Stone (Judge Hardy), Fay Holden (Mrs. Hardy), Sara Haden (Aunt Millie), Ann Rutherford (Polly), Cecilia Parker (Marian).
The Bowery Boys (1946-58): Leo Gorcey, Huntz Hall, Bobby Jordan, Gabriel Dell, Billy Benedict, David Gorcey.
Henry Aldrich (1939-44): Jimmy Lydon, Charles Smith (Dizzy), John Litel and Olive Blakeney (Mrs. & Mrs. Aldrich), Mary Anderson and then Diana Lynn (Henry's girl friend).
Francis, the Talking Mule (1949-56): Donald O'Connor
Also: *Lum and Abner* (Chester Lauch and Norris Goff); *Scattergood Baines* (Guy Kibbee); *Fibber McGee and Molly* (Jim and Marian Jordan).
The Thin Man: see Detective Series.

B . Medical
Dr. Christian (1939-41): Jean Hersholt.
Dr. Kildare (1938-47); from *Internes Can't Take Money*, 1937: Joel McCrea): Lionel Barrymore (Dr. Gillespie);

assistants: Lew Ayres (Dr. Kildare; 1938-42), Van Johnson (Dr. "Red" Adams, 1942-5), James Craig (Dr. Tommy Coalt, 1947).[1]

[1]From *Variety*, September 24, 1941, p. 1: "Andy Hardy Meets Dr. Kildare May Be Start of New Series"; the script "has already been worked out."

C . Jungle
   Tarzan (1932-70) Lex Barker (1949-53); Jane: Maureen O'Sullivan (1939-42), Brenda Joyce (1945-49); Boy: Johnny Sheffield (1941-47).
   Jungle Jim (1948-55): Johnny Weissmuller.
   Bomba (1945-55): John Sheffield.

D . Western
   Hopalong Cassidy: William Boyd (1935-48); California: Andy Clyde (1940-48).
   The Cisco Kid: Cesar Romero, Chris-Pin Martin.

E . Detective[1]
   Bulldog Drummond: from the silent era through *Calling Bulldog Drummond* (1951): Walter Pidgeon (also *Nick Carter: Master Detective*, 1939). Major series, late thirties: John Howard as Drummond; John Barrymore as Inspector Neilson. 1947: Ron Randell (2 BDs).
   Sherlock Holmes (1939-46): Basil Rathbone: Nigel Bruce (Dr. Watson).
   Charlie Chan (1929-49): Sidney Toler (1938-47 [death]), Roland Winters (1947-49); Number One Son, Jimmy Chan: Victor Sen Yung (Young); Number Two (not as regular in appearances): Keye Luke.
   The Falcon (1941-49): George Sanders (1941-42), Tom Conway (1942-46), John Calvert (1949-49).
   Boston Blackie (1941-49); Chester Morris.
   The Saint (1938-54, excepting 1943-54): George Sanders (1939-41), Hugh Sinclair (1941-43). The original 1938 Saint, Louis Hayward, made one in 1954.
   The Thin Man (1934-47): William Powell and Myrna Loy.
   The Lone Wolf (1935-49): Warren William (1938-43), Eric Blore as the butler Jameson: Gerald Mohr (1946-47), Ron Randell (1949).
   The Whistler: Richard Dix (1944-47). *Return of the*

Whistler (1948): Michael Duane, Ted Nichols.

Ellery Queen (1935-42): Ralph Bellamy (1940-41), William Gargan (1942); Nikki Porter: Margaret Lindsay; Inspector Queen: Charley Grapewin.

Dick Tracy (1945-47): in all but last, Morgan Conway: Dick Tracey; Pat: Lyle Latell.

Superman: (1948) Kirk Alyn.

Spy Smasher Returns (1942-46): Kane Richmond, Marguerite Chapman.

Crime Doctor (1943-49): Warner Baxter.

Joe Palooka (1934-44): Joe Kirkwood, Jr.: Joe Palooka; Leon Errol: Knobby Walsh (later, James Gleason and William Frawley); Elyse Knox: Anne Howe (1949 entry: Virginia Welles).

Michael Shayne: Lloyd Nolan (1940); Hugh Beaumont (19).

Big Town and *Big Town After Dark* (1947): Philip Reed: Steve Wilson; Hillary Brooke: Lorelei Kilbourne; Robert Lowrey: Pete Ryan.

[1]*The Great Movie Series*, editor-in-chief, James Robert Parish (New York and South Brunswick, N.J.: A. S. Barnes, 1971); *TV Movies,* 1975 edition. Edited by Leonard Maltin, et al. (New York: New American Library Signet, 1974).

IX. Character Actors (Major)
   A. Leads (i.e., could carry a picture)
      (Clifton Webb, Monty Woolley), Lionel Barrymore, Wallace Beery, Charles Coburn, James Dunn, Barry Fitzgerald, Sydney Greenstreet, Walter Huston, Charles Laughton, Peter Lorre, Claude Rains.

   B. Character Actors
      (Eddie "Rochester" Anderson, William Bendix, Robert Benchley, Eric Blore, Ward Bond, Joe E. Brown, Hans Conreid, William Demarest, Leon Errol, James Gleason, Bill Goodwin, Charley Grapewin, Edward Everett Horton, Herbert Marshall, Henry Morgan, Jack Oakie, Lynne Overman, Franklin Pangborn, Vincent Price, S. Z. ("Cuddles") Sakall, George Sanders, Lewis Stone, Guinn "Big Boy" Williams, Chill Wills), Walter Abel, Luther Adler, Philip Ahn, Frank Albertson, John Alexander, Leon Ames, Morris Ankrum, Robert Armstrong, Edward

Arnold, Lionel Atwill, Edgar Barrier, Richard Barthelmess, James Barton, Albert Basserman, Alfonso Bedoya, Ed Begley, Stephen Bekassy, Charles Bickford, Sidney Blackmer, Fortunio Bonanova, Walter Brennan, J. Edward Bromberg, Ed Brophy, Edgar Buchanan, Charles Butterworth, Louis Calhern, Joseph Calleia, Morris Carnovsky, John Carradine, Leo G. Carroll, Walter Catlett, Hobart Cavanaugh, Eduardo Ciannelli, Fred Clark, Stanley Clements, Ray Collins, Russell Collins, William Conrad, Elisha Cook, Jr., Melville Cooper, Jeff Corey, Lloyd Corrigan, George Coulouris, Jerome Cowan, Frank Craven, Joe Crehan, Donald Crisp, Roland Culver, Finlay Currie, Henry Daniell, Howard Da Silva, Harry Davenport, Ted De Corsia, Albert Dekker, Reginald Denny, Alan Dinehart, Charles Dingle, Ludwig Donath, Tom Dugan, Douglas Dumbrille, John Emery, Carl Esmond, Frank Faylen, Paul Ford, Wallace Ford, Victor Francen, William Frawley, Will Geer, Stephan Geray, Thomas Gomez, Paul Guilfoyle, Edmund Gwenn, Alan Hale, Jonathan Hale, Porter Hall, Thurston Hall, Sir Cedric Hardwicke, Raymond Hatson, Sessue Hayakawa, Richard Haydn, Juano Hernandez, Jean Hersholt, Louis Jean Heydt, Russell Hicks, Henry Hull, Rex Ingram, Burl Ives, Sam Jaffe, Frank Jenks, Victor Jory, Allyn Joslyn, Roscoe Karns, Robert Keith, Cecil Kellaway, Edgar Kennedy, Guy Kibbee, Percy Kilbride, Leonid Kinsky, Martin Koslack, Otto Krueger, Jack LaRue, Marc Lawrence, Canada Lee, Sheldon Leonard, Sam Levene, Gene Lockhart, Richard Loo, Burton MacLane, Horace MacMahon, George Macready, E. G. Marshall, Raymond Massey, Aubrey Mather, Mike Mazurki, Donald McBride, Frank McHugh, Victor McLaglen, Donald Meek, Adolph Menjou, Philip Merrivale, Thomas Mitchell, Victor Moore, Frank Morgan, Arnold Moss, Alan Mowbray, Conrad Nagel, J. Carroll Naish, Alan Napier, Robert Newton, Lloyd Nolan, Ramon Novarro, Henry O'Neill, Reginald Owen, Nestor Paiva, Eugene Pallette, Emory Parnell, Eric Portman, Tom Powers, Stanley Bridges, Frank Puglia, John Qualen, Charles Ruggles, Sig Rumann, Joe Sawyer, Joseph Schildkraut, Jay Silverheels, Alastair Sim, Walter Slezak, Everett Sloane, Art Smith, C. Aubrey Smith, Charles Smith, Lionel Stander, Henry Stephenson, Onslow Stevens, Paul Stewart, Milburn

Stone, Ludwig Stossel, Clinton Sundberg, Grady Sutton, Lyle Talbot, Akim Tamiroff, George Tobias, Regis Toomey, Henry Travers, Arthur Treacher, Tom Tully, Peter Van Eyck, Luis Van Rooten, Phil Van Zandt, Conrad Veidt, Harold Vermilyea, Erich Von Stroheim, Anton Walbrook, Raymond Walburn, H. B. Warner, Robert Warwick, Minor Watson, Henry Wilcoxon, Charles Winninger, Grant Withers, Roland Young, George Zucco.

X. Child Actors (Major)
(Scotty Beckette, Donald Buka, Darryl Hickman, Roddy McDowell, Dickie Moore)[1] Johnny Sheffield, Jackie "Butch" Jenkins,[1] Bobby Driscoll,[2] Dean Stockwell,[2] Skippy Homeier, Claude Jarman,[2] Ted Donaldson, Peter Miles,[2] Beau Bridges.[3]

[1] Early forties.
[2] Later forties.
[3] In *Zamba* (1949), jungle picture with Jon Hall.

If nothing else has convinced you, the pages of this Typology should: Our memories of the forties are overwhelmingly memories of men.

Bibliography

A book like this one necessarily rests on a broad web and a deep well of sources. Its subjects are several: movies, the American 1940s, women and men, remembering. Its approaches to these subjects are also multiple: historical, psychological, anthropological, aesthetic. In selecting this bibliography, I have included, in addition to works cited in the text, works that indicate the range of the book's subject and works that seem to me most accurate and most helpful in understanding the multifold subject of men-women relationships now and in less volatile times, particularly as these relationships are reflected in the popular culture.

In some areas I have sampled for the bibliography: in the autobiographies and biographies of Hollywood personalities; "The Films of . . . " type books; gossip texts; histories of the late forties Red Witch-hunt; anthologies of essays about film; and reference texts such as *Filmed Books and Plays, 1928-1969*. In other areas, I have chosen from a particularly large number, those I used most: contemporary film journals; magazines and newspapers of the forties; general film aesthetic; history; psychology; anthropology; sexology; contemporary studies of women and men in fiction and nonfiction; and the popular novels of the 1940s, which, like the movies, tell us so much about that era. Thus omitted from the bibliography but integral to the study are, for example, most of Freud; Jung; Mead; Erik Erikson; the Lynd's studies of Middletown (1929; 1937); Kinsey and Masters and Johnson and their critics and spin-offs; the memoirs of Errol Flynn; novels about Hollywood, such as Robert Carson's *The Magic Lantern*; contemporary novels about growing up in the forties, such as Herman Raucher's *Summer of '42* and David Madden's *Bijou*; and novels from the forties such as Richard Brooks' *The Brick Foxhole* (on which *Crossfire* was based), *Gentleman's Agreement*, and *The*

Chinese Room, an under-the-covers novel at least as popular in the 1940s as *Gone with the Wind*.

Agee on Film: Reviews and Comments by James Agee. Boston: Beacon Press, 1964.

Alloway, Lawrence. *Violent America: The Movies 1946-1964*. New York: The Museum of Modern Art, 1971.

Allport, Gordon W. "Eidetic Imagery." *British Journal of Psychology* 15 (1924-1925): 99-120.

Alpert, Hollis. *The Dreams and the Dreamers*. New York: The Macmillan Co., 1962.

Amberg, George, ed. *The New York Times Film Reviews: A One-Volume Selection, 1913-1970*. New York: Arno Press Book published in cooperation with Quadrangle Books, 1971.

American Film: Journal of the Film and Television Arts. American Film Institute.

Anger, Kenneth. *Hollywood Babylon*. New York. Dell Publishing Co. (Delta), 1975.

Anobile, Richard. The Film Classics Library: *The Maltese Falcon, Casablanca,* etc. New York: Avon Darien House Books, 1974, etc.

Appel, Alfred, Jr. *Nabokov's Dark Cinema*. New York: Oxford University Press, 1974.

Aumont, Jean-Pierre. *Sun and Shadows: An Autobiography*. New York: W. W. Norton & Co., 1977.

Balio, Tino. *The American Film Industry*. Madison: University of Wisconsin Press, 1976.

———. *United Artists: The Company Built by the Stars*. Madison: University of Wisconsin Press, 1976.

Barris, Alex. *Hollywood's Other Men*. South Brunswick, N.J., and New York: A. S. Barnes, 1975.

———. *Hollywood's Other Women*. South Brunswick, N.J., and New York: A. S. Barnes, 1975.

Barthel, Joan. "Ellen Burstyn Plays 'Alice' From the Inside Out." *New York Times,* 2 March, 1975, Section D, p. 17.

Barthes, Roland. *Mythologies*. Selected and translated by Annette Lavers. New York: Hill and Wang, 1972.

Bartlett, Frederick. *Remembering: A Study in Experimental and*

Social Psychology. Cambridge: Cambridge University Press, 1964.

Baxter, Anne. *Intermission, A True Story*. New York: Ballantine Books, 1976.

Beatty, Jerome, Jr., *The Girls We Leave Behind: A Terribly Scientific Study of American Women At Home*. Garden City, N.Y.: Doubleday & Co., 1963.

Behlmer, Rudy, ed. *Memo From: David O. Selznick*. New York: Avon Books, 1973 (1972).

Benchley, Nathaniel. *Humphrey Bogart*. Boston: Little, Brown & Co., 1975.

Bergman, Andrew. *We're in the Money: Depression America and Its Films*. New York: New York University Press, 1971.

Blum, John Morton. *V Was for Victory: Politics and American Culture During World War II*. New York: Harcourt Brace Jovanovich, 1976.

Blumer, Herbert. *Movies and Conduct*. New York: The Macmillan Co., 1933.

Bogle, Donald. *Toms, Coons, Mulattoes, Mammies, and Bucks: An Interpretive History of Blacks in American Films*. New York: Viking Press, 1973.

Bowers, Ronald. *The Selznick Players*. South Brunswick, N.J. and New York: A.S. Barnes, 1976.

Brackett, Leigh. "From 'The Big Sleep' to 'The Long Goodbye' and More or Less How We Got There," *Take One*, January 1974 (issue of September-October 1972), pp. 26-28.

Braudy, Leo. *The World in a Frame: What We See in Films*. Garden City, N.Y.: Doubleday Anchor Press, 1976.

Brownmiller, Susan. *Against Our Will: Men, Women and Rape*. New York: Simon and Schuster, 1975.

Bull, Clarence Sinclair, and Raymond Lee. *The Faces of Hollywood*. South Brunswick, N.J., and New York: A. S. Barnes, 1968.

Campbell, Kay. "Hollywood and the Slicks." *Variety*, 5 January, 1949, p. 14, columns 4-5.

Capra, Frank. *The Name Above the Title: An Autobiography*. New York: Bantam Books, 1972 (1971).

Carter, Randolph. *The World of Flo Ziegfeld*. New York: Praeger

Publishers, 1974.

Cavell, Stanley. *The World Viewed: Reflections on the Ontology of Film.* New York: Viking Compass Books, 1971.

Cawelti, John. *Adventure, Mystery, and Romance: Formula Stories as Art and Popular Culture.* Chicago: University of Chicago Press, 1976.

————. "Myth, Symbol and Formula." *Journal of Popular Culture* 8 (Summer 1974): 1-9.

Corliss, Richard, ed. *The Hollywood Screenwriters.* New York: Avon Books, 1970.

————. *Hollywood Rajah: The Life and Times of Louis B. Mayer.* New York: Henry Holt & Co., 1960.

Crowther, Bosley. *The Lion's Share: The Story of an Entertainment Empire.* New York: E. P. Dutton & Sons, 1975.

Davis, Bette. *The Lonely Life: An Autobiography.* New York: G. P. Putnam's Sons, 1962.

Deming, Barbara. *Running Away from Myself: A Dream portrait of America drawn from the films of the forties.* New York: Grossman Publishers, 1969.

Denney, Reuel. *The Astonished Muse.* Chicago: University of Chicago Press, 1957.

Deutsch, Helene. *The Psychology of Women.* 1: "Girlhood"; 2 "Motherhood." New York: Bantam Books, 1973 (1: 1944; 2: 1945).

Dinnerstein, Dorothy. *The Mermaid and the Minotaur: Sexual Arrangements and Human Malaise.* New York: Harper & Row, 1976.

Donovan, Timothy P. " 'Oh, What a Beautiful Morning': The Musical, *Oklahoma!* and the Popular Mind in 1943." *Journal of Popular Culture* 8 (Winter 1974): 477-88.

Dorsey, Helen. "I'm Louise Fletcher and I'm Somebody." Chicago *Daily News,* 31 January-1 February 1976, Section 2, pp. 19-20.

Dowdy, Andrew. *"Movies Are Better Than Ever": Wide Screen Memories of the Fifties.* New York: William Morrow & Co., 1973.

Downs, Robert B. *Famous American Books.* New York: McGraw-Hill, Inc., 1971.

Du Plessix Gray, Francine. *Lovers and Tyrants*. New York: Simon and Schuster, 1976.

Durgnat, Raymond. *Films and Feelings*. Cambridge: The M.I.T. Press, 1967.

Dyrud, Jarl. "Toward a Science of the Passions." *Saturday Review*, 21 February, 1976, pp. 22-27.

Eames, John Douglas. *The MGM Story*. New York: Crown Publishers, 1975.

Edwards, Anne. *Vivien Leigh: A Biography*. New York: Simon and Schuster, 1977.

Eisenger, Chester E., ed. *The 1940s: Profile of a Nation in Crisis*. Documents in American Civilzation series. General eds., Hennig Cohen and John William Ward. Garden City, N.Y.: Doubleday Anchor Books, 1969.

Ellis, Dr. Albert. *The Folklore of Sex*. Rev. ed. New York: Grove Press Black Cat Books, 1961.

Enser, A. G. S. *Filmed Books and Plays, 1928-1969*. Rev. ed. London: André Deutsch, Ltd., 1971.

Ephron, Nora. *Crazy Salad: Some Things About Women*. New York: Bantam Books, 1976 (1975).

Fairlie, Henry. "The American Woman and How She Got That Way." Chicago *Sun-Times,* "Views," 18 April, 1976, p. 3. Reprinted from the Washington *Post*.

————. *The Spoiled Child of the Western World: The Miscarriage of the American Idea in Our Time*. Garden City, N.Y.: Doubleday & Co., 1976.

Farber, Manny. "Underground Films." *Commentary* (November 1975): 432-39.

Farnsworth, Marjorie. *The Ziegfeld Follies*. New York: G. P. Putnam's Sons, 1956.

Fearing, Frederick. "The Screen Discovers Psychiatry." *Hollywood Quarterly* 1 (1945-1946): 154-59.

————. "Warriors Return: Normal or Neurotic?" *Hollywood Quarterly* 1 (1945-1946): 97-109.

Ferguson, Otis. *The Film Criticism of Otis Ferguson*. Edited by Robert Wilson. Philadelphia: Temple University Press, 1971.

Fiedler, Leslie A. *Love and Death in the American Novel*. New York: Criterion Books, 1960.

Fitch, Robert Elliot. *A Certain Blind Man: Essays on the American*

Mood. New York: Charles Scribner's Sons, 1944.

Fitzgerald, Michael G. *Universal Pictures: A Panoramic History in Words, Pictures and Filmographies*. New Rochelle, N.Y.: Arlington House, 1977.

Flamini, Roland. *Scarlett, Rhett, and a Cast of Thousands: The Making of Gone with the Wind*. New York: Macmillan & Co., 1975.

Fleming, Karl, and Anne Taylor Fleming. *The First Time*. New York: Berkley Publishing Corp., 1975.

Fordin, Hugh. *The World of Entertainment: Hollywood's Greatest Musicals*. Garden City, N.Y.: Doubleday & Co., 1975.

Forman, Henry James. *Our Movie Made Children*. New York: The Macmillan Co., 1933.

Frank, Gerold. *Judy*. New York: Dell Publishing Co., 1976 (1975).

Freeman, Lucy. *Fight Against Fears*. New York: Crown Publishers, 1951.

Friday, Nancy. *My Mother, My Self: The Daughter's Search for Identity*. New York: Delacorte Press, 1977.

Freud, Sigmund. *New Introductory Lectures on Psychoanalysis*, 1933. Standard Edition of the Complete Psychological Works of Sigmund Freud. Translated by James Strachey in collaboration with Anna Freud. London: The Hogarth Press and Institute of Psychoanalysis, 1964 edition. Vol. 22, Lecture 33, "Feminity," 112-35.

Freulich, Roman, and Joan Abramson. *Forty Years in Hollywood: Portraits of a Golden Age*. South Brunswick, N.J., and New York: A. S. Barnes, 1971.

Fried, Dr. Erdita. *On Love and Sexuality: A Guide to Self-Fulfillment*. New York: Grove Press, 1975. Originally, *The Ego in Love and Sexuality* (1960).

Friedman, Norman L. "American Movies and American Culture 1946-1970." *Journal of Popular Culture* 3 (Spring 1970): 815-23.

———. "Studying Film Impact on American Conduct and Culture." *Journal of Popular Film* 3 (Spring 1974): 173-81.

Fuchs, Daniel. "Writing for the Movies." *Commentary* (1962): 104-16.

———. and the Ladies Home *Journal* staff. *How America Lives*.

New York: Henry Holt & Co., 1941.

Furnas, J. C. *Great Times: An Informal Social History of the United States 1914-1929.* New York: G. P. Putnam's Sons, 1974.

―――. *Stormy Weather: Crosslights on the Nineteen Thirties: An Informal Social History of the United States, 1929-1941.* New York: G. P. Putnam's Sons, 1978.

Galton, Sir. Francis. *Inquiries into the Human Faculty and Development.* New York: E. P. Dutton & Co., 1911 (1883).

Gassner, John, and Dudley Nichols, eds. *The Best Film Plays.* New York: Crown Publishers, 1945.

Geduld, Harry M. *Authors on Film.* Bloomington: Indiana University Press, 1972.

Gerlach, John C., and Lana Gerlach. *The Critical Index: A Bibliography of Articles on Film in English*, 1946-1973. New York: Teachers College Press, Columbia University, 1974.

Gill, Merton M., ed. *The Collected Papers of David Rapaport.* New York: Basic Books, 1967.

Gladstone, Gabriel. "Hollywood, Killer of the Dream," *Dissent* 2 (1955): 166-70.

Goldman, Eric F. *The Crucial Decade—And After: America, 1945-1960.* New York: Vintage Books, 1960.

Goodman, Ezra. *The Fifty-Year Decline and Fall of Hollywood.* New York: Simon and Schuster, 1961.

Goodwin, Michael, and Naomi Wise. "An Interview with Howard Hawks." *Take One* 3 (March 1973; issue of November-December 1971): 19-25.

Gould, Lois. *Not Responsible for Personal Articles.* New York: Random House, 1978.

―――. "Pornography for Women." *New York Times Magazine,* 2 March, 1975, pp. 10-11, 50-51, 54, 57, 60, 62.

Gould, Mark, "Star-studded flashbacks from Howard Hawks, director," Chicago *Daily News*, 6-7 December, 1975. "Panorama," p. 17.

Goulden, Joseph C. *The Best Years, 1945-1960.* New York: Atheneum Publishers, 1976.

Gow, Gordon. *Hollywood in the Fifties.* The International Film Guide Series. South Brunswick, N.J., and New York: A.S. Barnes, 1971.

Greenberg, Harvey R., M. D. *The Movies on Your Mind.* New York: Saturday Review Press, E. P. Dutton & Co., 1975.

Greene, Graham. *The Lost Childhood and Other Essays.* New York: Viking Compass Books, 1962 (1951).

Guiles, Fred Lawrence. *Hanging on in Paradise.* New York: McGraw-Hill, Inc., 1975.

Hall, Stuart, and Paddy Whannel. *The Popular Arts: A Critical Guide to the Mass Media.* Boston: Beacon Press, 1964.

Halliwell, Leslie. *The Filmgoer's Companion.* Sixth ed. New York: Hill & Wang, 1977.

Handel, Leo A. *Hollywood Looks at Its Audience: A Report of Film Audience Research.* Urbana: The University of Illinois Press, 1950.

Harrison, P.S., ed. "A Motion Picture Reviewing Service... (for) Exibitors." *Harrison's Reports,* 1947-1950.

Hart, James B. *The Popular Book: A History of America's Literary Taste.* Berkeley: University of California Press, 1961.

Harwell, Richard, ed., *Margaret Mitchell's "Gone with the Wind," Letters: 1936-1949.* New York: The Macmillan Co., 1976.

Haskell, Molly. *From Reverence to Rape: The Treatment of Women in the Movies.* Baltimore: Penguin Books, 1974.

———. "The 2,000-Year-Old Misunderstanding—'Rape Fantasies.' " *Ms.* 5 (November 1976): 84-86, 92, 94, 96, 98.

Hayward, Brooke. *Haywire.* New York: Alfred A. Knopf, 1977. (Paper: Bantam Books, 1978.)

Hendin, Herbert. *The Art of the American Film.* Garden City, N.Y.: Higham, Charles. Doubleday Anchor Books, 1974.

———. *Ava: A Life Story.* New York: Delacorte Press, 1974.

———. *Hollywood at Sunset.* New York: Saturday Review Press, E.P. Dutton : Co., 1972.

———. *Kate.* New York: W. W. Norton, 1975.

———. "The Revolt Against Love." *Harpers* 251 (August 1975): 20-27.

Hendin, Herbert, and Greenberg, Joel. *Hollywood in the Forties.* New York: Paperback Library, 1970.

Higashi, Sumiko. *"Jane Eyre:* Charlotte Bronte Vs. the Hollywood Myth of Romance." *Journal of Popular film* 6,1 (1977): 13-31.

Hinshaw, David. *The Home Front.* New York: G. P. Putnam's Sons, 1943.

Hochman, Sandra. *Happiness Is Too Much Trouble*. New York: Ballantine Books, 1976.

Hollywood Quarterly. Berkeley: University of California Press.

Hoopes, Roy. *Americans Remember the Home Front: An Oral Narrative*. New York: Hawthorne Books, 1977.

Hopper, Hedda, and Brough, James. *The Whole Truth and Nothing But*. New York: Pyramid Books, 1963.

Horney, Karen. *New Ways in Psychoanalysis*. New York: W. W. Norton, & Co., 1938.

Hotchner, A. E. *Doris Day: Her Own Story*. New York: William Morrow & Co., 1976.

Houseman, John. "Today's Hero: A Review." *Hollywood Quarterly 2* (January 1947): 161-63.

———. "Violence 1947: Three Specimens." *Hollywood Quarterly,* 3 (Fall 1947): 63-65.

Houston, Penelope. *The Contemporary Cinema*. Baltimore: Penguin Books, 1966.

Howar, Barbara. *Laughing All the Way*. Greenwich: Fawcett Crest, 1974 (1973).

Howard, Jane. *A Different Woman*. New York: Avon Books, 1974.

Hunter, Ian M. L. *Memory*. Baltimore: Penguin Books, 1972 (1957).

Huss, Roy, and Silverstein, Norman. *The Film Experience: Elements of Motion Picture Art*. New York: Dell Publishing Co. (Delta), 1968.

Hyams, Joe. *The Biography of Humphrey Bogart*. New York: New American Library, 1966.

———. *Bogart and Bacall: A Love Story*. New York: Warner Books, 1976 (1975).

Jacobs, Lewis, ed. *The Movies as Medium*. New York: Farrar, Straus & Giroux, 1970.

———. *The Rise of the American Film*. New York: Teachers College Press, Columbia University, 1939.

James, William. *Principles of Psychology,* 1. New York: Holt, 1890.

Jarvie, I. A. *Towards a Sociology of the Cinema: A Comparative Essay on the Structure and Functioning of a Major Entertainment Industry*. London: Routledge and Kegan Paul, 1970. In America, *Movies and Society*. New York: Basic Books, 1970.

Jensen, Paul. "The Return of Dr. Caligari: Paranoia in Hollywood," *Film Commentary* 7,4 (Winter 1971-72): 36-45.

Jones, Dorothy. "Hollywood at War, 1942-1944," *Hollywood Quarterly* 1 (1945-1946): 1-19.

Jones, Ken D., and McClure, Arthur F. *Hollywood at War: The American Motion Picture and World War II*. New York: Castle Books. Originally published by A. S. Barnes, 1973.

Journal of Popular Film. Bowling Green: Popular Culture Association.

Jowett, Garth, for the American Film Institute. *Film: The Democratic Art*. Boston: Little, Brown & Co., 1976.

Kael, Pauline. "In Brief." *New Yorker* capsule reviews; and *New Yorker* essays.

———. "Empathy, and Its Limits" (review of *An Unmarried Woman*), *New Yorker*, March 6, 1978, pp. 99-102.

———. *I Lost It at the Movies*. Boston: Atlantic Monthly Press, Little, Brown & Co., 1965.

———. "Profiles: The Man from Dream City." *New Yorker* 51, 14 July, 1975, pp. 40-68.

Kanfer, Stefan. *A Journal of the Plague Years*. New York: Atheneum Publishers, 1973.

Keyes, Evelyn. *Scarlett O'Hara's Younger Sister: My Lively Life In and Out of Hollywood*. Secaucus, N.J.: Lyle Stewart, 1977.

Knight, Arthur. *The Liveliest Art: A Panoramic History of the Movies*. New York: New American Library Mentor Books, 1959.

Koch, Howard. *Casablanca: Script and Legend*. Woodstock, N.Y.: The Overlook Press, 1973.

Kracauer, Siegfried. "National Types as Hollywood Presents Them." *Public Opinion Quarterly* 13,1 (1949): 53-72.

———. "Those Movies with a Message." *Harpers* 196 (June 1948): 567-72.

Lake, Veronica, and Bain, Donald. *Veronica*. New York: The Citadel Press, 1971.

Lambert, Gavin. *GWTW: The Making of Gone with the Wind*. Boston: Atlantic Monthly Press; Little, Brown & Co., 1973.

———. *On Cukor*. New York: C. P. Putnam's Sons, 1972.

Lamparksi, Richard. *Whatever Became Of?* Vols. 1-4. New York: Ace Books, 1967, 1968, 1970. Vol. 4: New York: Bantam Books, 1975.

Landraum, Larry N., and Synon, Christine. "A Checklist of Materials About World War II Movies." *Journal of Popular*

Film 1 (Spring 1972): 147-53. Title on 147: "World War II in the Movies: A Selected Bibliography of Sources."

Langer, Susanne K. *Feeling and Form: A Theory of Art.* New York: Charles Scribner's Sons, 1953.

Larkin, Rochelle. *Hail Columbia.* New Rochelle, N.Y.: Arlington House, 1975.

Lear, Martha Weinman. "Of Thee I Sang." *New York Times Magazine,* 4 July 1976, pp. 48, 50, 52.

Life. 23 November, 1936 (first issue), through period.

Life Goes to the Movies. New York: Time-Life Books, 1975.

Lingeman, Richard. *Don't You Know There's a War on? The American Home Front 1941-1945.* New York: G. P. Putnam's Sons, 1970.

Loos, Anita. *Kiss Hollywood Good-by.* New York: Ballantine Books, 1975 (1974).

MacCann, Richard Dyer, and Perry, Edward S. *The New Film Index: A Bibliography of Magazine Articles in English, 1930-1970.* New York: E. P. Dutton & Co., 1975.

MacGowan, Kenneth. "A Change of Pattern?" *Hollywood Quarterly* 1 (1945-1946): 148-53.

Maddox, Brenda. *Who's Afraid of Elizabeth Taylor?* Philadelphia: M. Evans & Co. (Lippincott), 1977.

Madsen, Axel. *William Wyler: The Authorized Biography.* New York: Thomas Y. Crowell Co., 1973.

Mailer, Norman. *Marilyn: A Biography.* New York: Warner Paperback Library, 1975.

Maltin, Leonard, ed. *TV Movies: 1975 Edition.* New York: New American Library Signet Books, 1974.

Manchester, William. *The Glory and the Dream: A Narrative History of America, 1932-1972.* 2 volumes. Boston: Little, Brown & Co., 1973.

Mann, Klaus, ed. "A Review of Free Culture." *Decision* 1-3, 1-2 (January-February 1942).

―――. "What's Wrong with Anti-Nazi Films?" *Decision* 2 (August 1941): 27-35.

Marcus, Robert D. "Moviegoing and American Culture." *Journal of Popular Culture* 3 (Spring 1970): 755-66.

Markfield, Wallace. "Play It Again, Sam—and Again." *Saturday*

Evening Post 240, (22 April, 1967): 72-79.

Mast, Gerald. *The Comic Mind: Comedy and the Movies*. Indianapolis: The Bobbs-Merrill Co., 1973.

Mayer, Arthur L. "An Exhibitor Begs for 'B's.' " *Hollywood Quarterly* 3 (Winter 1947-1948): 172-77.

McCarthy, Todd, and Flynn, Charles, eds. *Kings of the B's: Working Within the Hollywood System: An Anthology of Film History and Criticism*. New York: E. P. Dutton & Co., 1975.

McClelland, Doug. *The Unkindest Cuts: The Scissors and the Cinema*. South Brunswick, N.J., New York: A.S. Barnes, 1972.

————. "Hollywood at War: The American Motion Picture and World War II, 1939-1945." *Journal of Popular Film* 1 (Spring 1972): 23-35.

McClure, Arthur F., ed. *The Movies: An American Idiom: Readings in the Social History of the American Motion Picture*. Rutherford, N.J.: Fairleigh Dickinson University Press, 1971.

McConnell, Frank D. *The Spoken Seen: Film and the Romantic Imagination*. Baltimore: The Johns Hopkins Press, 1975.

McCreadie, Marsha, ed. *The American Movie Goddess*. New York: John Wiley & Sons, 1973.

Mellen, Joan. *Big Bad Wolves: Masculinity in the American Film*. New York: Pantheon, 1977.

Milland, Ray. *Wide-Eyed in Babylon*. New York: William Morrow & Co., 1974.

Miller, Alice Duer. *The White Cliffs*. New York: Coward-McCann, 1940.

Miller, Don. *"B" Movies: An Informal Survey of the American Low-Budget Film, 1933-1945*. New York: Curtis Books, 1973.

Miller, Douglas T., and Nowak, Marion. *The Fifties: The Way We Really Were*. Garden City: Doubleday & Co., 1977.

Minnelli, Vincente, and Arce, Hector. *I Remember It Well*. New York: Berkley Publishing Corp., 1975 (1974).

Mitchell, Juliet. *Psychoanalysis and Feminism: Freud, Reich, Laing and Women*. New York: Vintage Books, 1975 (1974).

Mitchell, Margaret. *Gone with the Wind*. New York: The Macmillan Co., 1936.

Monaco, James. "That's Entertainment." *Take One* 4 (September 1974; issue of May-June 1973): 38-39.

Morella, Joe; Epstein, Edward Z.; and Clark, Eleanor. *Those Great Movie Ads*. New Rochelle, N.Y.: Arlington House, 1972.

Morgenstern, Joseph. "Will the Sequel Equal the Original?" *New York Times*, 1 August 1976, Section D, pp. 1, 13.

Morin, Edgar. *The Stars*. Translated by Richard Howard. New York: Grove Press, 1961.

Morris, Lloyd. *Postscript to Yesterday: American Life and Thought, 1896-1946*. New York: Harper Colophon Books, 1965 (1974).

Movie magazines of the 1940s and 1950s.

Ms. "Special Issue on Sexuality." 5 (November 1976).

Münsterberg, Hugo. *The Film*. New York: Dover Publications, 1970. Originally, *The Photoplay: a Psychological Study*. New York: D. C. Appleton & Co., 1916.

Murray, Laurence L. "Complacency, Competition and Cooperation: The Film Industry Responds to the Challenge of Television." *Journal of Popular Film* 6,1 (1977): 47-70.

Nabokov, Vladimir. *Speak, Memory*. New York: Grosset & Dunlap Universal Library, 1960. Originally, *Conclusive Evidence* (1947).

New York Motion Picture Critics Review. 3 volumes. New York: Critics Theatre Reviews, 1944, 1945, 1946.

Null, Gary. *Black Hollywood: The Negro in Motion Pictures*. Secaucus, N.J.: The Citadel Press, 1975.

Panovsky, Erwin. *The Fox Girls*. New York: Castle Books, 1972: Originally published by Arlington House.

————. *The Great Movie Series*. South Brunswick, N.J., and New York: A. S. Barnes, 1971.

————. "Style and Medium in the Motion Pictures," in (e.g.) Daniel Talbot, ed., *Film: An Anthology*. New York: Simon and Schuster, 1959, pp. 15-32. Originally, "Style and Medium in the Moving Pictures." *Bulletin of the Department of Art and Archaeology,* Princeton University, 1934. Revised as "Style and Medium in the Motion Pictures." *Critique* 1 (January-February 1947).

Parish, James Robert, ed. *Hollywood's Great Love Teams*. New Rochelle, N.Y.: Arlington House, 1974.

————, and Bowers, Ronald L. *The MGM Stock Company: The*

Golden Era. New Rochelle, N.Y.: Arlington House, 1973.

——. *The Paramount Pretties.* New Rochelle, N.Y.: Arlington House, 1974.

——. *The RKO Gals.* New Rochelle, N.Y.: Arlington House, 1974.

——, and Stanke, Don. *The Glamour Girls.* New Rochelle, N.Y.: Arlington House, 1975.

——, and De Carl, Lennard. *Hollywood Players: The Forties* New Rochelle, N.Y.: Arlington House, 1976.

——, and Lennard, William T. *Hollywood Players: The Thirties.* New Rochelle, N.Y.: Arlington House, 1976.

Payne, Robert: *The Great Garbo.* New York: Praeger Publishers, 1976.

Pines, Jim. *Blacks in Films: A survey of racial themes and images in the American film.* London: Studio Vista, 1975.

Powdermaker, Hortense. *Hollywood, the Dream Factory: An Anthropologist Looks at the Movie-Makers.* Boston: Little, Brown & Co., 1950.

Pratt, William, including the collection of Heub Bridges. *Scarlett Fever.* New York: The Macmillan Co., 1977.

Pyle, Ernie. *Brave Men.* New York: Henry Holt & Co., 1944.

Quirk, Lawrence. *The Films of Ingrid Bergman.* New York: The Citadel Press, 1970.

——. *The Great Romantic Films.* Secaucus, N.J.: The Citadel Press, 1974.

Ragan, David. *Who's Who in Hollywood.* New Rochelle, N.Y.: Arlington House, 1976.

Read, Herbert. *Education Through Art.* New York: Pantheon Books, 1958.

Ricci, Mark; Zmijewski Boris; and Zmijewski, Steve. *The Films of John Wayne.* New York: The Citadel Press, 1970.

Riesman, David; Glazer, Nathan; and Denney, Reuel. *The Lonely Crowd: A Study of the Changing American Character.* Abridged edition with 1969 Preface. New Haven: Yale University Press, 1973 (1950).

Ringgold, Gene. *The Films of Rita Hayworth: The Legend and Career of a Love Goddess.* Secaucus, N.J.: The Citadel Press, 1974.

Rivkin, Allen, and Kerr, Laura. *Hello, Hollywood! A Book About the Movies by the People Who Make Them.* Garden City, N.Y.: Doubleday & Co., 1962.

de Rougemont, Denis. *Love in the Western World.* Translated by Montgomery Belgion. Rev. New York: Pantheon Books, 1956 (1938). (English edition: *Passion and Society.*)

Rosen, Marjorie. *Popcorn Venus: Women, Movies and the American Dream.* New York: Avon Books, 1974 (1973).

Ross, T. J., ed. *Film and the Liberal Arts.* New York: Holt, Rinehart and Winston, 1970.

Rosten, Leo C. *Hollywood: The Movie Colony, The Movie Makers.* New York: Harcourt, Brace & Co., 1941.

Sargeant, Winthrop. "Fifty Years of American Women." *Life,* 2 January, 1950, pp. 64-67.

Sarris, Andrew. *The American Cinema: Directors and Directions, 1929-1968.* New York: E. P. Dutton Paperback, 1968.

———. "The High Forties Revisited." *Film Culture* 24 (Spring 1962): 62-70.

———. *Interviews with Film directors.* New York: Avon Discus Books, 1969 (1967).

———. *The Primal Screen: Essays on Film and Related Subjects.* New York: Simon and Schuster, 1973.

Saxton, Martha. *Jayne Mansfield and the American Fifties.* Boston: Houghton-Mifflin Co., 1975.

Scheurer, Timothy E. "The Aesthetics of Form and Convention in the Movies Musical." *Journal of Popular Film* 3 (Fall 1974): 307-24.

Schickel, Richard. "Growing Up in the Forties." *New York Times Magazine,* 20 February, 1972.

Seldes, Gilbert. *The Great Audience.* New York: The Viking Press, 1950.

Sennett, Ted. *Lunatics and Lovers: A Tribute to the Giddy and Glittering Era of the Screen's "Screwball" and Romantic Comedies.* New Rochelle, N.J.: Arlington House, 1973.

———. *Warner Brothers Presents: The Most Exciting Years —from the Jazz Singer to White Heat.* New York: Castle Books. Originally published by Arlington House, 1971.

Sexton, Anne. *A Self-Portrait in Letters.* Edited by Linda Gray

Sexton and Lois Ames. New York: Houghton Mifflin Co., 1977.

Sheehy, Gail. *Passages: Predictable Crises of Adult Life.* New York: E. P. Dutton & Co., 1976. (Paper: Bantam Books, 1977.)

Sight and Sound. Quarterly.

Signoret, Simone. *Nostalgia Isn't What It Used to Be.* New York: Harper & Row, 1978.

Sklar, Robert. *Movie-Made America: A Social History of American Movies.* New York: Random House, 1975.

Slater, Philip. *The Pursuit of Loneliness: American Culture at the Breaking Point.* Boston: Beacon Press, 1971 (1970).

Smith, Julian. *Looking Away: Hollywood and Vietnam.* New York: Charles Scribner's Sons, 1975.

Spearman, Charles. *Abilities of Man: Their Nature and Management.* New York: The Macmillan Co., 1927.

Springer, John. *All Talking! All Singing! All Dancing! A Pictorial History of the Movie Musical.* New York: The Citadel Press, 1966.

Steen, Mike. *Hollywood Speaks! An Oral History.* New York: G. P. Putnam's Sons, 1974.

Stine, Whitney, and Davis, Bette. *Mother Goddam: The Story of the Career of Bette Davis.* New York: Hawthorn Books, 1974.

Sullivan, Harry Stack. *The Interpersonal Theory of Psychiatry.* Edited by Helen Swick Perry and Mary Ladd Gawel. New York: W. W. Norton & Co., 1953.

Sumner, Cid Ricketts. *Quality.* New York: Bantam Books, 1947 (1946).

Susman, Warren, ed. *Culture and Commitment, 1929-1945.* The American Culture series; General Editor, Neil Harris. New York: George Braziller, 1973.

Sweeney, Russell C. *Body and Soul: The Story of John Garfield.* New York: William Morrow & Co., 1975.

———. *Coming New Week: A Pictorial History of Film Advertising* (through 1940). New York. Castle Books. Originally published by A. S. Barnes, 1973.

Swindell, Larry. *Spencer Tracy: A Biography.* New York and Cleveland: The World Publishing Co., New American Library Book, 1969.

Take One. Published monthly by Unicorn Publishing Corp.,

Montreal and Toronto, Canada.

Talbot, Daniel, ed. *Film: An Anthology*. New York: Simon and Schuster, 1959.

Taylor, Elizabeth. *Elizabeth Taylor*. New York: Harper & Row, 1964.

Tewksbury, Joan. *Nashville: An Original Screenplay*. Introduction. New York: Bantam Books, 1976.

Thomas, Bob. *King Cohn: The Life and Times of Harry Cohn*. New York: G. P. Putnam's Sons, 1967.

Thomas, Tony. *The Films of the Forties*. Secaucus, N.J.: The Citadel Press, 1975.

Thompson, Clara. *On Women*. Selected from *Intersponal Psychoanalysis*. Edited by Maurice R. Green. New York: New American Library Mentor Books, 1971 (1964).

Thompson, David. *America in the Dark: Hollywood and the Gift of Unreality* New York: William Morrow & Co., 1977.

Tiegel, Eliot. "Contemporary Artists Score with Old Songs." *Billboard,* 27 September, 1975, pp. 17, 78.

Tomkins, Mike. *The Robert Mitchum Story*. New York: Henry Regnery Co., 1972.

Tornabene, Lyn. *Long Live the King: A Biography of Clark Gable*. New York: G. P. Putnam's Sons, 1976.

Trent, Paul (text) and Richard Lawton (design). *The Image Makers: Sixty Years of Hollywood Glamour*. New York: McGraw-Hill, Inc., 1972.

Trumbo, Dalton. *Additional Dialogue: Letters of Dalton Trumbo, 1942-1962*. Edited by Helen Manfull. New York: Bantam Books, 1972 (1970)

————. *The Time of the Toad: A Study of Inquisition in America* [1949] *and Two Related Pamphlets*. New York: Harper & Row, 1971.

Twomey, Alfred E., and McClure, Arthur F. *The Versatiles: A Study of Supporting Character Actors and Actresses in the American Motion Picture, 1930-1955*. South Brunswick, N.J. and New York: A. S. Barnes, 1969.

Tyler, Parker. *The Hollywood Hallucination*. New York: Creative Age Press, 1944.

————. *Magic and Myth of the Movies*. New York: Henry Holt & Co., 1947.

Tyler, Ralph. "Literary Figures Offer Plots and Quips." *New York Times,* 1 August, 1976, Section D, pp. 1, 13, 16.

Updike, John. *Picked-Up Pieces.* New York: Alfred A. Knopf, 1975.

––––––. "Suzie Creemcheese Speaks." *The New Yorker,* 23 February, 1976, pp. 109-14. (Review of A. E. Hotchner's *Doris Day: Her Own Story.)*

Vallance, Tom. *The American Musical.* New York: Castle Books. Originally published by A. S. Barnes, 1970.

Van Druten, John. *Old Acquaintance.* New York: Random House, 1940.

Variety. All issues, 1940-1952.

Vidal, Gore. "Who Makes the Movies?" *The New York Review of Books* 23, 25 November, 1976, pp. 35-39.

Vizzard, Jack. *See No Evil: Life Inside a Hollywood Censor.* New York: Simon and Schuster, 1970.

Von Stroheim, Erich. "Movies and Morals." *Decision* 1 (March 1941): 49-56.

Walker, Alexander. *The Celluloid Sacrifice: Aspects of Sex in the Movies.* London: Michael Joseph, 1966.

––––––. *Stardom: The Hollywood Phenomenon.* London: Michael Joseph, 1970.

Wall, W. D., and Simpson, W. A. "The Effects of Cinema Attendance on the Behavior of Adolescents as Seen by Their Contemporaries." *British Journal of Educational Psychology* (1949), pp. 19, 53-61.

The Warner Bros. Golden Anniversary Book: The First Complete Features Filmography. Edited by Arthur Wilson with a Critical Essay by Arthur Knight. New York: A Dell Special Published by Film and Venture Corp., 1973.

Warner, Jack L., and Jennings, Dean. *My First Hundred Years in Hollywood.* New York: Random House, 1964.

Warshow, Robert. "The Gangster as Tragic Hero." *The Immediate Experience.* Garden City, N.Y.: Doubleday & Co., 1963, pp. 89-107.

Wayne, Jane Ellen. *The Life of Robert Taylor.* New York: Warner Paperback Library, 1973.

Weinberg, Herman O. "Axis to Grind." *Decision* 2 (October 1941): 89-92.

Whitman, Howard. "What Hollywood Doesn't Know About Women." *Colliers* 123, 5 March, 1949, pp. 18-19, 46.

Wiese, Mildred J., and Cole, Stewart J. "A Study of Children's Attitude and the Influence of a Commercial Motion Picture." *Journal of Psychology* 21 (1946): 151-71.

Wilson, Earl. *The Show Business Nobody Knows.* New York: Bantam Books, 1973 (1971).

Wilson, Edmund. *Classics and Commercials: A Literary Chronicle of the Forties.* New York: The Noonday Press, 1967 (1950).

Wolfenstein, Martha, and Leites, Nathan. *Movies: A Psychological Study.* Glencoe, Ill.: The Free Press, 1950.

Wood, Michael. *America in the Movies, or "Santa Maria, It Had Slipped My Mind."* New York: Basic Books, 1975.

Wood, Robin. *Hitchcock's Films.* International Film Guide Series. Number Two. Edited by Peter Cowie. New York: Paperback Library, 1970 (1965; 1969).

Wylie, Philip. *Generation of Vipers.* New York: Farrar and Rinehart, 1942.

Zeligs, Meyer A., M.D. *Friendship and Fratricide: An Analysis of Whittaker Chambers and Alger Hiss.* New York: The Viking Press, 1967.

Zierold, Norman. *The Moguls.* New York: Avon Books, 1969.

Zinman, David. *Saturday Afternoon at the Bijou.* New Rochelle, N.Y.: Arlington House, 1973.

Index